THE LEADER

The Mortar That Defines the Leader

Gregory Philip Niven

Copyright © Gregory Philip Niven

First Edition Published 2021

Published by Publicious Pty Ltd – Big thank you to Andy
https://www.publicious.com.au/

All rights reserved. No part of this work may be reproduced or utilized in any form or by any means, electronic or mechanical, including photocopying, recording or by any information storage and retrieval system, without the prior written permission of the publisher.
Readers should be aware that Internet Web sites offered as references or citations for information may have been removed, changed or altered between the time this was written and when it has been read.
The contribution from many sources is used to support arguments or concepts within this book, all respect goes to these people, past and present for allowing me to use their words to better give context to my book, I hope to one day also be referenced by other avid readers and writers.

Edited by Jon Reyes
Email: jonreyes1006@gmail.com

Print: 978-0-6452044-0-7
Ebook: 978-0-6452044-1-4

Printed in Sydney Australia.

Cover Art design completed by Rebecacovers

Cover photo credits goes to Brad Harris
Email: bradharris@ozemail.com.au

Official Website: https://www.gregoryphilipniven.com/

Contents

Chapter <I> - Hyper-Care 12

Section One – In The Beginning 15

Section Two – Leg Strength Is The Benefit Of Sinking 30

Section Three - Where a Vision Comes From 40

Section Four – The Wrap-Up 51

Chapter <II> - When to Flip the Switch 54

Section One – When Opportunity Is Thrust Upon Us 56

Section Two – Perception is Reality 62

Section Three – What Does Our Body Language Mean? 71

Section Four – The Wrap Up 78

Chapter <III> - Tough Love 81

Section One – Through the haze into the fog 83

Section Two – Our Journey And The Ecosystem We Must Rely On 95

Section Three: Fall For What We Stand For 104

Section Four – The Wrap-Up 114

Chapter <IV> - Throw You a Bone 118

Section One – It's Not Always Because We Are Sinking 119

Section Two – Flexibility and a Step Back 130

Section Three – Planning And Enacting Our Goals 140

Section Four – The Wrap-Up 154

Chapter <V> - You're on Your Own Now 157

Section One – The Old and the New 159

Section Two – What Is Your Motivation To Be You? 173

Section Three – Reading the Room 187

Section Four – The Wrap-Up 200

Chapter <VI> - The Wolf amongst the Sheep 203

Section One - Empowering You 205

Section Two - Accepting Who You Are 218

Section Three - A House Divided 231

Section Four – The Wrap-Up 243

The Conclusion – The End – A New Beginning 246

References 251

About the Author 255

My Ode 261

THE LEADER
The Mortar That Defines the Leader

Target Audience

This book's audience wants to understand what leadership is—not just the definition of leadership but the very fabric of who we are as leaders. There is no one true leadership style. This book is a depiction of one view considering other styles and interpretations, and presents a case that we must be open-minded in our leadership approach to be great leaders. Most predominately in the world, the old and the new, but there are so many layers that comprise what it means to be a leader, somewhat in the gray.

To connect is part of what it means to be human. To develop foundations of love and support with those that you associate with is part of pro-social human interaction and development. This book will help to improve the personal and professional capabilities of the reader.

My mission in life is to be someone that can be relied on to help when there is a need for assistance. To be respected for the things that I have been able to or unable to achieve in my life to have an impact in the lives of others for the good of humanity.

Acknowledgments

I first need to acknowledge my wife for supporting me as who I am and partly for whom I am becoming. Without her support, I would not be who I am today. Eva has taught me so much about myself how I come across—reminding me that sometimes the way I say things can be perceived different in my head than how people 'take me.' Eva has taught me that physical activity and fitness provides more benefit to my mind than putting all my time into my mind. That it is everything in life that comes together to make a complete package, that to focus on one thing, and one thing alone, is isolation, that a multitude of things come together and develop a better package than any one idea could.

Secondly, my brothers, are my rocks, they keep me grounded, and they will not go anywhere. I know even when each one of us has been offered jobs in separate countries or cities, we all come back to the fact, in the back of our minds, that if you want something, you've got to take all. It's an unwritten rule. One that my wife recounted in her wedding vows. Both of my brothers are intelligent, strong-willed people capable of anything they put their minds toward. I have learned so much and been awarded so much of their exposure in my younger life that I believe that the reason I am quite mature is attributed to them. Whom I have associated myself with has helped me become who I am today. Being just over eight years older than me, I think I also learned to be at their maturity during my teens, so I never found myself 'clicking' in many groups. I see now that most of my friends are older than me, which I attribute to my brothers and my level of maturity or understanding.

Now for me to be able to have written this book, I would have had to be born so both my mother and father deserve credit. It has been a rocky and interesting start to my life, but the lessons I learned from my upbringing have taught me a lot of things that I will not do and some things that I can take into my future. I have become someone who takes a lot of what I see with a grain of salt, I haven't been a true believer of anything really other than my faith in God, and I think that is part of how I was raised. It's not necessarily a bad thing, but it also takes a bit of joy out of some of the most simplistic things in my life.

My mother and father have given me opportunities to get to places that many people of the world wouldn't ever get the opportunity to see. I must acknowledge this because it would be remiss of me to cry "poor me." The past is gone and what I can do is use it to help better my future.

What Motivated Me to Write This Book

I was walking the other night,
It was cold, and I was caught in the rain,
But I said to myself,
Pull yourself away from your life and look at what it means to live,
Do all the little things really matter,
Should they really cause me frustration,
I continued to walk, music in my ears,
Rain on my shoulders,
And I couldn't help but smile,
When I realized that I am alive,
And at this moment,
Nothing can take that from me,
How lucky am I,
I am a social creature,
If I were alone for just one day,
I don't think I would last,
And this moment in the rain alone by myself,
Really was a great moment,
But it is just enough to let me reflect on what I have,
And to accept that there is a time and place for all activities,
That this short-lived moment of walking in the rain,
Has given me more perspective on my life at present,
Than all the advice that someone could have given me,
Because life needs to be lived,
And the little moments of peace make all the difference,
In this expansive life that we have,
What makes the most impact,
And what does it matter,
And to who,
Whom am I trying to get the attention from,
And that is where it matters,
If you know where and whom you are focused on,
Then this will answer your question when life gets hard,
Is where I am currently,
Where I want to be,
Or should I be somewhere else,
Because it matters now,
Not later,
Where I want to be,
Is where I should already be,

And if I'm not,
It's time to take a walk.

...Steel is forged in fire...

Introduction

I was told once, in essence, that people will look for direction, and if they cannot find that direction in you, they'll find someone who will give them something they want. We're all driven by something—the "id" as Freud alludes to is our instinct. Our basic needs for survival are what drives us. In modern-day life, our instincts still play a distinct part in our lives. The need for survival drives us to self-protection. Our need for survival is motivated by having a job, which provides us food, shelter, protection, and the necessities of everyday life.

We are driven by a cause our causes differ, yet all correlate in the fact that we all have a purpose, whether it is known or yet we may not be aware of it yet, humans are like a pack, and we are prone to follow the direction of people who motivate us. The exact example I was given was, "These people will either find leadership in you, or they will take direction from the Union." (O'Loughlin, 2014), which was in the case of Union membership and the leaders causing a clear delineation between management and the workers.

Well, you see, that's just it. As human beings, we will always find direction. Whether the cause is just or outrageous, we all find solace in our causes in life. Society or, in the case of a professional environment, the kind that is potentially frowned upon is the direction that people wonder how it got to that point. How did the direction or leadership of a place get so bad that people turned to a support network over their primary environment?

But it is not always one person who stands up in a crowd that is a leader—we are all leaders. Yes, we are all leaders. In different situations, we take on the leadership role. This book is not just for someone who thinks they are a leader. It's a book for everyone who wants to grow and become better for themselves, their families, or their workplaces.

Some of the ideas that are expressed within this book are references to great authors and great historic leaders. Complimenting this are my own insights and perspectives on leadership and what makes a leader, who I am and how you can use it to become better equipped.

What I will explore in this book is the stages of development that give direction to leaders or what I perceive it to be. Like the title of the book suggests, a leader is not an epiphany or something that magically appears. A leader is molded over the course of seconds, minutes, days, weeks, and decades.

The development of a leader continues to change. Like Play-Doh, we continue to shape, and evolve in reaction to our environment. Leaders, in my opinion, are not born, although someone might be dealt with a better set of cards. The way in which you maneuver, dodge, lift, and take stock of your situation, do you appreciate how much control you have over your life and its direction? The engine might get you there quicker, but sometimes the smaller engine lets you appreciate the journey for what it really is. But then again, it's a matter of perspective.

- **Leadership:** the process of influencing others toward achieving a goal in which they are empowered in such a way that people will achieve the outcome by their own will to succeed.

- **Management:** the structure, rules, and pathway in which the goal is to be achieved, management is the set of standards that form the process and set the strategic plan for leaders to enact.

Before You Begin This Book

You need to find your happy place. Somewhere you cannot be disturbed, that you can fall into this book—to forget about life's troubles, hardships, and challenges. To be fully absorbed into the moment.

This is how it works for me—I plug in my headphones and listen to a set piece of music. Every time I read a book, I put on the same loop of music. I have trained my brain to understand that when I put this music on, I sit in this seat and I read these books and that I am in my happy place—that I am in a location where I am ready to absorb and allow the book to take me away on its journey. To be in the moment, and be nowhere else but this space and time, right here.

Every person has their own place, and it may not be the same as mine, but if it works for you, then I've already started to make an impact. B.F Skinner developed the theory of operant conditioning, which is a method of learning through rewards and punishments for certain behavior. As individuals, we make associations with certain sequences, and as such, the continual use of the same scenario develops a conditioned emotional response. In my case, it is my place in time where I am most able to switch off from the outside world and be in the moment with the book that I am reading. We will touch on operant conditioning later within the book.

Chapter <I> - Hyper-Care

"No matter who tries to teach you lessons about life, the only one who can really make you learn, is yourself."

(Niven, 2017)

Introduction

We don't all get to the top, and those that do, don't make it there by their sole intentions. What is the top? In this example, it is the very best outcome of all of your efforts. What is it that you see as being a massive achievement, yet it's going to take quite an effort to get there? Much the same as when we are a child, we are taught in stages how to walk and how to learn. The same applies to how a leader is developed over time, and as such, becomes the person that they have been driven to become either by intention or chance. I don't necessarily think that we learn entirely new things. I think that when we learn, we draw the information out through what we already know. We somehow piece it all together by our understanding of the world and our place in it.

The nurture effect is the theory that our behavior is determined through our upbringing, environment, social, and life experiences. That how we are cared for, or the latter, we are conditioned to behave in a certain way.

I am a firm believer that what someone learns as a child can generally predetermine their behaviors for the rest of their life. This is not to say all people end up this way, but a fair assumption can be made, showing the future of someone based on the indicators from their past actions, reactions, or things that have been placed onto them. It's the same as our first introductions with someone new. Within the first couple of minutes, you have already judged this person and made your mind up based on your first impressions. Much as with children, our first memories of events in our lives shape the way in which we deal with situations in our present and future. Of course, with awareness, we have the opportunity to change these things if we want to. You just have to want it badly enough to exact changes in yourself. The easiest person to change is yourself. Hard to believe, I know.

The way in which we see our parents can also determine our future. If you come from a family that at one time or another struggled financially and you saw your parents struggling to get by. You might find that your urge to make copious amounts of money is due to this early childhood memory. That your urge is driven from your past, that you never want to be in that same situation, that you will rise above your circumstances and become what your parents were unable to become.

This chapter is called "Hyper-Care," a term coined and used in project management. It is used to define that stage in which support is provided and where it is most needed. If hyper-care was to be summarized in one word, that word would be "guidance." The purpose of the hyper-care stage is to provide a helping hand, as such providing much needed support. That is why during project management, hyper-care is to ensure that the people involved in the project, or roll out, are provided enough guidance so that the success of the project in the "Go-Live" stage is achieved.

Much the same as being a parent, leader, or mentor, we must set up our kids, colleagues, brothers, and sisters so well that their journey is achieved with our guidance. Not just by our forcing them, but by allowing them every opportunity to succeed. I will touch on it throughout the book, but by reading this book, you are responsible for providing the truth and transparency to these people, regardless of whether they like it or not. It is all of our responsibility to succeed. I have had people whom I have mentored who have become lazy and lose focus on what it is they are trying to achieve. You only get as much as you put in, and for that, the work comes from you. The mentor's job is to guide and aid. This doesn't mean the job is done for you.

It is your requirement that you commit your heart to the development of others, and in turn, you will receive in yourself happiness, overwhelming contribution, and desire. Though strain does come with this because you have to invest your time, which can be hard to find at certain points in our lives. You must commit those around you to help them succeed and become better by giving. You will it fulfilment in tenfold. Hyper-care is the early stages of development, where there is a genuine need for your time and energy that you will invest into the bank of trust between both parties. It is a two-way street in some respects, but a leader who wants to become more than they are must exude their experiences on those around them and within their focus to help others achieve their goals, which in turn will help leaders with their own personal achievements in life.

For a leader, this is a frustrating stage of development. and it is quite easy to lash out or expect that people should just know the right answers. But with a stable hand and lots of patience it pays off. Well, most of the time. But when it does, it is all that much worth it. What I hope you learn from this section is my approach, and another perspective other than your own, on the importance, as a leader, or as someone who wants to learn what their leader is doing to them. That to truly succeed, it takes time, respect, commitment, a lot of determination, and patience. As a leader, it is your responsibility to grow and take those that are around you on the growth journey. If you keep it all to yourself, you will find that your job or role in your group will not be sustainable long-term.

Most importantly, forget what you currently know, open your mind, and absorb.

Section One – In The Beginning

We don't always find ourselves in a position of leadership because we sought it. My first experience in a leadership position was when it was thrust upon me. At the time, I thought I had a choice. But there was no choice. This was the path I was to follow, one which would set me up for the rest of my professional and personal life.

The company I had applied for a traineeship through had just taken on a new contract, something that would challenge me beyond my current capacity. Not only from a professional perspective, but it would test the borders of my emotional well-being, setting a threshold of tolerance that would translate into patience that I am lucky to have.

The company would retain all the previous employees from the old contract, essentially everything was the same, yet the shirts had changed color. At first glance, everything remained the same. But, the ruse of first appearances soon wore off, and the truth came to light. I now understand that to win contracts, it comes down to a few considerations: service and cost.

The old contract, amongst "supposed" service issues (as I was not there at the time and can only refer indirectly, had only a small part to play), the cost was the inherent and driving factor for the change. The people whom I had originally only thought had changed shirt colors, had also changed the color of their money. In staying over with the new contract, the pay grade would change. This change would not be an increase in certain areas.

My initial interview for the traineeship was with the state manager. A man who knew all too well how to talk his way out of any problem. I felt as though I was drunk. I couldn't get my words out properly. My thoughts couldn't even keep up with the rate at which I was speaking. Most of what I thought came out of my mouth was white noise. I couldn't even make sense of what I was saying. Why was I so unable to control myself? I would look all around the room and be unable to keep my eyes focused. It's no easy feat to stare into someone else's eyes—especially when I had no experience and barely a clue of what I was saying.

I was in a large lunchroom, the walls were a bland white, and there were previous outlines of flyers and banners that had since been removed. My interviewer sat back in his chair, I spoke, barely moving, all the while sweat drip down my brow. I wore a tie that my mother had helped me weave, yet by the time I was in the interview, it was strained, pulled down with my anxiety by the impending interview. I said to myself, once it is over, it's over. Something I continue to tell myself in stressful situations.

The man sat across from me, leaning forward as if to suggest he was ready to talk. I ceased speaking. He slowly slinked toward me and sat forward, telling me that I have the job and asking when I could start. The words came out, and I heard them, yet I didn't understand what he meant. It was happening all too fast for me to comprehend. I had prepared myself for other interviews as I didn't expect to get this job. It was in the logistics industry. I remember that I had to look up in a dictionary what the word meant only hours before my interview. Yet I went into the interview, and I still didn't know what the word meant *(lucky for me, it wasn't a question in the interview)*.

Not being able to restrain myself, I smiled and said I could start Monday. I recall inside, I was chastising myself. What had I agreed to? It was Thursday on this day that I accepted the job, not knowing even what I was going to be doing. In four days, I would start a new job, an entirely new life.

At the time of the interview, I was living in Albion Park Rail, a part of the South Coast of Australia, about one hundred kilometers from Sydney. The job was located in Port Botany, which, if I was to commute from the South Coast, would be about one and a half hours trip back and forward to work. At the time, I owned a basic car that got me from point A to point B, and I had a loan on the car for about five thousand dollars. An amount of money that was way beyond my ability to pay back on what I was earning prior to the interview.

The decision to go for the interview in Sydney was a huge decision in my life. Many times in my mind, I had decided not to turn up for the interview, stay where I was, and forget about moving. My mother didn't want to see me go. I had my brother living with me, and I had my two best friends only a couple of hundred meters away. I was very comfortable, but something inside of me was yearning for more — something I can see now, but not something I was aware of at the time. I was seeking direction, something more for myself beyond what I had at the time.

I walked out of the interview in a daze. I had just accepted a job that would pay me about twenty-five thousand dollars a year. This was the kind of money that I thought (at the time) that I could live on for the rest of my life.

It paid about eighteen thousand per annum. Looking back, this was a lot of money for me. I worked as a warehouse hand—a trainee role. I would bind books, take phone calls and deliver printing. Yet, the status quo was challenged. Something had changed the way in which I saw my income. I recall a conversation with a lady that used to come into the store often. She had some influence over my boss at the time. And this influence made me listen to what she had to say. At the time, I didn't know why what she said made so much of an impact. But I do now.

The lady was having a conversation with my boss. In Australia it was at the time of the Federal budget coming out and it generally gets people talking about the minimum wages. She said, *"I cannot believe that some people are not even on minimum wage. It's impossible to make a living on anything less than five-hundred dollars a week."* (Unknown, 2009).

To this day, those words are with me. I fabricated a necessity within my mind. I thought over these words for days and nights. I couldn't understand their meaning at the time, but something inside of me then had yearned for more. I now had a goal to be earning five hundred dollars a week—at minimum. I had heeded the call.

What I know now is this, indirectly this conversation I had heard was one of the first goals I had ever set myself in life. I had challenged the status quo. To aspire to something, more than just going with the flow. I also held in high regard what had been said due to the influence of this person over my boss. Looking at my boss, who was an established business owner, I subconsciously knew that if he was influenced by what she had said and that what she had said matters.

The four days that ensued after the interview were the longest and shortest days I had encountered at the time in my life. Every night I had laid awake in fear of what was to come. I would continue to tell myself that I could just call them up and tell them that I wasn't going to come anymore. But I was too weak to even make the call. I knew in my heart that I didn't have the stamina to call them to tell them I wouldn't be coming in anymore. I didn't even have the words equipped to be able to talk to them. What would I say?

Each day I would spend most of my time with my mother, brother, and best friends to savor the time as much as possible. I promised that I would be living on the South Coast on the weekends and only work in Sydney Monday to Friday. Yet this would be impossible when I had fully grasped the responsibilities of my role.

On Sunday morning, the day before I started the new chapter of my life, I packed my car and began to say my farewells. This car ride was one of the hardest things in life I had ever done before. I left in the rear vision mirror my life that was for the first twenty years of my life. As a child, after my parents divorced, I was unable to go to school camps without fits of separation anxiety from my mother. And now I was expecting to move away from my mother, whom I had spent the majority of my life beside. Someone whom I had rebelled against and still came and slept in my same room every evening.

And so, I bid farewell to the life that was and powered up on the highway to start a new journey. I struggled all the way not to just turn around and forget this big change for me. Life was too easy where I was. Why challenge it? But I persevered. Somehow, something inside of me pushed onward.

In the following two weeks, I worked alongside an older gentleman who taught me all that he knew. Unbeknownst to me, he would be the man that would teach me all that I would know about what logistics meant at the start of my career. This man was a hard worker, and he would come in almost every Saturday and plan out the week's work in advance. Planning is now something that I cannot stress enough to this day. He taught me how to talk to freight brokers, truck drivers, managers, store people, and executives. I was his shadow for several weeks, During the course of this time, he was fair to me. While he would continue working into the later hours of the evening, he never expected me to stay with him. He would tell me what I needed to know and let me go. He would become my mentor.

Learning a new role is hard, and my mentor had an appreciation that I had talent but I wasn't confident. He was a grandfather, which was part of his patience. While he was patient with me, he was not with others. He would lose his temper when things didn't go as planned, yet when I would ask him what had gone wrong, he would slow his pace and explain to me in detail why it didn't go to plan, he would explain at what point in the process it didn't go the way it should have.

One day I was told by my mentor that he had put in his notice and was retiring. So it was time that I stepped up and took over for him. I froze, I was stuck for some time trying to contemplate what this meant for me. I felt like I had to quit now or do something drastic. It was just my adrenaline at the time, but I knew that this meant my support network was soon to leave and I had a heavy weight that would be added to my shoulders.

This is where for me, at least, *hyper-care ceased,* and the walls began to close in on me, or so I perceived at the time.

Analyzing Our Experience Origins

One way or another, we are all being mentored. Every day we learn something from another person. If you don't think you learn from others, then you're about to learn something. You learn something new every day, even the bad habits that people have teach you what not to do, and what to do better. Sometimes we just copy what other people do. Have you ever mirrored someone that you were learning from? I know I have. When you sit side by side with someone who teaches you something they are doing, you try your best to do it exactly as they do.

Without even realizing it, you may subconsciously begin to copy parts of their personality. Have you ever found yourself saying words that someone you have been working with? You might pass the moment off as coincidence. But if you take some time to think about it, you'll find that you are copycatting.

"Copycat" is a term used for people mirroring each other. It originated from observing kittens learning the basic habits by imitating the behavior of their mother. It is nothing to be concerned about. Copying someone can show a level of empathy toward someone. We tend to mirror the body language of people we like or look up to. It is an essential part of learning to sit in the seat of another person and learn from their perspective, although we learn at our own pace and in our own way, people are predisposed to be a certain way, by way of their childhood, and the way they were taught.

Although we might not think it, at certain points in our lives, we have safety nets but they come and go depending on your circumstances. At different times we lift ourselves up. The safety net either adjusts upwards or downwards. The people that we associate with form part of our safety net, although we sometimes think that we are completely on our own. We have all had a hard day, and someone just seems to say something that helps you adapt and overcome the problem. Even if you have done this yourself, the empathy of those around us contributes to our success. As a leader, it is your responsibility to do your best to do the same for those within your influence.

Within the continual parts of hyper-care that are in our life are complemented by people's level of empathy. When we learn, we learn by being told, by doing and experiencing, by seeing, and by making mistakes. If you have a boss that smacks you on the hand for making a mistake, you might ingrain it in your mind to never do that again. But in retrospect, you might make a mistake, and if your boss guides you through the process, you might find it more beneficial as you have respect for how you made the error and how to overcome it next time.

We all learn differently. Some ways in which we are taught works for people in different scenarios. Operant conditioning, which B.F Skinner theorized that *"rewards are introduced to increase a behavior, and punishment is introduced to decrease a behavior"* (Skinner, 1938), can be identified in many parts of our lives, where people who are seen to be doing the wrong thing are punished, and generally will reduce the behavior that causes these results. Along with that theory is the idea that if we do the right thing, we are rewarded, and our behaviors are reinforced.

This is not to say that operant conditioning is the only way to operate when mentoring or helping to support and develop others. But it is a good example of a simplistic approach to rewarding or punishing behaviors. This is also a good tool for leaders. The empathy that you provide to the person you are training or supporting is fundamental in the person's development. If you are cold, shut off, and uninviting to a person, they will be worried about your intentions, which will affect the way in which they learn. Whereas if you are engaging, optimistic, and inviting, you are more likely to get a positive result from your support and training, which will generally be mirrored by the other person. Empathy forms the foundation for how we are perceived or perceive another person and their intentions.

There are three core types of empathy that we can use and understand in our journey:

1. The cognitive, which is about understanding another person's perspective or side *"if we could look into each other's hearts, and understand the unique challenges each one of us faces, I think we would treat each other more gently, with more love, tolerance, and care"* (Ashton, 1992).

2. The social empathy, which is to perceive and interpret what another person is <u>feeling</u>, *"When people talk, listen completely. Most people never listen"* (Hemingway, 1996).

3. The empathic concern is the feeling you feel for another person, which could be <u>sympathy</u>, or concern for the person that you feel, in which you are able to relate to that person, *"It's like a parent's love for a child. If you have that love for someone, you're going to be there for them"* (Goleman, 2016).

Without even knowing it subconsciously, you will learn better from someone that you think understands you. You are able to connect more seamlessly. It is not something that you will understand without being aware of it, but you will emotionally connect with another person who is quite similar to yourself. The same as you mirror another person, they also mirror you. Have you ever noticed when you walked up and spoke to someone that when they took a step back, you instantly felt like you had done something wrong, or there was a problem?

When you are talking with someone, notice the direction they have their feet pointed. Usually when you want to move on from a conversation, your feet are pointed away from a person. You are turning or turned and creating an invisible block between yourself and the other person. It is our body language that also factors into our empathy with another person, and it is our body language that gives away how we feel or how we are reacting to a situation.

It is important to understand the way in which we come across, to be mindful of our body language, and be in the moment. This is a conflicting ideal, to be aware of yourself whilst also being relaxed and in the moment. But if you let it happen naturally, it will happen, so long as we are with people who are similar in behaviors to ourselves, we will slip into a similar pattern and connect easily without too much consideration of our body language, mirroring, and empathy. But if we find ourselves in a situation with a person, we are not easily able to connect with, we then need to be more self-aware. You can change yourself easier than you can change someone else.

This is where cognitive empathy is important because it is the ability to be in the shoes of another person—to step outside of our own skin and traverse the normal boundaries of our social skills. If you find someone is quite glum, concerned, or sad, try to mirror their tone. Try to talk at their level, don't stonewall them with your positive vibes because it will just increase the chasm between you and them.

Pro-social consideration is the concept of doing things that benefit everyone, not with any intention of deception but to do what you are doing in the best interest of everyone.

To use cognitive empathy is to be one with others—to match their emotional state, or at least have a good understanding of their mindset. So next time you are with someone who is quite down, slowly slide into that tone. Use their body language and mirror them, but be subtle. With some practice, you will connect with people you wouldn't normally get along with. This technique needs to be used with a pro-social consideration, and I expect that this form of empathy will be used to improve your connection with a person, not to manipulate them, because then it is a deceptive form of communication.

It is important that cognitive mirroring is used slowly. If you change your body language, tone and mirror them instantly, they will catch on. Although even subtle changes will be noticed, you may notice on a subconscious level, you might just have a feeling that something doesn't feel right. What you will find is that the other person will connect and open up more easily with you.

Consider a time where you have been out with your friends. Everyone is in a good mood, and just one of your friends is quiet and down. The group will connect more rapidly together, but the person on their own, if they don't connect with the group, they will become even more isolated. You may make attempts to appease them. You are only doing it out of empathic concern. But you won't be motivated to lower down with them. You are inclined, generally, to stay with the group. This is a part of leadership because, in most cases, people go with the majority, not the minority, this is called a social group empathy. People's moods operate around the same level as each other (although there's always that one guy).

In our culture, there is a groupthink, the group think is essentially what we consider are our boundaries, morals, ethics and what we would consider a good result. This is also called social empathy. There is consistency that people generally fit into groups because they are similar. Diversity still exists, but people who do things that are similar together find it easier to stick together. With hyper-care, the culture of the organization or social group needs to also be considered. How the majority operates factors into the way you connect with people. This can be changed over time, but to do so, it takes subtle and slow changes to make it the norm. Social empathy is the ability to interpret the way that other people feel and think—no easy task.

But by being aware of how other people might feel you could pick up on cues that other people wouldn't so easily be aware of or notice. These are advantages that you can use to connect with people because if you are able to understand how a person feels, you might be able to relate to their feeling. By doing so, you are more rapidly able to connect with them. You might notice during the conversation that they turn their body toward you and copy parts of your mannerisms. It is important in social situations to pick up on the way in which someone emotes something or expresses themselves as you might be to catch on to some of their cues.

How this relates to hyper-care is that if you are aware and looking out for the cues of other people, you are more easily able to focus yourself and, in turn, are able to attach yourself to other people's emotions.

Your empathy can be grown the same as you learn to read. Awareness is the foundation of this skill development. If you are in the process of mentoring someone which as a leader, you should always have this mindset, and you find that they are disconnecting, you might be able to put your empathy development skills to practice.

Consider that when I had my interview for the logistics traineeship, I was able to control myself more effectively and hone in on my interviewer's level of clarity, maybe I could control the interview more effectively. Much the same for yourself, you might think back to a situation where you have subconsciously stored memory, and you might look at it now and think to yourself, *Actually yeah, I recall now that he actually copied the way in which I crossed my arms.* The ability to be aware gives you the opportunity to change your situations and the situations of others. One of the three most critical values a leader can have is awareness. Make it a value so that it is an unperishable quality.

When you train someone on something, if you are rushing and disengaged, it's obvious that the result will be less desirable as compared to when you provide someone with an opportunity to be trained in a manner that best suits their empathic style. A leader must be aware of the most effective training environment. When I was joining the Army, I had an interview with a warrant officer. He had been around a long time, and when he asked who I was, I spoke for over five minutes. Rather than a long-winded speech, I should have been short and sweet, militant. It is important to understand the style in which you need to portray in different settings. If I read his body language, I may have been able to create a connection.

Regardless of the situation, you need to read the room before you jump into the hot water. Much like my example above, I should have read the room better, but it is a lesson in the end. As a leader, the imperative is on you to upskill those that are around you, regardless of the scenario. How do you know the way they want to be trained? By the visual cues at first, seeing the way in which they take you, their mirroring of you, or how you mirror them. Either person can create the connection by way of mirroring—being aware doesn't mean you will do it. Instinctually we do this. What it will do, though, is if the connection is not being made, you have the ability to find a solution to the problem, pick up the cue and develop a method that will create the connection that works best in the scenario.

I haven't touched on goal setting or desires, which will be discussed in the next few chapters, which is the focus on self-actualization. The focus of this chapter is on being able, adaptable to your surroundings, the human empathy surroundings. Because connecting is a psychological need, *belongingness, and love needs* relates to Maslow's hierarchy of needs, *"he contended that humans have a number of needs that are instinctoid, that is innate. Maslow chose the term instinctoid instead of instinctive to demonstrate the difference between our biological heritage and that of nonhuman animals"* (Maslow, 1943, p. 507).

Along with developing your ability to connect from a leadership perspective, this development will also help you to understand the empathic needs and wants of your friends and family. Empathy is developed not only by experience but by the want or need for progression in one's self. As humans, we constantly want to be better. It's part of who we are, that we continue to want for more, for better than what we had. Empathy is also more prevalent with people with whom we actually connect. If you are in a team environment, and you don't have any reasonable connection with the people in the team, you will be less likely to embrace your empathic concern for their well-being. Although you will have an inherent approach, your direct connection with these people won't endorse you to take the risk of showing your true empathic abilities.

In the United States Marines, it goes in this order: "Respect and protect your unit, respect and protect the Corp, respect and protect God, respect and protect your country." Your unit, your team, is the first priority. Teams that not only connect professionally but those that connect emotionally (empathically) form deeper bonds. The bond that means you would risk your life or career for. You need to understand each other beyond that professional surface level if you want to really understand the motivations of your team.

Empathy is a connection. It is part of opening up, listening for what is really said, and being in the moment. Empathy isn't just about nodding your head and thinking to yourself, *They must think I'm a good listener.* Consider that true listening is when the voice in your head is not developing a quick response to their sentences. True empathic listening is when they finish their sentence, and you have to pause to think of a question or answer. This shows that there is no ulterior voice inside preparing a script. It is true listening, that you are focused on hearing, not speaking—a level of cognitive empathy that is hard to obtain. But by taking into consideration that we aren't the best and that there is true room to grow and become better, do we work toward the attainment of the better, the more strengthened version of ourselves? The answer of course is yes.

"When the individual is willing to fulfil the demands of rigorous self-examination and self-knowledge. If he follows through his intention, he will not only discover some important truths about himself but will also have gained a psychological advantage: he will have succeeded in deeming himself worthy of serious attention and sympathetic interest" (Jung, 1957, p. 89).

Basic building blocks

Body Language – In golf, when you get lessons, they film you hitting the ball, your swing. You then watch yourself and improve visually. If you can film yourself in an interview or in a practice scenario, you might see easy cues that you can improve. You don't know how you come across until you see yourself from the third person.

Our body language should be watched, then we can evaluate how we come across and that will explain our perception based on the circumstance. You would either want to video yourself or get someone who can give you honest feedback on your body language to help you understand how you can present yourself in a way that is presented better in different circumstances. In everyday life, body language is what helps to convey our message with either more emphasis or meaning. We connect more effectively when we are connected in physical proximity. A voice over a phone loses its personality. It is just words played out with a response awaiting, whereas body language speaks volumes. The body can translate entire frustrations or intention more effectively than someone's words. Being a leader means that you need to be self-aware, being aware of your body language is important. Find a way to view how you are presenting yourself, either by video or asking for feedback from people. This will help you in understanding your own ticks and physical responses.

Conditioning – This is one of my favorite things to look at, we are an object of our surroundings, there's always people in our circles that don't conform, but it is so hard when we all determine what is socially acceptable, and it can be felt in many ways. But conditioning, or known by B.F Skinner puts it, Operant Conditioning, is very much like an electrical circuit. Simply, it is determined by a positive and negative response process. Generally, if someone does something bad, and they are hit, each time they do this, they are less likely to conduct this action. The same goes for reward. If you do something and are rewarded, you will associate this activity with reward and will continue to do so long as the reward continues to come through.

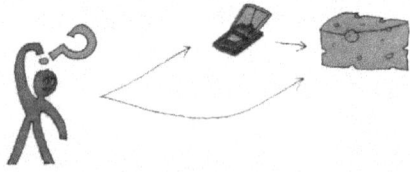

Observational Learning – This is similar to operant conditioning, but is a way of learning by way of observation. When you see someone say to another person, "You need to set a good example for your kids." We mirror people around us. You will see a group of kids walking the street in a group, and you will find they are clothed and walking in a way that associates the group as a collective. This is a basic building block of a leader, people want to aspire to leadership, and if a leader dresses well, communicates well, and presents well, the people within that group will slowly mirror the attributes of that leadership. It is not always instant, and sometimes it is a passive activity, but it is important to understand that what we say and do, is heard by those around us. I know when my manager has said something that annoyed me, such as critiquing the way in which I presented to a customer, I recall this event from several months prior and think, *Why bother, I know what he will do*. And therefore, I have shut the door before allowing an opportunity to play out, the result might actually be different, but the examples we set and their severity confirms the tone of those around us.

Think about what you say and do and what effect this has on your teams. Self-awareness of what you are doing is important because you set the tone for those around you.

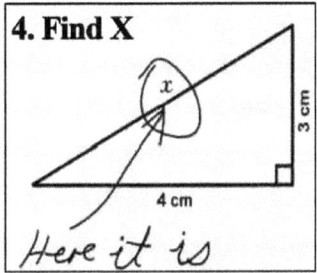

Empathy – This is critical to everyone's development. Some people might think empathy is a form of weakness, but I can assure you that it is a strength. To empathize with someone, to understand their perspective, their point of view allows you to grasp a more diverse perspective on circumstances and events. There is a clear reason why people say that "two heads are better than one." Our success requires collaboration. If we go about tasks without any involvement from the stakeholders or people who might have exposure to different experiences that could influence our decisions, we will surely die by our own swords.

Empathy is a tool. When used correctly, it can make people jump over mountains for the leader. If you can understand someone's perspective and allow them to contribute, you will gain their respect, along with their input, and therefore the person will become invested. Investment means that someone has skin in the game. They have a level of risk to themselves if something fails. They will work harder to make sure the mission succeeds—more than someone who isn't invested. Empathy is not only about getting results out of people. It is also a personal connection point. Empathy can be used to gain a better awareness of another person's circumstances and allow each other to be respectful of each other's situations in life. How do we improve our empathy? By listening to someone, by turning our phones off, and being in the moment. It is quite hard these days, but if you want to learn, then listen, keep quiet, and let someone talk to you, and you shall learn. Remember that you have two ears and only one mouth.

These basic building blocks can be linked to all other facets of our behavior, and I am sure there are other ways of presenting them, but what is being provided here is a simple set of blocks to consider, even do your own research on these concepts. Gathering data from a range of sources will give you a better and more robust understanding of the concepts. Multiple sources mean multiple ideas and, in turn, the ability to mix them all together and find the most consistent approach.

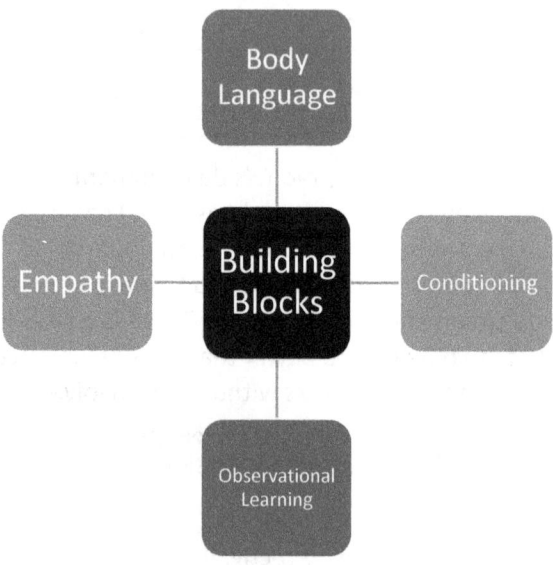

Section Two – Leg Strength Is The Benefit Of Sinking

Hyper-care. What I consider this to be is the phase in which a leader is guiding others or being guided by someone else. This stage requires a lot of attention, focused essentially on holding someone's hand and leading them from in front and beside. Much like the concept of mirroring, which was discussed in short in the last section. In this stage, you are learning the ropes. For now, what it means is that you have the opportunity to learn by example.

This stage is something that comes naturally to human beings. If you use the example of when a mother gives birth to a child, the early stage of life is when the mother spends the entirety of her time ensuring the needs of the child are fulfilled. The child in this stage is unable to care for themselves, and as such basic human instinct leads the way. Much the same in business, when a person sees a "deer caught in the headlights," nine out of ten people will provide aid. This can be as beneficial as it can be a disservice to the said *deer*. Firstly, why might you ask as to why it is a potential disservice? This is something I will explore in greater detail in chapter two, but in a short summary, it is natural for humans to find ways to survive. The majority of people, when backed into a corner, will have no choice but to fight their way out. Others, either knowingly or unbeknownst to them, will use a plea to others to help them out of a situation. The second being the wrong type of Defense, due to the fact that the person is unable to deal with their own problems, which has the potential to manifest into more facets of their life— we label them as unable to stand up for themselves. In some way, shape, or form, this person was rescued, and as such was caused a disservice for this person in the long run. This is not an irreversible thing, but it takes a remedy to resolve.

Now back to the second point, why is it a benefit to help someone who is a deer caught in the headlights? Well, this person is potentially in the hyper-care stage. Not everyone is able to stand on their own two feet unless they are shown. We learn to walk by seeing people around us do the same. This stage is where the nature vs. nurture debate comes into play. In my opinion, the hyper-care stage is the nurture part of our lives. The nature stage is chapter two and onwards, which will be explored in further detail.

How is it that someone is in hyper-care, and how were they identified as someone who should be in this stage? As a leader, you must be someone who is able to identify where they are in their development stage. But that can be said of some, but others, it is based on sole instinct, much like the nature debate, some leaders are more aware, yet less perceptive of their own identifications. What this means is that someone might lead the leader through the stages of development, unbeknownst to themselves that they are following the pathway that most mentors take their people or themselves through, *"There are no mistakes in life, only lessons"* (Anderson, 2015).

Hyper-care to me, is the stage in a person's life where they need a helping hand. They need guidance and expectations set upon them as to how and why things are done as they are. There is no set parameter that makes a leader who they are, and this chapter is not designed to give a specific expectation. What this is designed to do is to make you think and understand that self-awareness and the awareness of others are key to the development pathway.

Guardrails are a visual cue to how hyper-care should work. As a leader, we have the responsibility to help those around us to be better. The more we teach, the more we even learn. The guardrails can be likened to management. It is the structure and rules to the process that you, as the leader, must bring to your team. A leader must also use effective management to ensure that your structure is clear and consistent. This is a quality of a mentor.

One For The Mentor

For this stage to be effective, you must understand where your people are in their path, it might come instinctually to some, but like others, such as myself, I find it effective to step out each stage of the process to visually see what comes together to make the process work. This can also be called the discovery stage. In this stage, the focus is on understanding how our people understand themselves. This identification stage requires you to devote critical time to put together the pieces that make the person. These pieces are all dependent on the role that they undertake, along with projections of where they see themselves in the future. This is their investment.

The expectation is that you provide a large amount of time to the people you want to invest time in, focusing on providing them with clear examples of how you would do the same things in their position. If you are distant from the person, it will cause them to make decisions on their own or fall into the trap of procrastination. You must make yourself available. Sometimes a person might think that they don't have a mentor because we haven't been privileged enough to have someone devote their time to us. But it is a mistake to think that we cannot continue learning. Just in reading this book, taking the time to think about oneself is development. I know I have postulated to myself, *Who is my mentor?* Well, I don't have one. Though this statement in reflection is incorrect, you draw information from everywhere, be it good and bad. I set goals for myself through pictures, such as how I want to build my fitness. I find a picture of someone who has made it, and I use them as an example to learn from. You can take lessons out of every source. I am a visual learner, and I use pictures to give me guidance. I see a strong person either in my workplace or within my social network, and I motivate myself to be like that person. These things work. They aren't foolproof, obviously, but we must continue to seek direction, and it comes from a range of sources.

What Are Our Greatest Achievements?

Consider what we think have been our biggest achievements in our lives. One thing I have experienced is that most people place their greatest achievements on them having children, especially their firstborn. This is due to the amount of stress and pressure that comes from it. Seeing my sister-in-law have her baby, my nephew. It was apparent the time before the baby was due and after the birth during the new born stage was a challenge. Yet, after all that stress and anxiety, the challenge was worth the sleep loss. I understand the power this brings to a person's life. Through all the struggle, there is a light at the end of the tunnel. Simplify this: nothing worth having is easy.

Most people don't comprehend how much strength it takes to have a child, especially if there are complications. I challenge people to think retrospectively. I never ask someone what their greatest professional achievements are. I ask them what their top three greatest achievements are. You will find that most people will focus on their personal lives. In essence, that is where they find their drive for their professional life. There is no clear line separating work from our personal life. There is no complete separation in the modern age. We are always somehow connected, and we must be mindful that the decisions we make in either facet of our lives affect the other.

"It is not the bricks, but the mortar that defines the ~~(man)~~ leader." (Pacino, 1996)

It is our responsibility to ensure that our people are informed enough to understand the connection of their personal achievements to their professional careers. If a leader can successfully connect great achievements to strengths in their professional life, people are likely to start to consider their work differently. Attaching personal afflictions to work, and vice versa, make you and the people you are leading more passionate about work life and what you are achieving together—that our personal and professional lives are a reflection of our personal achievements.

The Power Triangles

I recall a time during my traineeship after my mentor had resigned, and my managing director was visiting the site. At this time in my life, I barely knew what an "MD" was. During the day, my MD asked if he could have a chat with me since it was the first time we had met in person. He spoke to me about the company and what we did overall. His presence was well known. He filled the room with an aura of confidence. I was nervous and trying to make a good impression. I focused my thoughts as best I could. At the end of our conversation, he asked if I had a question for him. I asked him, "What's it like being the big man in charge?" Without being able to even think of an answer, he grinned and laughed. When I look back on this moment, I can now see that he knew I was smarter than even I could comprehend at the time.

He responded by leaning back in his chair, comfortably, saying, "Just fine." And for a few moments, we sat there on the same metaphorical level. He then asked me if I would like an extra five thousand dollars in pay. My face answered the question straight away. What I didn't know at the time was that he had a long-term goal. Good leaders look at the long-term, and this is where we must remain. If we get stuck in the short term, we forget what the end result looks like and we lose sight of what we need to focus on to get there. He could see that I was the right person for the job, the discussion we had must have given him some indications of this but also what other people who had met me also had confirmed within his mind. I might have been inexperienced at the time but my want to achieve highly was enough for him to give me a shot at the title.

And this example shows that a leader must be willing to have a card up their sleeve, and when our team is ready, they must be given the carrot so that they feel entirely empowered. Because in the long-term, the extra money meant nothing, it was an insignificant amount in comparison to the output achieved. Most leaders get stuck in the *now* and forget about the *why*. To achieve this, we must learn to take a step back and look at where the person we are instructing is headed, not where they are now.

I was provided many exceptions by my previous mentor. I had to learn by stumbling, and I did it a lot, it is impossible to learn effectively without first learning how to fail, or at least get close enough to failure to know what not to do in the next situation. He guided me through many situations, providing the theory behind the issue and the practical steps to resolve it. My manager was very focused on the power triangles theory. I recall the first day of my employment, he sat me down in his office and provided me with his expectations, and advised me that he would like me to focus on my leadership using the power triangles.

My manager explained this theory by Eric Berne's: Transactional Analysis, in which we must be as a teacher to our people, focused on showing how to do something, then allowing them to own that process. With this, the person becomes empowered and becomes the owner of that role. An area where most leaders begin to fail in their leadership is when they rescue the person from their troubles. Much like the hyper-care phase, this chapter is akin to the rescue phase of the power triangles.

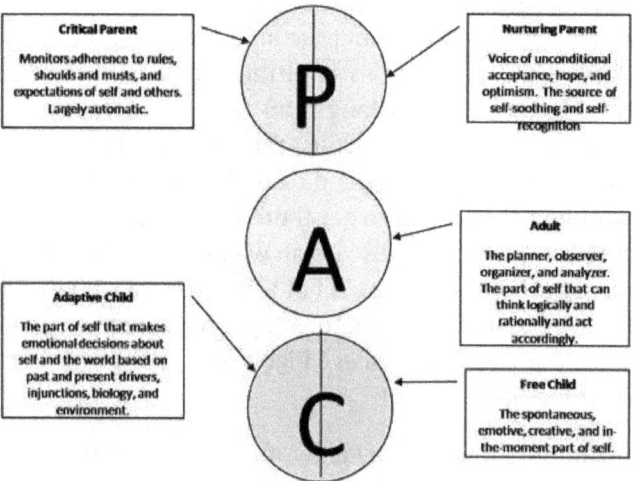

The Rescue State

This phase is effective in the early stages of development of a person being led or learning from those that are around. Though, much as I have previously said, if we revert to rescuing, people become dependent on their safety net and the ability to reference back to their mentor but this will make them lose their ability to take ownership of their role. Much like my mentor expressed, it is for us to guide and mentor, not to do their job. This was something I learned quickly whilst under the leadership of my mentor, that rescuing people causes dependencies, ones that, when formed, become hard to break.

I have fallen for the rescue trap many times. It is easy to say, "Don't do it," but it is very easy to do, and it is hard to get out of. Even being experienced in this, I have still learned better ways to move forward with each different situation. Unfortunately, I can consider myself as someone now directly "mentor less," but that's not to say that I don't consider different people as sources of mentoring. Such as when I think of boating, and how my father-in-law teaches me about ropes, knots, and portside/starboard. Although it's not a mentorship, the essentials of boating have taught me the processes involved in being a skipper. That for example that something in boating is not directly relatable to a project plan, but the steps you undertake and the minute details that you have to factor in when setting off in a boat, you can apply this logic into the business world and take this as an opportunity to translate experiences from one field into another. Even when they are not directly relatable, you can look at the concepts and share the experiences between different scenarios. I can relate or shift my understanding of boating into the concept that I speak about, which is relatable. I can even use this to create a connection with someone interested in boating.

How do we learn to be relatable? By learning to appreciate our mistakes. Reflection is required to better ourselves. Sometimes, in life and business, we don't get the time or availability to take stock of what has occurred so we can plan better for the next scenario. Reviewing our actions or decisions is hard but important in learning to address a situation differently. Although different occasions call for different approaches, everything is relatable. This is a hard skill to master. If you can relate your experiences, skills, and knowledge to different industries or sections, you can show a different approach to people who are set in their ways.

You are a mentor, regardless of the title. If you have the perspective that you are teaching people, then those people are helping you. In a way they are also mentoring you. If you have this mindset, you will open yourself up to learning from every available source and teaching others with this mindset.

Therefore collaboration is critical to everyone's success. I am sure there was a time when you were going to do something, but a person popped up in your mind, and you thought, *What would they do?* We all approach things differently, and it is important to know that how we approach things differently, determined by the circumstances, is a critical success factor. This comes from experience and exposure to different ways and concepts in our lives. What is important is that even if we are sinking, as we kick harder to reach back to the surface, our legs, our arms get stronger. And each time we start to sink, it gets a little bit easier with each stride to reach the surface again.

What Is A Telling Point?

We've all been there before, where the chaos just doesn't seem to end, and no matter how hard we try, how many hours we put in, we just don't seem to be able to get ahead. Sometimes the easiest answer is accepting that it may never change. And that your ability to deal with the fact that it will never change might be made all that much easier to accept and move on from. If you can accept that you cannot change everything, then you can focus on the things that you can change and move beyond the things that you cannot change. You can go a couple of ways, and in the past, I have gone a different way each time. There is no correct way. I have had a situation where no matter what I did, I just couldn't get myself out of the hole, and the only way out was a way through. I changed how I approached the situation. I took a step back and put each problem into categories. It was the best decision I had ever made. It led me to a much more structured role, and I was all the better for it.

I took the problems, wrote them on a whiteboard in priority order, and then took a physical step back. The issues got smaller—visually and emotionally. Sometimes we need to take these challenges and put them into the context that they deserve. It is quite easy to get frustrated and think that the world is crashing down on you, but when you put it into the context of your life, is it that big of a deal? Is being at work to fix a problem for a customer worth not seeing your daughter before she goes to sleep? This is not to say that you must disregard work, but it is to say that if you take all problems in life and put them into context, you will be more structured in your ability to prioritize and conduct yourself professionally.

On the flip side, I have persevered through some serious issues and somehow kept on going, yes, the nights were very hard on me, and I just felt completely exhausted by the start of each day. But I continued through it even though the end was never even near enough for me to gather enough motivation to continue. But I learned so much from this experience. I realized that I was letting everything affect me and that, in the end, I am one component in the cog. As a leader, heavy is the head that wears the crown. We cannot take all the responsibility, no matter how some people might expect us to do so.

I set a goal that it would be my year to learn to become resilient. I said to myself every day that I would learn to be resilient and not allow things in my life that are out of my control to affect me. It is not so simple just to say it, and it happens. You must continue to convince and bend your arm until you start to think this way. Habit is the natural extension of learning, and if we recite what we want day in and day out, in time, we will form a consistent structure, and things will go the direction we want, and it will happen. It is always as we are just about to give up that things finally change and come around the bend.

The telling point is when something goes beyond a point where we can put up with it. If you truly don't want to work your way through something as you feel your efforts will end up futile, then decide. As a leader we don't want people to see us as undecided, leadership expects a clear direction from us. I have failed to find an alternative to a role I had and, on multiple occasions, backed out of leaving. This decision to stay affected the way people had seen me and how I had seen myself. I doubted my abilities as I had gone against what I had stood for most of my life. I had always thought I was someone who made decisions and stuck to them. But putting things into consideration in our personal lives also adds to the stirring pot.

During this time, I had found out my wife was pregnant, so my decision to walk away had now made it hard to think this was a sufficient way out. Along with that, our additional home and house we lived in were undervalued, and if we wanted to sell and have some money to carry us over, I had another thing coming. We were in a spot of trouble. My only decision was to break my life-long fundamentals and go against whom I thought I was. But in all of this, it is character building. I took away my selfish need to feel valued at work and the pain associated with being there—and realized that I am responsible for my growing family.

We must put everything into perspective. All too often, we have a team member who just cannot grasp why we are making a decision that affects their world. But when you take all perspectives and put them into play, the decision becomes easier, yet some people cannot understand the gravity of our decision-making. There sometimes are bigger things in play that not everyone can see at the surface level. I have been on the flip side where simple decisions are being made that I couldn't understand. When I moved into more strategic planning, I could grasp more detail from all different sides and would have to make decisions that didn't always benefit everyone around the table. Communication is critical in these situations.

Leadership is not about keeping everyone happy but making decisions vital to the group's survival, not just the self, but the group as a whole. Even if we go against what we think is the best way out, sometimes we have to put all of life's little challenges in the mix and come up with the decision that suits the group over the self. I know the struggle of staying in my situation, but I knew that I was making the right decision to stay on as I was no longer thinking just about me but another chapter in my personal life. Much the same as some decisions cannot be made in the heat of the moment—some decision-making requires reviewing and questioning your values. What we do today might be different tomorrow. What we need to consider is what happens six months from now. Will today's problems even matter anymore? What gravity does this issue hold if in six months it's all but forgotten? But if I make the wrong decision now, what happens in six months? Consider all the points of contact before making any rash decisions.

The upside of making poor decisions is that you will quickly learn what not to do in the next occurrence. Much like the operant conditioning concept, we will learn one way or another. Have the mindset that everything is a lesson and you will never fail. You will never fail if you never give up.

Section Three - Where a Vision Comes From

Where do you see yourself in five years? Close your eyes and picture it.

If that image is too blurry, or you just picture a shadow in the darkness, well, guess what? You're not alone. When I look at my life mission statement, my goal for twelve months from now is a colorful picture. Then two years is nice to have, three years is a black and white mural, and my five-year plan reminds me of a dark Van Gogh painting.

We all want the best in our lives. Some of us want to help others, some of us want to help ourselves, some of us want to do a bit of column A and column B.

"Everybody ends up somewhere in life. A few people end up somewhere on purpose." (Stanley, 2001, p. 34)

You are not alone if you think that you don't have a vision if you already do, and that could already be the case since you are already reading this book and on the self-development journey.

But even if you think you have it all figured out, we lose sight of our visions at times, hard times, work changes, realizations, and a myriad of reasons why things change or why you can lose sight. But first of all, it is important to determine your fate. If you have even a glimpse of where you want to go, I guarantee that you will succeed in all of your goals, so long as you write it down and continue to chip away at it day in and day out. It is not the big leaps but the small steps each day that brings you closer to your goals.

Goal-Setting

Goal setting is easy, and if you attribute enough time to understanding how it all works, from there, it will get easier each time you do it. The standard goal-setting tool is SMART, specific, measurable, achievable / agreed on, realistic, and timed. When you think of your goals, can you use these headings to place parts of what you are trying to do into each of these boxes? If you cannot, I am sure the book will inspire ideas on how to do so. But right now, have a go and see if you can use this simple template to compartment your goal(s). Your goals should align with your vision. Your vision is your long-term you. And your goals are milestones to achieving this. Your vision is not just something you reach, and your journey is done. Your vision is the day in and day out, who you are, and who you aspire to be.

Your vision is who you are, where you are standing, how you feel, and what you can smell. It is the result of your values and the direction you are going. Live and breathe this moment daily so that you continue to progress in the direction of your vision. If it has a smell, a taste, then it will feel even more real, give it an aroma of success, gratitude, and happiness.

So where does a vision come from, you might ask? Well, for me, it came from me asking someone where they wanted to be in five years. Funnily enough, I didn't have a five-year plan myself. When they asked me what mine was, I had to be creative and fast. I felt dishonest asking someone for a plan I didn't have myself. Though what I said is what I still want today, I knew all along, yet I had never said it out aloud. I spent some time and did some real research on goals. I wanted to understand if there were any benefits to setting goals and achieving what we set out to do from now till then. I realized while doing this research that I was achieving goals. By doing the actual inspections of what a goal is, I created a goal during the process. I set myself a goal to set a six-month, twelve-month, two-year, three-year, and five-year goal.

I then used these goals as discussion points during interviews that I went to for the next couple of years. It's now become a basis of why I move to a new role because my end goal is to achieve or attain a certain position. To achieve that, I need to move into roles that will give me exposure to certain elements that will support my career advancement. As of recently, though, I had a goal that conflicted with this goal, I wanted work-life balance, and things in my personal life changed. My focus shifted to a family with children. My focus required reanalysis.

Although I have conflicting goals, what is important, is that still, I can achieve all of the things in my life that I put my mind to. Yes, I might have a goal that is now the priority, but it doesn't mean I cannot have both. It just depends on when I want it. Sometimes people think that if they change their mind or a situation gets in the way, it's all over red rover. But that is far from the case. If I remember people I have developed, I recall them stating their greatest achievement in their lives was becoming a parent. If that is their greatest achievement, and I can achieve that myself, I will only be stronger. And the position I am aiming for might end up being easier to obtain than it would have been if that was my only focus.

Life changes. Things change. What is important is that we are flexible. A vision is where we want to end up, what we want to be, breathe it in and out, and live in that moment when we think about it. There are always obstacles in life, and accepting this at face value will make your planning so much stronger. In project management, change is considered "scope creep," where what was initially indicated as the plan has now crept out of where it should have been. Scope creep is planned for yet not completely controllable—it is anticipated. Much like when you set yourself goals, you need to set some specific, tangible goals, but fluid ones, that can be perceived in several ways. So that when you think you are at a point where you deserve ticking that box, then make that decision and do so.

It sounds strange, but I find it invigorating when I tick a box to show that I have completed something that I have put my mind to. Sometimes even when it has come about by chance, somehow, I feel like the stars have aligned, and I have achieved something by my focus. It is good to keep a record of this so that you can look back and see how much you've achieved in a short period.

Your vision can also come from someone else. You don't necessarily have all of the answers. It could be that you see someone in your workplace, family, or on television doing great things in their life. You could mirror them and look at what they are doing. You might take their template and use it as your own. I have always considered that someone who copies another person considers them as someone who's in a place where they know what they want. No one copies another person so that it would disadvantage them. "What is the difference between the smart man and the wise man? The difference is, the smart man learns from his own mistakes. Whereas the wise man learns from the mistakes of the smart man." (Tucic, 2016)

You can start from scratch. You might have an idea based on your family environment and friends as to what you aspire to in your future. Your personal and professional vision will come from anything and everything. If you are like a sponge, don't deflect but absorb from around you, I guarantee that you will achieve many things in your life. People, even those who don't know what they want in life, still achieve great results. We all do. What is important is tracking what you have achieved and writing down the things you want to achieve. What I want you to do is list down your goals. If you don't have them, then think of someone that inspires you. They don't have to be a personal mentor. But is there someone on television, or a parent or friend? Do you aspire to be Batman? Now that is a stretch, but even Batman has goals, cleaning up the streets of Gotham, perhaps? This takes careful time and planning. Each day the streets need a presence. He doesn't necessarily need to fix things every day. By the fact that he exists, and people know he does, he makes a difference. Have you had a boss in the past who you didn't know if they did anything, but just somehow, when they were around, the business ran?

Get a piece of paper, or use your computer or phone. What do you consider to be your most important thing in life? Are you at university? Are you working a job where you desperately want to get promoted? Think of your top goal right now and use it to map out the below. You shouldn't spend more than ten minutes filling this in, but if you'd like, you could spend more time on this—that's your decision. They should be a stretch while still achievable within the time available.

My six-month goal is... twelve-month goal is... two-year goal is... three-year goal is... five-year goal...

Now, if that was painful, remember, like all things in life, the more we do it, the less onerous it becomes. A goal or vision without emotion and passion are just words on a page. If you want to be a leader, you need to want it. You have to want it. If you see someone else who is successful and think they have it made, it doesn't necessarily mean that it will be right for you. When I spoke previously about mirroring someone, what I didn't touch on was that you need to have a shared perspective of that person. Wanting what someone else has is good, but it needs to fit you and who you are.

Add A Bit Of Passion

Having a drive is the second step of achieving your goals. First of all, having a vision is stage one. If you are emotionally connected to something, you will do anything you can, above all odds, to achieve or obtain what you hold so tightly in your mind or heart. You have seen it yourself when someone is at a gym, and they are doing the bare minimum, the results are very low. But when you put your heart and soul into it, you can see the intensity level. You even burn fat from using your mind. In return, your body releases endorphins, which are peptides that activate the body's opiate receptors, causing an analgesic effect. The same goes for achieving your goals. Your goals are the stepping stones toward achieving your vision.

I need to clear this up. Your vision must continue to be in front of you. If you complete your vision, you will, in essence, lose your sight. The reason it is called a vision is that you can see it in front of you. There is a reason why we continue to seek out self-development, the gym, diets, health and fitness. We always want more. We want to continue to grow. No matter who we are, it is a basic human function to continue to develop. You can see it yourself when you get into something, and you feel like you are going nowhere. It's tragic, but when you think about fundamental human needs, if you are solid and going nowhere, it's the essence of complete consistency. You can't go wrong, can you? Of course, you can, because we always want for more than we have now. You hear about the rich getting richer, don't you?

I find that fulfilment comes from a complete package when it comes to goal setting and defining, or at least working on my vision in life. The package consists of setting your goals, monitoring your goals, aligning yourself and refocusing on your goals, reviewing your progress, adjusting your milestones, and rewarding yourself for your goals you complete. I will go into greater detail on these in the final chapter. But goal setting is not just about the actual achievement itself but the journey and the package that makes up the entirety of the journey. Much the same as your vision, we are here. Now, there is no time machine to jump us to the future. We only have our mind, which gives us the ability to imagine what could be, and although we can dream about it day in and day out, we have to live our lives in each moment, which comprises each second. I think the goal is a by-product of the journey you set yourself. Each moment of your life is the greatest happiness you can experience.

It is very easy to say this, but it is also very hard to do so. I struggle with finding fulfilment in every single moment, sometimes I rush forward to the end goal, and when I get there, it's a letdown. What I have become effective at, though, is continually reminding myself to appreciate the moment for what it's worth. I think it's part of age, but it also comes down to your focus. When you seek it out, it comes about—much the same as reminding yourself to appreciate the little things in your life. In my diary for the whole year, I have listed on each page what is my day's biggest success, the greatest challenge, and the top three goals I have achieved.

These together provide a daily package of what I believe to be my best success which can be a personal achievement or professional, along with a challenge I have overcome which has been the biggest issue of the day, and listing the things that I achieve each day. If you were to track ten days like this and look back, you would see much progress. You would see how much you and most people achieve. And I cannot stress enough how important it is to reflect on your achievements. I review my week each Friday. I look at my work week and see what I have achieved. If I don't see a large number of tick boxes, I am surprised. Because it is really easy to achieve many things but seeing how much, in fact, we have achieved is a hard feat. I challenge you to take stock each day of the things you conquered, and wake yourself up, that you and I and everyone can achieve great things, and you already do it, but you just don't realize it. And meaning, fulfilment comes from the little steps. It's in each moment of life that you achieve and develop that brings you closer to your goals.

Needs

What are our needs? In his 1943 article "A Theory of Human Motivation" in the Psychological Review, Abraham Maslow identified a hierarchy for human needs. The bottom of the pyramid is the basic human physical requirements, such as food, water, shelter, and rest. The next tier is safety pertaining to our security and safety level in our lives, whether at work or home, financial or emotional. The next tier is friends, family, lovers, and those we use as a support network. The next tier is our psychological esteem or feeling of accomplishment, gratitude, and worth for what we have done or will do. The final tier is our vision, what we want to achieve, what we think ourselves to be. Self-actualization is the psychological want to be what we aspire to be.

The largest human requirements, the things that keep us alive at the bottom of the pyramid, require constant renewal and replenishment. And although they are the biggest factors to the physical human existence, they hold a lot less weight in retrospect to the top of the pyramid, yet they hold the least requirement from a physical human survival. But being the smallest in the pyramid, it has the heaviest level of gravity. If we do not actualize ourselves, we will find despair and depression. Even if we are meeting our physical human needs, our psychological state has the potency to destroy our character much easier and more effectively than our basic human needs.

Animals do not have the same level of brain development as humans, this of course isn't hard to see. Our psychological health is more important than our physical health. Because our psychological health can deteriorate our entire physical being if it is not kept in check, we might have the physical capacity to go for a lengthy run, but if we are not motivated to do so, then we won't. The same as a team that plays in a game that has already accepted defeat generally loses. We are easily able to self-defeat ourselves before we have even run the race. Our psychology is very important, and what we think determines what we do. Our bodies, in essence, are vessels. Our minds are the harbingers and deciders of what the body will do.

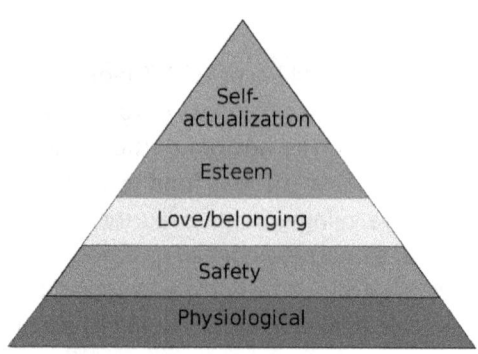

Maslow's hierarchy of needs is a good tool to show the level of gravity that each need has, yet the volume it holds does not necessarily include its importance. Doing things that benefit our bodies is important, but feeding the mind is a much more important factor, and understanding this is important. If you think of a task that you don't like doing, the more you say how hard it is, the harder it gets. But when you fight this feeling and do the task, it is easier than we had anticipated. Our mind is a barrier, and turning our mind, arguing with ourselves is important to overcoming even our thoughts and barriers. Your greatest enemy is yourself because only you can decide what or how you will feel.

If you can harness your mind, and we will over the course of this book, you will be more aware of yourself, your needs, and who you can be so that you can overcome great things. Look at the great many people who compete in the Paralympics, people who have overcome great physical battles have also overcome even greater psychological battles. The battle of the mind and the ability to overcome it takes great personal strength. This strength comes from our core values, the things that make us who we are. Overcoming our psychology is a commitment to becoming better every day. You cannot stop the bad thoughts, but what you can do is find ways to overcome them every day.

Your vision is not without its challenges. There is no easy way to achieving great things. Nor should there be. You would not appreciate the daylight without the night-time. Nor would you appreciate the magnitude of your achievements if you hadn't overcome great obstacles.

Core Values

Your vision is who you are. It's who you aspire to become or where you want to be. But if you live by your set of values, you are already there. You just can't be in it just yet. Because it's in your headlights, you're on your way to it. Sometimes we are already there, everyone around us can see it, but we cannot. We don't want to become stagnant. We continually aspire to more. Once we have reached a certain level, our drive pushes us to the next level. As I mentioned before, the rich get richer. This touches on fulfilment as well as you continue to drive forward. People in this world could stop working tomorrow and still have enough money to last ten lifetimes. But then why do they continue to work to get richer?

Because of their vision, their mindset is to continue to grow, and for some people, that is financial. There is no level at which you cannot earn anymore. There is no system like a game where you reach the top cash flow, and it stops. We can continue until they create a new number to define the amount of money some people aspire to. We will touch later on the unrelenting need for fulfilment. But know right now that a vision must comply with your set values. Generally, these are predetermined in the foundation of your childhood, they can change, but normally speaking, they are ingrained in us through our nature and nurture.

Your Core Values are what you have at the core of who you are. Your values make up the what, how, and why of what you are and what you will become. Our values are not just words on a page. They are what we are made up of. When you ask a friend what they think of another person, they might say, He is quite honest, or He is quite dishonest. That is a person's value, and whether it is true or not, it is a part of their character. If you have ever called someone very passionate, this is a value. This is part of what makes them up as a person. Consider your values. What do you think people would say your values were? Are there any values you don't think you have, yet you think you would like to have them? Let's discuss this later, but firstly, consider what values you have. Do they align with your life vision? If you think you don't have a vision, you're wrong because you do, and you just don't know it yet. Whether you have realized it or not, our nature determines a pathway. Our nurture decides which way we walk it.

You have a vision, you just might not know it yet, and your vision must comply with who you are, what you want, and how you will achieve it. Don't feel hopeless if you lose sight of your goals and vision. We all hit a slump. If our lives were only on the upward spiral, we would never appreciate the hard times for what they were worth. We wouldn't see the great challenges that we could overcome and learn from. The hard times bring out the best in the good times of our lives. And it is always the hard times that we reflect with friends on what we went through to get to where we are now. Whether you are in them now, or they are around the corner. Know that all things come to pass.

Where does a vision come from? From you, from those around you, from your environment, from everything. If you are sightless, don't worry. Just by seeking out this book, you are already setting yourself a foundation. If you haven't found your vision or aren't setting the paving for your vision by the end of this book, then I still wouldn't be worried because it is there. You just don't see it yet. Again, just by reading this book, you are setting yourself some clear expectations. This book and others like it are part of self-development. Your want, your need to develop, is an emotional connection, and it will drive you toward your goals any which way.

Now that I have a good appreciation of my own personal vision and my goals in life, I believe that I have helped others with finding their own. Since that first development conversation with one of my employees, I have helped many people to set goals that would set the foundation to work toward achieving their vision. By understanding my own vision, writing my goals, and enacting them, I now have the experience to be able to help others achieve their goals, as well as my own. I have learned so much more from listening to my employees and colleagues on what they want and what they have achieved, and how they did it. I've even changed my approach to things in my own goal setting based on these conversations.

The takeaway is that it is important to understand yourself, your character, and what you want in life. And an effective way of doing this is listening to others about themselves. You will find consistency in what they think about themselves and in how you feel about yourself. And if you see someone who has got it all figured out, then mirror them, and meld what they do to how you would like it done instead. There are no set criteria for what you want in life, you might think that there is, but you determine your fate, you determine who you are, regardless of how you are perceived, what you think and feel that matters most.

Because it is you who has to live with you for every waking moment of your life, so make sure it's what you want for yourself. Consider what you and other people have failed to find what you want. If someone else has a nice car, is that what you really want? Maybe living in the country debt-free is what you really want. Enact your vision by living and breathing what you want every single day.

Section Four – The Wrap-Up

To learn to walk, a child must first learn to fall. We all start from somewhere, and it is our experiences and challenges that we have overcome or will overcome that make us who we are. It is our differences in a group that makes us strong. It is the differences that we bring to the table that makes working as a leader or in a group as a collaborator exciting.

The ideal hyper-care stage is when we have been given ample time to learn the so-called ropes and given enough support to develop into a strong leader. But much like my own circumstances, I was put into a sink or swim situation, and I would suggest that it is often the case for most leaders. In my favor, I made it, and I think it has made me all the better. But for others, it has the chance to really punish or test them, even beyond their bounds. Leaders are not meant to be the same, and we, or they, all operate in different capacities. To come out the same would be a misconception of the realities of human nature.

The basic building blocks are essential parts of all of our character, but in researching body language, conditioning, Observational learning and empathy you will find out more about the things that we all do, yet we are so unaware of them. That what makes us different, what makes us special is so unknown to people, we just accept someone as they are without understanding the motivation behind it all. It is the want to understand more about ourselves and those around us that develops the emotional intelligence that is important to a leader. Being aware of ourselves and others is critical to the learning journey of a future leader and your ability to seek out development in those behind, beneath, and around.

We need to ensure that we do not get trapped by thinking that we are ready for the next stage, sometimes you might think that you are ready, but you're just not there yet. It is our responsibility to monitor our own progress and to know when the right time for the next step is to occur. A trap example is when we are performing well and autonomously, but when an issue occurs that isn't familiar, we make the wrong decision, and we feel swamped. When in fact, these are the best learning experiences, when we are out of our depth, most times you will absorb from those around you that are succeeding, even without being aware of it, you will mirror them. Even if you have to step back, I can guarantee you that you will have learned heaps from this experience, and you will be armed for the next occasion.

The most important thing you can do whilst you are in the process of learning is to actively listen. Don't just stop talking and allow them to talk, listen and really take into consideration someone else's experiences and see how they addressed a situation. Try and learn from others and how you can meld it to your own processes. Gathering from a range of sources prepares you for the uncertain, allows you to be aware and responsive to things that most people would find outside of their comfort zones. To be observant of the basic building blocks and do your own research into what they represent. These are the foundations for great leaders, those who have strong emotional intelligence and continue to develop themselves. Once you have a grasp of what they mean, challenge the norm, challenge the perspectives of others. How? By getting people to understand the other side of an argument and teaching them your perspective.

A trap for young players is that they are one-sided. You can see it in the personal afflictions of people. The goal is to get them to broaden their horizons and take stock of both sides of the conversation, but this takes time. There is no quick solution. And time, seemingly if you cannot give time, they, or we will seek direction from influences around them or us, what is important is that conflict seeks to bring about resolution. Try and learn to change people's perspectives by testing your skills.

Exercise: Consider who in your team or environment you are in the process of mentoring or teaching. Take a few moments and write down their top three strengths and their top three weaknesses. Now write down beside each weakness what you have observed are their failings in these areas. Now write down simply what you have been doing to help them in these areas. Now consider this, have you taken the time to speak with this person or persons about these weaknesses and directly advised them that you have been working with them on improving these areas? Transparent communication gives the person an indication of your focus areas for them, and if successful. the person will seek you out when they have made errors in these areas and tell you what they have done to fix it. This may not always be the case, but there are results in having these one-on-one conversations with your people. This must, though, be considered with empathy. The last thing I would want is someone coming to me telling me all of my issues and that they will fix them for me. If you don't feel ready for this stage, just do the exercise on paper but leave the person until you think you have the support and familiarity or confidence to do as such.

Chapter <II> - When to Flip the Switch

"Be of your word, for it is all that you have when you speak."

(Niven, 2017)

Introduction

In this chapter, the discussion will be relative to when we are ready for that next step. What is the next step? Is when someone is ready to progress out of hyper-care. Is it that we know that we are ready to take the next step in our careers? Maybe the biggest question is if someone is ready for the next stage, how do we identify that correlation between ready and untested, as such, the appearance of being ready when not faced with major challenges. What I mean by this is that when someone is not tested by many different challenges, issues, or errors, they lack those experiences, and dependent on the person's role, certain challenges may not be met until later in their career.

How do we prepare ourselves for the next stage? How do we provoke ourselves to make the necessary errors during the guidance or 'learn to walk' stage so that we can move onto the next stages? I think the most important thing we can do is to identify what we want to achieve during our journey. When we know this, we are ready for the next stage. It is important that it is prepared and timed. If it is rushed, the decision is not made on enough merit. The onus is on ourselves to ensure that we are tested prior to moving on.

The transition between phases can seem abrupt. We can feel as though people give us the cold shoulder. The familiarity of comfort and support is being taken away. We feel as though we are being punished or have done something wrong. This stage is important as it makes us strive to impress those whom we get support, and we try over-communicating to try and get some admiration. But the flip of the switch is designed to test us, see how we react to change. The reality of life is that the people around us that we learn from can move on and never come back, so the onus is on ourselves to learn on our own merits. And to use this as an opportunity to teach others during and after this stage.

When we are given the opportunity, the overall success is based on your input, and that will give people around you an appreciation of your output. If we expect the people around us to do what we must do ourselves, to do more of their work, we will surely stay in limbo, potentially in decline, with the chance that we will fail to achieve and pursue our goals effectively. If you want to succeed, get used to doing it yourself because in life, we have the guidance and the lanes that we can work within, but only we have the arms that swim the lane.

Section One – When Opportunity Is Thrust Upon Us

I recall an example when my site manager had just resigned, mostly because he was pressured enough that he "made a choice" to move on. In this instance, I heard that my managing director was flying to the site to have a discussion with the team. I remember the fear—my palms sweating—I felt as though I was next on the chopping block. Much like you see in the movies when the boss goes, *The rest of you go with him*, and they start clean. In the weeks preceding this day, the site manager then was telling me that the site was losing money. That our jobs were at risk, that the site couldn't make money and that they expected the impossible.

I sat nervously watching the front of the site for a car to make an entry through the front gates. The minutes felt like hours, and the hours felt like days. I stared into the space at the front of the parking lot, waiting. Fear, in my opinion, is counterproductive. Although I have been advised the opposite by other colleagues but take it as you may. A car began to drive into the car park from the front gate. My heart rate doubled in a matter of milliseconds. My thoughts began to race, and I started to prepare myself mentally for my next job. The car pulled slowly into the car space and docked. It felt like a long time for someone to get out of their car. I could see through the front screen the person in the car was on the phone and continued to sit there for many minutes.

I looked to my site manager, who had his hands in the air and was pacing back and forth in his office. His annoyance or fear was with us all. It translated from the boss to us. It was a shared feeling. We all felt the angst of our leader. The car door opened, and we watched as the site manager sat in his seat and started to browse his screen, looking for a way to distract himself.

A large presence entered the front access to the building—a tall, wide-shouldered man with silver hair and a strong facial expression. He opened the front door and entered the main room where we all sat. In a low tone, the man asked, "How are we all?" To which we all responded in unison with a warm but concerned welcome. The man was the company owner, a man who held himself with such confidence that you knew he was of importance. He was a man sure that he could seal any deal. He was so passionate about his business that it came across as ruthlessness against those who would cause him harm or that of his business.

His presence filled the room as he greeted each of us. He paid no attention to the site manager. My empathy for my boss was in full force. I could feel his angst from being ignored. He was cornered in his office, and the managing director was parading around him with leisure. The MD spoke with each of us in detail about our weekends and what we had been up to recently. After his parade, he set his sights on the site manager. He grabbed his overnight pack and wheeled it into his office, closed the door behind him with a thud, and sat directly opposite the site manager.

We expected a blaring rage and that both parties would begin screaming at each other. But the opposite happened, the managing director spoke, and we could hear him through the walls, more the tones of his voice than the actual words. But we could feel what was going on. The MD was in control of this conversation. The site manager thought he had control by resigning.

This situation showed me that not all battles are won through hostility. This is something that I respect—to take control of a situation and not be the loudest, but the most strategic. I had no understanding of what it meant to be strategic at the time.

The conversation between the two continued for some time. Then the MD stood and left the room, walking out into the warehouse floor. The site manager walked past me and said, "Be careful of these guys, they will sell you the dream, but they will screw you over." I had no idea what he meant at that time. I was confused by why he was telling me this. The site manager proceeded to the front door with the state manager. They were emptying the company car that was given to him.

When Opportunity Comes

After the MD's walkthrough, he requested that I go upstairs and have a conversation with him and the state manager. He was casually sitting in the board room upstairs while I sat with an almost army upright seated position. He asked me about where I would like to be and where I saw myself. Midway through my story, he interjected and said that he would give me twenty thousand dollars extra and the company car if I take over as the site manager. The MD said he believed in me and that a manager from Queensland would become my mentor.

The conversation felt like it was a lifetime before it was over. I remember sitting in the board room expecting that I wouldn't have a job any longer. My palms were sweating, and even though I tried my best to be confident, the two men that were with me could sense my nerves. Experience in the game gives you a greater sense of a person's feelings in a situation, and in this situation, *they had me pegged.*

I recall saying that I would need to talk with my father (whom I was living with at the time) and that I would need the evening to make my decision. This is something I have never said, I was always reactive, but for some reason, I was so fearful of the job. The words that the previous site manager said to me made me contemplate the role. The MD said he would return in the morning for my decision. That night after work, I returned home and told my brother and my father. They supported my decision. I was going to accept but wanted to know more information about the role. I was unable to have a good sleep that night. My thoughts continued to be my worst enemy.

"Take aim higher than the mark, not to reach by their strength or arrow to so great a height, but to be able with the aid of so high an aim to hit the mark they wish to reach." (Machiavelli, 1532, p. 30)

The next morning came, I was in the main thoroughfare of the warehouse. The MD came to me and asked, "Have you made your decision?" I said that I had considered it last night, and he interjected and said, "Good because I asked payroll last night to have your pay changed and the car put into your name." I didn't even get to say what I was going to say, he was not taking no for an answer, and I didn't resist. I accepted, regardless of my queries or of what I was going to say. The MD, satisfied with the decision, left and headed to the airport, leaving me stunned by what had just occurred.

The MD instinctually knew, beyond awareness for others, he was by nature or nurture someone who knew that I was the man for the job, I might have been the only person there that could do the job due to so many other site managers failing, and yet I was still there. But that was because my first ever mentor brought me through my hyper-care. And when it stopped, I was onto the next stage, which was the time to stand up for myself or be stuck wanting help from everyone around me. This being one of the hardest times in my entire life, professionally and personally since my job, was my life at this point in my life.

Deciding On Yes or No

I think that a driving factor in the success of us all is belief—what it means when someone believes in you. Take a moment and think of someone who believes in you. Now think to yourself, why?

I would think that it would be because they care about you, and if someone cares about you, they will invest time into you. And if your mentor is someone who is investing time in you, then consider them someone who cares for you. And if they care for you, well, I am sure that they believe in you. If I can take you back a moment to when my MD essentially made me take on the role. I didn't know it then, but he believed in me, in what I had done previously, and in some instinctual way, knew I had what it would take to achieve the role.

This was a fast-tracked opportunity for growth. Others may end up with an easier career start and can become complacent. As such, they will make natural progress and grow over an extended timeline. In my example and past, I was given the fast track. I can see now that a lot of what I did was less focused on quality and more on putting out spot fires and quantity. My role now is about quality, so I have ground out the areas where it was required. There is no right or wrong way of things being done, but what is most effective is dependent on the participant and how they engross themselves in the change.

This is not the best example of the time to flip the switch, as some people can sink, and then the entire plan falls to pieces. This is how some people flourish—they persevere through struggles.

Almost everyone has the drive to have better than what they have or have had before. We continue to aspire to greatness. I don't think anyone reading this aspires to lose money, get into debt, fall out of love and feel disappointment. There is the unrelenting need for fulfilment when someone continues to attempt to achieve better than before, the continual drive for better than the current situation. In my situation, I was at a point where I didn't know I was ready for the next experience, but I recall a couple of months after this, when we started to achieve some great results, we turned the business around. But I wanted more. I couldn't suffice with what I had. I needed more. The normality became boring. And so, we sought new clients. We looked at different work with existing clients. And so, we took on a great many services. But I learned from this, I rushed into this and took on more than I could physically work with, the revenue was great, but I had realized I had bitten off more than I could chew.

But I learned a great deal from this. The greatest benefit of failing is that you will have learned from the experience.

Learning From This

When have you had a massive opportunity thrust upon you? I am sure we have had a time where we have either raised to the occasion or kicked ourselves for not giving it a shot. But when you did rise up and failed, what do you tell yourself? I won't be doing that again. In essence, you have learned a great deal from this experience. You know the situation you fell for, and next time you will either be more prepared or able to deflect and attain fulfilment elsewhere. Even if you accept every time and fail, I bet you each time you have learned something from it, haven't you?

I know that I continue to say yes to a lot of things that I don't know the answers to, but I seek them out, and in return, I teach them what information is newly acquired. I think I forget more than I have learned, and sometimes I relearn things that I had thought I knew a lot about. These are all opportunities. When someone asks you to do something, next time, if you don't know the answer, try and ask for clarification about their question. You might find they will answer the question themselves. If they ask you what something means, why not question them and ask what they think it means themselves and try and work it out together. It's not always the case, but sometimes someone will ask you a question about something they know, but they are self-conscious and ask the 'dumb' question to reinforce themselves.

You even do it yourself without realizing it. I am sure you have asked someone a question about something you are doing, you know the answer, but for some reason, you don't know the answer until someone actually confirms it back to you. You will also find that these situations bring about opportunities. The more people can rely on you, the more things people will throw at you. Embrace it. It's an opportunity to better yourself and learn more about anything and everything. It was the same in the case with my MD, who already knew my answer before I told him. Although this was partly coercion, it was also something I knew in advance. The body language and aura that I presented in that conversation with him was enough of an answer as any.

That is why in chapter one, I speak about the basic building blocks. A critical factor in how you present yourself is in your body language.

Have you ever seen when someone is talking, and the other person has their body turned, and they are nodding profusely? They sharply answer with, "Yep, ah. Yep, okay." They are trying to get out of the conversation, or they are busy. Some people just cannot see this, and they continue to wage war on their ear until they finally get away. Understanding body language is very important as a leader as you can determine who is comfortable and in what situations. Now the standard crossed arms theory of 'that person is closed off' doesn't work effectively. It's interesting to see the most prevalent body language during a conversation is mirroring. Next board meeting or group conversation you have, look at the body language of each of the people. If you see a couple of people who are talking or listening, if they are all consistently crossing their arms, you will find that they are mirroring each other. Why do we mirror people? Because we have a connection with them, like the wise man and smart man, we learn from the best in the group, or as best as possible.

What we need to understand is each other. Once you understand someone, you can pick up on their 'tells' you will know that a certain type of body language is representative of their mood. It is very hard to mask our body language, and generally, our body language gives us away. It is so very hard to fake. The most obvious feeling is when someone is uncomfortable, you have even experienced it yourself, you sit in a seat, and you continue to pull your phone out and look at it. Generally, you have no messages, and you are caught up on everything, so you put your phone away again. Then you shuffle in your seat, cross your legs, uncross them, pull out your phone, look around at people and do it in repeat. You feel like everyone is looking at you, and the more you try to hide your nerves, the more it shows.

There are two sides to the coin. There is the perception of what you represent and how people perceive that image of you. And how you perceive yourself, and what persona or mask you put out for people to view and what you think it represents.

Section Two – Perception is Reality

A phrase I heard continually throughout the time I worked with one of my previous managers was: Perception is reality. That the way in which people perceive you is generally something that they see in you or about you. Something that people find hard to deal with is that they can be perceived in many ways, such ways that are not benefiting their own perceived characteristics. I have told many people since, that if they are perceived a certain way, that there must be some truth in it, and even if there isn't, if the outside world thinks that, then this is you. Then the only person that disagrees is you, so what is reality?

This is a concept that a lot of people find hard to understand and deal with. No matter who you are or where you come from, someone at some point in their life will perceive you in a way that you will not appreciate. The perception concept is a good one to use to direct and meld yourself into a better leader. If you are perceived to be lazy or not pulling your weight, people seem to gossip, and the rumor mill generally comes around in strides. When it comes back to you in one way or another, this is an opportunity for you to learn that the way you are perceived is something you need to manage.

Generally, a perception is blown beyond the actual event starting as simply as the person is on their personal phone when people are around. The perception could be that the person is always on their personal phone and is seldom working. How do we manage this perception? Is it that you need to be mindful of your surroundings? I say yes, mainly because I said it. But think about this. The way in which we act or project ourselves around people changes, so wouldn't it be reasonable that as a leader, the expectation is that you lead by example. It is not so simple to say that other people do it. The expectation is that a future leader is more aware of their surroundings and if they really want to achieve better than they have, grow or step aside.

People will either want to be you, be around you or tear you down and see your weaknesses and proclaim to people that you are, in fact, mortal. This is excessive, but people are self-conscious, and if you show weakness, people will take advantage, and can you blame them? We are always looking out for an opportunity ourselves to progress, so this in itself is an opportunity. So never give other people the opportunity to tear you down. As a leader, you must display all of the greatest characteristics that people desire. You don't hear people say to a leader that, "Ah, it's ok, you don't need to set the standard," whereas you will continue to hear, "You need to set a good example, don't let them see you doing that."

I have had people I have mentored and led who had found their anger in these issues—being outward and blaming the issue or perception on those around. The root cause is the self. As a leader people are attuned, people don't always have the best intentions for others at heart, and as humans, we are the jealous type. As a successful leader, you must learn to manage your perceptions and understand which battles need to be fought and on what grounds they need to be contested.

A good example of managing perceptions is the life of a Prime Minister, the perception, generally, is that they are open to all opinions and that they must lead the nation without emotion. Focus on what the people want, not what they need. But the reality is that the responsibility of the role is to focus on what we need and give what the people of the nation want without sacrificing what they need and then show the people that the leader is balancing everything equally. The media, being the perception changer, can change the opinions of people in just one to two short sentences.

There is a clear difference between the word or direction of a military leader as compared to a politician. As a military leader, your followers are regimented and will follow the direction, normally with little objection. Whereas in the position of a politician, everyone has their own agendas and representations. In that, there is a large area for misdirection and continual politicking. It is easy to see a top politician as misguided or unable to make a clear stance from the public eye, but in reality, it is no easy job. The same goes for the private industry, we are paid for our job or output, but there are areas that can be maneuvered for each individual's own goals. The way in which we perceive our situations, the autonomy we are given, or sometimes a poor leader's inability to manage their time and as such you are given the absence of their exposure. It will affect the way in which you see people that are relative or similar to your current leadership.

"My own definition of leadership is this: the capacity and the will to rally men and women to a common purpose and the character which inspires confidence." (Field Marshal Bernard Montgomery, n.d.)

The Make of Different Leaders

Why is it important to understand that there are differences between the types of leadership styles? Because no one leader can be the same, in each establishment or industry sector, different leadership is required. We are molded by the environment that we are within. We are all leaders in different scenarios, and it is important to take this into consideration when we perceive someone in a certain way. I know I have seen some of my previous leaders as weak, but when I have really understood what they were doing, they were in a position where they were unable to make a decisive change and just being there was the crux of their position. This is just one example, but I am sure you had had a boss before that you didn't get along with, but when they moved on, you found that you lost their counsel and their presence in certain situations. Perception is the basis of a leader's success, whether we believe it or not, how we are perceived will affect our future prospects, and it is a hard road to revert to our once-great stance in people's minds if we have fallen from grace, as it may be perceived.

I like to use the term perception swaps. Where you can be polarized in just a few visions. I am sure you had seen it before when you greatly appreciated someone's opinion, but at some point, someone tells you that they have been speaking behind your back. This goes one of two ways, you either take the benefit of the doubt and consider before judging or getting agitated to go speak with the direct source. But the general way that most people deal with this situation is to start to get on the defensive, you start to question this person's integrity, and it clouds your judgment. The same as a significant political figure on the television—this comes down to who's opinions you trust.

I use the example of George W. Bush, who was portrayed by the media as a baffling moron. For years my brothers and I would watch the news, and when they showed him, they showed events where he just made a fool of himself. I couldn't believe that this man could run the largest empire in the world. I recall any conversation where politics would come up. I would shake my head and laugh when he was in charge. But not until many years later did I actually challenge myself on my opinion of that leadership style. I thought more about it and questioned whether someone whom I had thought was dumb could make it into a high-powered role such as being the president.

I watched a documentary on body language, *Secrets of Body Language,* which showed a different side of the former president. It showed where the media had made him look silly, such as walking the wrong way around a path to get to the Russian president. Now every other leader followed the same path, so naturally, the media portrayed him as confused and incompetent. He walked around the path to get onto the other side of the other president, which opened my eyes. When they took the photo from the press, he stood on the other side of him and had his hand in a dominant position in front of the other man. To the untrained eye, it was nothing.

I was impressed. What was perceived as stupidity was actually a cunning ploy to disarm or change the power position of both these men. What this made me realize is that while the basic building blocks are critical to each leader, we aren't great at them all. In this case, Bush had a keen idea, and he used a simple plan and body language to support this. In the early term of his administration, he relied heavily on his cabinet as you don't need to be great at everything. As a leader, he excelled in certain areas whilst his cabinet made up for the other areas of expertise to create a complete package. There were other sources I reviewed, but this really shook up my understanding of perceptions.

What it did do was make me question what was being put in front of me every day on the news. I even questioned how I had perceived certain events and how they could have been flipped around. This was a good example of how there was an agenda presenting a picture and story to me, and rather than considering possible alternatives. I took it at face value. A good leader needs to be aware of possible biases and try and understand both sides of each story. And much like the basic building blocks, not only through this book but other sources will a retrospective understanding come about. If he could have improved how he was perceived, maybe the whole world would see a different leader. Again, perception is reality.

Changing Perceptions

Taking all of this in, how would you or I do it better? By knowing how you are perceived means, you have the ability to make changes to improve this view from others. Awareness is a success factor in the ability to influence how you are perceived.

Where does this ability to change perceptions come from? Is this something that people are just born with, or is it that they are taught through vast knowledge or experience? That leads to the nature vs. nurture debate. There is no definitive answer as to which is right. In my opinion (I am an enthusiast behavioral theorist), it is a combination of both. The nature theory is based on genetics and the assessment that people's personalities and traits are predetermined at birth. The nurture theory is based on the person's environment and influences during their life that makes them who they are.

"In all my years of research and dealing with violent offenders. I've never yet come across one who came from a good background and functional, supportive family." (Douglas, 2017, p. 408)

How does this relate to the business world? Well, we have all had a bad manager at one point or another in our career, right? I believe that although we are predetermined with certain genetics, those of our parents, how we act, and our values are driven by our family environment in the majority of cases.

When I talk with new leaders, I always ask them to refer to their personal life achievements. When you ask people what they have achieved in their lives, rather than in business, people are more passionate, rightly so. But what this does is draws from their personal achievements and gives an outlet into their work environment. A good example is when a person states that their greatest achievement in life is the birth of one of their children. What does this show? Is it patience, resilience, a level of selflessness, and commitment? To have a child is a huge feat, one which requires a lot of work. Generally, there is a need for the man to support the wife during the process, before and after. Now, how it is described in their achievement also gives away other details. The person will explain the struggles, but what is most important is for all the struggles, they appreciate the good and the bad. You can also help direct them to be this way. Translating this perspective from a personal achievement into business is the key to creating a professional passion and ability to transfer their skills into other components of their life.

Now you might ask, why am I using an example from a serial killer book? Because these are people who are on the very opposite end of the scale. A well-documented series of cases to provide realistic behavioral perspective or predetermination. Our actions are generally reactions. We react based on our circumstances. In some cases, people will provide a bad event as their greatest achievement because they got through it and learned from it. That is important for you on this journey to understand that almost anything is translatable. It is your responsibility to find your life goals and try to translate them from personal achievements to career strengths. Where do the strengths from your personal goals come through into your work life? That is your job to help create translations. If you have someone who is supporting you now or you are supporting someone, ask them how the greatest life events can assist you in a working capacity, and another perspective gives you more options.

With that in mind, sometimes it is your responsibility to learn from your leader, manager, or people around you in two ways, one in which you learn from the examples of a mentor or people around you, and sometimes to learn from their words. Not always will you learn by the actions of these people or people you surround yourself with. You may hear the theories from these people and, as such, apply them in instances that suit you. People think that you must always lead by example and that the example you set is what must be applied. But a true leader understands that you will best learn what is most relevant to yourself, rather than following blindly in the footsteps of the people that are around you. Yes, you will be influenced, but what interests you most will be what you follow suit on the most and the best applicability to your situation.

Much the same as every person goes through their own childhood, if we reflect on some of our personality traits, where did we get them from? I can recall times where my mother would say, "Your father used to do the same thing," or, "You remind me of your father when you do that." There are many cases in life where we are referred to as being similar to someone else. As such, what we learn in our early life, generally shines through the remainder of our lives. Much the same as in our early career life, a lot of our habits continue to shine through. That is why the stages of development are so important to ensure that you are given every opportunity to succeed, on the best timeline that suits your development pathway, you set your times, you set how you want to learn. It's easy to change things if it isn't going your way, walk away, don't quit, just know when it's time to walk away.

Something's Got to Stick

Drawing back to our perceptions, much like those when we are referred to as being similar to someone else, the perception of who we are sticks. As they say, *if you throw enough mud, eventually something sticks.* How we are perceived also has the potential to make or break our professional persona, sometimes prior to someone meeting us, they have an image in their head of who you are, based on how you are perceived by others. So, it is important that you focus enough attention on the perception theory.

"Perception is reality." (Hayes, 2014)

My manager was very aware of the teachings of this statement. That perception is what makes you, or at least how you are perceived and can bring you down emotionally and professionally. This is teaching. The perception of my manager was not in the same position that he stipulated to others as to where it should be. That is to say that he told me to portray myself a certain way, yet he struggled himself with his own portrayal, but regardless the lesson still has much value. It is much easier to point out the areas where someone else can improve. On self-reflection, though, it is hard to change ourselves. That takes a lot of effort and time.

What I am trying to get you to understand in this section is that although we might speak of something, we don't always follow the pathway of what we have said. And that is not to say that someone is who speaks like this is a hypocrite. What it shows is that the theories behind what people say can be applied in different instances. And are not always relevant, but it is our ability to actualize theory in the practical that most benefits our situations. So, these theories are great, but they need to be applied to your current situation to better you.

What does that mean? It means that theory is not everything, and practical actions do not make up everything. It is the combination of the two that makes a good leader. A theory provides support to the practical activity. The old way of thinking is that practical activity is the best way forward, but the good leader is able to identify the most beneficial way forward. There is no one way to do anything. People get stuck in their train of thought and think that there is one best way to conduct themselves. Be mindful that achieving anything can take many approaches. A good leader is persistent and perseveres.

"Obstacles can't stop you. Problems can't stop you. Only you can stop you." (Gitomer, 2015)

A really important point for everyone to understand, and this comes down to perceptions, is that when you size someone up, don't just consider who they are and their individual attributes. A 'trap for young players,' it is foolish to think that just because someone is weaker than you, that they cannot overpower you in many other ways. A good example of this is when you consider a person that seems small and weak (and this can be physically or mentally proposed). You just don't know whom they associate with. Their friends or business colleagues might hold considerable might. And in times of trouble, their allies become your enemies. Much the same as when war breaks out across the globe. Leaders of the 'allied nations' are influenced to support each other as a united front. So, it is ineffective to think that when you pick a fight with someone that they won't call in for backup. You just don't know who is around the nearest corner.

Section Three – What Does Our Body Language Mean?

In the next conversation that you are in, consider your own body language. Look at the next three conversations you have with different people. Try with your boss, colleague, wife, husband, partner, or employee. Try and see how you position yourself. I had previous employees film me when I had presented in front of a large crowd. After reviewing the video footage, I saw that I was agitated, moving around, I seemed confident, but someone who was analysing me would be able to see I was nervous. My exterior was a mask trying to permeate a level of confidence that just wasn't there. I saw that I was talking quite rapidly, and my words were getting mixed together. But it wasn't all bad. I had thought that it was a lot worse than I saw on playback. I actually learned from this situation. The next time I presented, I had a cue card with only a couple of words on it. It forced me to focus on the key points.

When you are speaking with someone that you are close to, and you think they have done a good job, next time you talk with them, give them a pat on the shoulder. I am sure if you think back, there was a time where someone said something to you, and they patted you on the shoulder. I can guarantee that in that instant, you felt invigorated, that you had a close personal connection. As humans, our greatest way to be empathic to another person is through our touch. Why do we love to hug each other so much? It releases oxytocin through our pituitary gland, lowering both our heart rates and our cortisol levels. Comfort is linked to our touch. Try it next time when you are with someone. If you are congratulating them for something they have achieved, finish it off with a pat on their shoulder, and you will find a better result.

What about when you are speaking with your boss, have you sat at the other end of the desk and your employer had the layer of the desk, computer, and other items, you can already see it. A layer between the two of you, now you might have a great relationship, but the layer creates distance. The separation creates a professional puppeteer relationship. Whether it is intended or not, there is a truth to this—a cover that identifies you as two different persons in an office. But I recommend that you try getting your boss to sit with you but without the barrier between the two of you. You will find that you will cross your legs either out of comfort or as a protective layer in replacement of the desk. You will sit across from each other without the desk covering you both, and you will find a different feeling as part of the conversation. I have changed how I am in my office. I put my desk against the far wall and leave the middle of my office completely open. From there, I sit with my fellow managers, and I find the conversations to be more open and transparent. This is in part because of who I am but also because of what I surround myself with. The more you practice and associate yourself with things that are similar to whom you want to be or how you want to present, the more your behavior and personality are reinforced.

Now before we go on, it needs to also be understood that you can take from these situations a form of deception. My brother says, "All forms of communication are deceptions." He wasn't completely wrong. In some way, shape, or form, we are all influencing each other's decisions. Look at sales. It is to sell something that will benefit them, and of course, in return yourself. I consider this to be true in respect of understanding, that we must look at all situations from all sides of the story. It is nice to have, but don't feel like you are deceiving someone. The reason I add this in is that there are people who are malicious and that will use these techniques to manipulate. There is much power in understanding these techniques and being aware of how they can be used in different situations. Being aware or observant of your surroundings is important.

When you next have a conversation with your partner, consider your body language. If they have their arms crossed, try crossing them too, but subtly, of course. You will find that the more you mirror your partner, the more open they will be to you unless they realize what you are doing. Then you will find the opposite. But if you can get the formula right, you will find a more open and meaningful conversation. When two people are attuned and mirroring each other, it shows that there is comfort, trust, and a form of respect for one another. Sometimes it can be envy that you want to be like that person, you think it, but your body is more outward in its representation. This is also a part of empathy where we show our level of interaction during the conversation. The more mirroring, the more the connection. Now it is important to understand that you shouldn't use your body language to manipulate your partner. Empathy and your body language should be natural when you are at home. But it is useful to understand that you can influence anyone in your life. From a professional capacity, social or home, but it is not recommended. It is just good practice outside of a work environment.

What is most important is that you understand your body language and that of those around you. If you look at your partner, you might pick up on some nonverbal cues that you hadn't seen before. When you spoke about your sports and the things you like, but you know they don't, you can see they are looking around the room, not super attentive. But in retrospect, when they talk about their passions, I can assure you that you do the same. So, what you can learn from this, is maybe when you are annoyed, they haven't listened, think about a time or the next time they talk about their likes, maybe try to be a bit more attentive. I guarantee that you will see a difference in their reception of your ideas next time.

Use Experiences You Can Control

Consider someone that you know well. When you look at them when they tell you something dishonest, you somehow just know, don't you? Next time this happens, just take a step back and look at their body language. I will use my brother as an example. Every time he tells a lie, or if he is caught out for it, he yawns and says, "Anyway," and runs his hand down his face along the bridge of his nose. I did a bit of research on tells that people have, and what is most important about a person's body language is the pattern of behavior. It comes in threes, if you see someone yawn, it doesn't necessarily mean they are lying, but if you see the same pattern for the type of event you think it is, it has more merit. It goes the same for each one of these things occurring at different times. I would suggest that if you see these in isolation, don't discredit them, but first of all, take the situation into perspective.

With body language, you can articulate what a person is almost thinking. There are some people out there that can naturally read a person's body language without ever having to study it. These are sometimes what we consider the confident men. But if you're like me and you have to study to understand things better, it's a large amount of us in this together. When you go into another meeting, and you see someone react in a certain way, in your notebook, just write down the situation, potentially the emotion and their body language. Next time it occurs, do the same. I can be certain that you will notice a pattern of behavior. Like I mentioned before, it comes in a series of events, they don't necessarily have to be in exact order, but the patterns are much harder to hide as it is a natural expression. Body language is something that is very hard to change if it is passive, meaning, without us being completely aware of every movement we make, we outwardly present feelings without even realizing we are doing so.

Why is this important? You also have patterns of behavior. Even without realizing it, you give off signs when you do things. Nonverbal cues give away your position many times throughout the day. If you asked someone who knew you well if they knew when you were lying, I bet you they would say, "Oh, because when you lie, you look around the room," or, "Well, you scrunch up your face a bit." Or there could be one hundred other ways, but what is important to understand is we all display our emotions one way or another. Now it's not about suppressing our emotions because we are aware of them. It is about channeling them the best way we can. And that means that we will always express ourselves one way or another, but how they are perceived is equally important. A large part of our perception is how we portray ourselves, and nonverbal expression, I would say, is the largest. You can say a thousand words in a single shrug of the shoulders, that is, to the right person. Familiarity is also essential to understand the patterns of people's behavior.

As a leader, how we present ourselves makes a substantial difference to those that are around us. Confidence and arrogance sit on a line close to each other. When you see a manager or person that you think is of importance, you see them walk in confidently, shoulders back, standing tall, and seem to walk with a sense of purpose. Have you seen other people walk around quite the opposite? Your level of appreciation for them deteriorates, right? They might actually be a harder worker than the other person, but again it's about the perception. The body language of a person emits whom they are without even having to say a word. First impressions are hard to break, and since we are such a visual society and human race, it's hard to get away from this.

You must teach people about their body language, use yourself as an example to show them how you have reflected inwards. They will also respect that you are willing to give something away to them as part of the learning experience.

Discipline is a daily requirement

Leaders must be disciplined to make certain that they exhibit only the types of behavior they want others to pick up. The bad characteristics are what gets picked up, so discipline is essential. This goes hand in hand with body language. The way we dress, walk and present ourselves sets the standard for everyone around us. I am sure that you will have a time where you have come into work a bit more casually, and everyone has picked up on it? I know that from Monday to Friday each and every week, I try my best to ensure I present myself as a confident professional. But sometimes, on a Friday when I need a moment of space away from this, I wear more casual clothes, and people make mention the moment I walk into work. Their first comments are, 'what's with the casual wear?' and many other comments. If it were someone else, it wouldn't really be a second thought, but people put their leaders under a microscope. They want to see the best and worst in them. It's the same as when you see a brand-new car, and you squint just to spot the minor scratch or rip in the upholstery.

We look for imperfections. Nothing is perfect, we all know this, but there is a belief in our heads that our leaders must be perfect. I've had a meeting with a client before, I had my site manager standing beside me, and the customer would only look at me. It was a bit embarrassing. Although, it's not uncommon in my current environment. And with my eyes, I try to look over at my colleague so as to direct the client to look over at my colleague. Then I turned my feet toward my colleague. I directed my body toward this person. It still didn't work. I then mirrored my colleague. I copied their stance and slowly their posture. Noticeably, the client started to look between us both, and I had included my colleague in the conversation more actively. Unbeknownst to them, I had influenced them but also provided them with no option but to include both of us in the conversation. The reason for this was because of the familiarity between myself and the client.

And it wouldn't have just been about body language. It sometimes is position and title. The person wants to talk with the person who makes the final decision, and with that, they direct all of their attention toward that one person. But in this situation, I made them nonverbally realize that there are more people in this conversation, and I respect the person I am with; therefore, my decision will be collaborative. Subconsciously the person included us both because I had directed them where I wanted them to go. This is just one simple example of how being aware of our situations allows us to influence and change the situations around us. What did I get out of this?

I got the underlying respect from my colleague because I am aware, I pointed it out, I'm not super modest, so I made sure they were aware of what was going on. In this situation, once you point it out, you get, "Actually, yeah, I noticed that." Once you make people aware of what they feel at a deeper level, they become observant of the previous experience and learn from it. I also realized just how much influence you can have in situations through some subtle changes to the circumstances. Being aware of your circumstances is a very powerful tool that can be used in a great many ways. And teaching others this is important as they see what you did and can use this technique in future situations.

Mirroring Body Language

I've also found the way in which one of my previous superiors held his pen in his hand. Even years later, I started to mirror that position. I got to the same position as this person, I began to mirror his posture in certain ways. I associated his stance with that position, and when I became a state manager, I started to emulate previously viewed body language. This is part of observational learning, where I have taught myself to be a certain way but stored in my deeper memory bank—where or when I acquired the same position and acted in the same way. The same goes for bad behavior, we've all had a bad manager before, and I am sure you see someone that when they get to this same role, and power gets to their head. Not always, but sometimes it is part of mirroring. The bad habits are emulated and stored in the memory bank for the same position that this person has acquired.

That is why it is critical as leaders to be aware of how we portray ourselves. Our body language expresses our emotions, and it is no easy feat to hide how we feel. In some situations, we have to try our best to mask our stresses or the pressures that we are under to ensure that the people around us see us as strong leaders. The last thing you want people to do is to think you are crumbling as they will start to feel the pressure themselves. A leader must be able to read the situation that is around them and deal accordingly. When you look at World War II heroes, you don't see a timid leader hiding and unable to plan. (You see the ones that survive, that is) that will make decisions, direct their team members, use each person to their greatest strengths, and defy the odds. Now it's not always a war situation where we bring out the best in our people, but it is a good example of the extremes of leadership.

A lot of our communication as a leader is nonverbal. We present all of our emotions in our physical presence, along with our use of gestures, stances, or power poses and our aura.

Section Four – The Wrap Up

A leader must be aware that they will change how they operate in different circumstances. With that, there are many considerations prior to doing so. There is no exact formulation. It is a multitude of theories and practical experience that helps each one of us to make the decision for change. It is a consideration of our circumstances. It may be the change required to get us back on track or to propel our employees or colleagues forward.

Sometimes we can never be ready for when an opportunity is thrown our way, and sometimes people become parents without ever expecting to be. Humans are versatile. We are survivors. I always think of ants when I think of human survival. The location of the ants is determined by the location of the best resources for their communal survival. We move to where there is opportunity, and most of us want to continue to grow. Some of us get a new opportunity just by chance, while some of us seek out these opportunities and grasp them. Wherever we begin and end, we are all given opportunities, and it is our decision whether we take them or leave them. What is important is being aware of the best possible situations and choosing what suits your situation best. Luck or chance is when preparation meets opportunity.

Being aware requires us to be aware of our personality and abilities. We have to be understanding of how people see us and how we are perceived. When people say that first impressions matter, they really do. I have had conversations in the past where someone might refer back to when they met me and how they thought I was something that I wasn't. Perception, which was discussed previously, is a big factor. Because your perception has the ability to precede you, if you have a reputation, you are perceived to be a certain way. Even when you first walk into a room, the way you dress says something about you straight away. When you meet and shake hands, if someone nearly breaks your hand, it tells you a bit about them. I've found, though, sometimes people present themselves a certain way as they are making up for their own lack or perceived lack of control.

When people get in their safety blanket, of our own control, we tend to always take it for granted. When you move from hyper-care to the next stage, there is a big gap to fill, a lot of learning that is lacking, and there is an expectation that we will always have to rely on our safety blanket. This falls within the realm of our control. Much of the time, people that are in control are level-headed, but when they break down, their mean side can come out, and they cling to whatever control or lack of control they can get.

This is not always the case. I have had previous people I have mentored who became lazy. When given the opportunity to move forward, they would step backward. I felt poorly, thinking that I had failed the person and that my advice wasn't working. But as part of my own learning, I realized that I must continue to put the work on my pupil. Their ultimate success or failure is heavily reliant on them, not on me. My role is to provide support and the basis of theory to help them with their role in their development. It's very hard to let go of your control, even when it is on the development of someone you have a good level of oversight on. But letting go has its benefits. You get to see if the relationship is one-sided.

What you should take out of this chapter is that a successful leader is one who is aware of his or her surroundings and presents a persona of whom we want people to see of us. If you act with confidence, you will find that more than likely, people will treat you as a confident person. If you slouch and talk to the ground, expect people to feel taller and superior in your presence. How you portray yourself is how you are perceived. We all have the capability to change how we are seen. Our body language is a big part of this. Just look at yourself in a mirror and raise your arms out wide, feel wider?

Exercise: Write down what opportunities you have been given recently. What did you do? The example could be the same as a night you went out with a friend anticipating a quiet night, which then turned out to be one of the best nights of your life. Does saying yes to an opportunity make it all that much better, that you have grasped the situation and made the best out of it? What did you think after this situation? Did you want to do it again next time? Also, consider a time when you took on an opportunity, and it blew up in your face. Did you think that next time you will be more hesitant? Write down a good story and a bad story where you have learned from each situation. I can assure you that in each situation, you have learned something that has made you more resilient and the ability to identify these situations makes you stronger and stronger. Now write.

Chapter <III> - Tough Love

> "Sometimes it is better to have lost in love than to have never loved at all." (Tennyson, 1861)

Introduction

What is tough love and how it allows us to understand that we need to rapidly take up the slack, there is no longer a grace period. If we cannot deal with this tough stage, we will not be able to rise above it.

"That men ought either to be well treated or crushed, because they can avenge themselves of lighter injuries, of more serious ones they cannot; therefore, the injury that is to be done to a man ought to be of such a kind that one does not stand in fear of revenge." (Machiavelli, 1532, p. 9)

This is such an example of how people need to be tested, pushed to their boundaries, but not always the case do we need to break someone down. We cannot brutalize our people. Guidance requires a level of care and a form of empathy with the person. To truly call one's self a leader, we must know that we are not perfect, but we want them to be, and it is the unwavering expectation that we set upon them and ourselves that drives us all to want for more.

An effective leader is not one who operates in isolation. When a leader operates as part of a group, that leader and the members of that group develop each other. As the saying goes: "Two heads are better than one." The same goes for leadership practices. It is important that new leaders understand the importance of developing their own circle of safety or being a part of one. A circle of safety is a system of trust developed by each of its members.

"Only when we feel we are in a Circle of Safety will we pull together as a unified team, better able to survive and thrive regardless of the conditions outside" (Sinek, 2014, p. TBA)

I will also draw a connection between a leader's determination and resilience that I believe is a pivotal success factor for a leader's journey. These two activities are each supported by the other. These are part of our emotional intelligence as a leader. To experience first-hand pressure is the way to develop resilience which is improved more so by being forged in fire and to be at the coal face. Being in a position where you give it everything, and yet you just cannot climb your way out of the problem. Resilience teaches you to have thicker skin, bounce the problems off to a certain extent, and focus on what is most important.

"You will continue to suffer if you have an emotional reaction to everything... True power is sitting back and observing everything with logic. If words control you, that means everyone else can control you. Breathe and allow things to pass." (Bruce Lee, N/A)

Note that resilience is when you go beyond your level of toughness. Toughness is your skin, sometimes physical, but it is the layer before you cut into resilience. Resilience is your emotional strength to persevere once you have gone beyond your limits.

There are many times in my career where I have continued to fight the battle and continued to get nowhere until I finally gained resilience and held out long enough to determine the cause and really focus on what will stop the problems. Because fighting the fire builds your resilience, and your resilience stems the fire from where it first starts.

What this chapter focuses on is the development stage, where we find that we need to begin to rely on our own abilities. At this stage, we could have had a mentor who has left our lives, moved away, had a falling out, or in the intention of this chapter, the mentor has identified that this time now is the best time to give the participant the opportunity to rely on their own judgment. The ideals that we initially expected of our teachers or support network and the way in which we as leaders present ourselves are the drivers of ourselves and people. It will come one day at some stage, and if we are able, it is good to be dropped cold, which allows us to sink or swim in this environment. A hard stage for us all to learn to take a step back and allow things to come to pass, to learn to swing, without your push.

"Risks are learning opportunities, and you will see a variance as a window into possible new directions and unforeseen benefits." (Govindarajan, 2016, p. 41)

Section One – Through the haze into the fog

"In order to mold his people. God often has to melt them." (Amish Proverb, n.d.)

If you can understand that a deer in headlights can also be the way in which a leader is visualized, then you can understand that in order for someone to learn to become something more than they currently are, they need to be brought down to be lifted back up again.

It's not always as easy to think that every person goes through the stages of their journey without any kind of trouble or conflict. With the consideration that we could be halfway through our journey and if we bring them back to phase one of their journeys. We could affect, improve or stunt their progress toward their goals.

An interesting consideration of this was one presented by Myamoto Musashi. The case is where a university professor meets with a famous Zen Master to learn the way of Zen. While the master quietly served the tea, the professor talked about his notions of Zen. The master poured the visitor's cup to the brim and then kept pouring. The professor watched the overflowing cup until he could no longer restrain himself. "It's full! No more will go in!" the professor blurted. "This is you," the master replied, "How can I show you Zen unless you first empty your cup." (Musashi, 1645, p. 8)

The Desire to Be Better

The purpose of this is to show that sometimes we build ourselves or others up so much that we consider ourselves as our best selves. A concept I consider one of my strengths, alongside one of my weaknesses, is the predilection of self. This is the idea that we, or in this case, I, want to be better than I am, always, and in everything, I do I want the best and better result possible. But it comes at a price that I continue to question myself. I even question my values at times which is a dangerous area to be.

In the best interest of becoming better, if that is something you so desire, here is a point to consider. We cannot go into a conversation wanting to learn, with preconceptions in our mind, nor the feeling that we already know more than the person we are asking the questions of. We have all done it, and in different social situations, we have misread or over anticipated our level of understanding, only to find out we knew not that much all along.

A part of a leader is to understand what it is to doubt oneself. If we think we know too much already, we have already stopped learning. And this happens along the journey. Much truth is in the saying, "Pride comes before the fall." (Proverbs 16:18, B.C). This is an essential part of the learning journey. We all have bouts of exuberance, where we liken to being overconfident. Dogmatism is a concept that people somehow introduce into their leadership when they get influenced by others along their journey. To be dogmatic is to be completely invested in your own ideas and that it's either your way or the highway. We've all seen managers like that, set in their ways and sure and steadfast that their way is the only way to do it.

In a prior role, we tried to get our projects across, but it just didn't have the engagement of the people working in operation. We engaged with our national improvement manager to try and figure out a more productive and inclusive way of planning. We came to the decision to roll out an 'ideas board.' The ideas board was designed to be visual, in a location that all of the employees could see throughout the day, along with it being designed to take their ideas and roll them out. Of course, there would be some ideas that would be silly or that weren't to be taken seriously, but the ideas that some people put in are generated from years of annoyance, and the people doing the job are able to identify the problems that sometimes are never raised, and they just continue to work day in and day out, without ever raising them.

The ideas board was designed using the similar style of the "Kanban" design by Taiichi Ohno whilst working at Toyota. The board is a visual management tool used to show the progress of small, medium, and large projects. The use of this board is only limited by the user. Involvement is a big part of leadership, dogmatism may be effective for some areas of an operation, but I haven't found somewhere that it is effective. I have found in my travels that the most effective leadership style is one that is open and transparent whilst being firm but fair. Visual management boards are just another way to express transparency to the people that you work with. There are many other ways to do this, such as consultation groups which is another form of collaboration. Whichever way you choose to go, what is most important is that you are not dogmatic. You will find that people shut down or provide only the information that they think they want to hear when dealing with this type of leadership.

I have had plenty of dogmatic leaders, and I would only present ideas or concepts that fit their selection criteria. I didn't go outside of that spectrum, nor did I keep them informed on things I was working on if it was contrary to what I would think they would approve of. Dogmatism stifles inventiveness, and to expect that people will keep you informed is based upon your ability to create a two-way communication. If you are transparent, people will mirror you and also, in some way or facet, be transparent with you.

Being Retrospective

It is important that, as leaders, we consider all aspects of an argument or concept. I have fallen for a concept and driven it all the way till I realized that it only benefitted the objective of others' self-interests and not for the good of the group. This is not to say that a portion of dogmatism is not good quality, but everything must be utilized in moderation. I continue to visualize a parental figure using this term against me in my youth.

As leaders, we cannot always be loved for all our decisions. Sometimes it is our responsibility to make the hard decisions, and not everyone wins in the end. But that is not to say we are dogmatic. If we have factored in the components of each person, sometimes the correct decision is our own. But our decisions need to be made with respect to all considerations from all parties. What is misunderstood is that many bad leaders make decisions without understanding the ramifications of their actions, without consideration of those whose opinions matter. The difference between a manager and leader isn't always clear to many. That is the poor part of dogmatism.

Leaders who make decisions without consultation do not understand what their actions mean, and even if, in the end, the activity brings great success to them and everyone around. In the case where it doesn't, the leader is the one who is ultimately responsible. As the saying goes, Heavy is the head that wears the crown This is not to say that if you understand all points of contention that you will always be successful. What it means is that we are then more informed and able to make decisions that make more sense to the grand scheme of things. When you make a decision without all the facts in place, when you decide blindly and a guess is not really a good reason to fall on your sword. I know if it were me, I would much prefer to have decided with all the facts at my disposal than to have guessed and covered my eyes when I fired the shot.

This is part of the concept of empathy. *"Empathy often is defined as an emotional reaction elicited by and congruent with another's emotional state or condition."* (Eisenberg & Fabes, 1999)

Empathy is akin to the concept of awareness of others, which is linked to emotional intelligence. A leader doesn't always decide solely based on the statistics. A good leader is able to decipher all the corresponding information, then make an informed decision. Not all decision-making is based on the weighing of the evidence in favor of one side. Sometimes information that is presented to us is ambiguous and directed to achieve the desired outcome.

Such an example is when I have been presented with financial savings for a major project I was leading. I have seen the weighing of the data go against what my plans were. But I skewed the information (within boundaries and remaining ethical) to show favor for the result I was trying to achieve. My manager at the time, a leader adept at problem-solving and cutting through the ambiguity of information, challenged what I presented. Without knowing the details, he could realize that something wasn't right.

It's funny because this same manager was someone to whom I continued to give feedback. I would say that he needed to improve his levels of empathy. That the way he came across to his employees showed a lack of empathy. But in reflection, what I understand from this experience, is that empathy comes in varying degrees. Each leader has a different quality of empathy. That is why every leader can operate at different levels of an organizational structure. There is no one person who can do everything. It's a physical and emotional impossibility.

Empathy doesn't necessarily require a leader to share due care for everyone to the maximum level at every moment of every day. What a good leader can do is understand the right level of empathy for the role that they fulfill. In a supervisor's role I had, I worked as a contractor on behalf of the Australian Defense Force. Something might I add that I was very proud to be doing. A warrant officer said to me during a conversation, "Which leader would you rather follow into battle? The one whom you know cares for how you are feeling? Or the one who will make the hard decisions? Get you and your buddies out and, in the end, make the right decisions for the best of the group." Well, I am sure we all know the answer to this question.

I had the opportunity to interview a Senior Military Officer. I asked him, "What are the top three things that make up your style of leadership?"

He answered, "I think if you treat people the way you want to be treated (don't be a knob), you go a long way to achieving good outcomes. From there, I think the other two things that define my leadership style are humor and humility."

Who Has All the Answers?

Sometimes as leaders, we think that people just want the right answer out of us, and that is all. A good leader can give the answer that is best for the organization or group. Empathy goes beyond the surface level of a simple 'yes or no' answer. Most people respect a leader who decides based on all the facts and communicates truthfully to the person. At face value, the leader will face angst. But a good leader will remain true to their answer and provide a transparent response.

People look to a leader to provide them with the answers. No one in their right mind expects that they will get their way all the time. This would only be the case for people who have had a certain type of upbringing or dogmatic people. But that is the exception rather than normality. What we must do as a leader is we must emit versatility in everything. A good leader is someone who doesn't act as if they know everything, but someone who has many avenues to acquire that said information. A leader who celebrates the expertise of his or her people is one that people will see as a leader who doesn't take the credit for things (not all the time). This type of leader is one who refers to their people as keys to solutions, and a good leader will rely upon and trust their team.

How do we learn, and continue to learn, even when we know so much? Well, in my opinion, I think it comes down to a level of respect. If you respect that you are not always the smartest in the group, that there are others that you will rely on, but maybe what the leader has is their determination, you already have the advantage. There is always going to be someone better than us at something. But where we make up for this is in our determination to grow from every experience, learn, and share our own knowledge. If we can learn from those around us, appreciating their best qualities, we have the capacity to become versatile by the sheer fact that we are able to refer to them for information that is required.

Something I remind those around me is that no one is perfect, but a good leader is someone who learns the good qualities from those around them. The bad qualities are things that we need to keep away from, but to understand what not to do. If we are aware, I mean contemplating and continually assess those and the situations around us, we can take stock and absorb information. We should aspire to greatness, but it is important to understand that to be perfect is to be a failure because perfect doesn't exist. And if we set ourselves a goal that is impossible, we will continue to fail. The more we fail, the more we either grow, but in this circumstance, the more likely we are to become tired of failure and find a way to improve. It is important to realize that we must continue to aspire to the best. It is the same as in my operations, and the site was always immaculate. Although I was never content with it, it always had something that needed fixing. But this unrelenting desire for me continued to impress visitors. They would see the site as a well-oiled machine.

Leadership, when I close my eyes and visualize it: I'm in the center of a circle with my team surrounding me. There are links between us all, not just from me to each one of them individually, but all of us are linked to each other. An effective team works between each of its members. The leader is part of the communication process but is not the be-all and end-all. A leader that is aware of what their role really is empowers their people and considers them as equals in the decision-making process. Ultimately the accountability of the decision falls with the leader, but the responsibility is on each member of the team.

This is not to say that all leader roles happen this way. This is just my interpretation of what I have based my career on, and it has worked so far. Being a good leader also requires a consistent approach toward change. We must embrace it. Change will always be.

"Go and open the door. Maybe outside, there's a tree, or a wood, a garden, or a magic city. Go and open the door. Maybe a dog's rummaging. Maybe you'll see a face, or an eye, or the picture of a picture. Go and open the door. If there's a fog, it will clear. Go and open the door. Even if there's only the darkness ticking, even if there's only the hollow wind, even if nothing is there, go and open the door. At least there'll be a draught." (Miroslav, 2006)

When we become complacent, time passes us by, and we lose our advantage. As previously noted, our advantage is determination. To be determined requires a commitment to one's self to continue to work toward the best results that one can obtain and beyond. To remain determined, we must remain resilient.

"More than education, more than experience, more than training, a person's level of resilience will determine who succeeds and who fails." (Coutu, 2018, p. 9)

Sometimes lacking or worn-down resilience is part of the reason why we become complacent. We cannot be our best every day. We as people need to have a strong support network within our bounds to help us maintain the best of who we are on the worst of days.

Sometimes Moving on Is Best

I had the worst career three months of my life, and I recall saying to Eva, my wife, at least we haven't had any personal tragedies in our lives. Surprisingly that very next morning, at 3-am Eva found out that her grandmother had passed away. Well, what a surprise it was to us. Understandably Eva and her family were distraught. Many weeks afterward, we both laughed our heads off. It was laughing that almost seemed completely crazy. We looked at each other and just couldn't stop laughing. Once the laughing gas had worn off, we both spoke about this moment. We had realized that we had gone through so much, and what matter most in our lives was this, that we could weather the storm and continue on. We both decided in our lives that we would find roles that would focus on the work-life balance, more focus on our family. We both were at this current stage earning great money, and we could afford anything that we wanted. But what we both wanted was to be with our families, and that money didn't mean what we thought it should mean to us. We laughed because we realized we had gone off course. We laughed because we knew we could fix it easily. I think we also laughed just because of the connection and the moment we had together.

Our security was making sure we could afford to pay the mortgage and enjoy going on holiday, but all the extra money was just being burnt away. By the lack of time we both had with our families, we ended up spending most of our money on dinner every night. We got some enjoyment, but what fulfills us the most is time with our family, not the money or the dinner that we ate. These moments are many, but the time we have with our families is important.

I remember waking at three in the morning every day, crying on the way to work, shaking with stress, and feeling more and more hopeless every day. When I had come to a moment in a day where nothing had gone wrong, I stared at my phone, waiting for the next problem. And it came, constantly, all at once and all day from early morning to late evening Monday to Friday. This was the most extreme career pain I had ever felt, but along with it, it started to affect my family, my life. I would go home and only talk of work until I passed out on the couch. Waking up, struggling to bed, and waking up again at three in the morning with thoughts racing about what I will do at work that day, knowing all of the problems I hadn't fixed from the day before. I was so exhausted I couldn't even get out of bed. I just laid there.

I put up with it for three months until my wife agreed with me, and we both told our bosses it was time to move on. I felt such a release, all of my friends said they could just see a completely different person. We both had become very resilient, but it had only lasted as long as it could. There are only so many things that we can put up with. I was very lucky that my friends and family were very supportive. But it was easy for them to say, "Just leave." I had two mortgages, and we were in the process of trying to have a child—what a great time to add having no job. I had to be smart about it all. Time went on, and it finally broke me. I couldn't take the work pain that was, in turn, affecting my personal life. I had stopped reading, training, running, building, creating, and I had stopped all of the things that fulfilled me.

I had to eliminate the one thing that was causing all of this—my current role. That way, I could continue to advance my life in the direction I promised I would in January. What I had to do was walk away, not quit, and do what was most important in my life at that time. To be resilient doesn't just mean to put up with things and hope they go away. My resilience was my ability to determine when I had enough and that change had to come. I am not against change, but the circumstances required me to hold on till a certain point. I don't think that resilience means putting up with the norm. Part of resilience is being able enough to make a change, to decide that things need to change on your terms, not someone else's. I said to myself, no more sleepless nights, it's not worth it, it's time to push back on myself, to make myself aware that I would not take it anymore.

I am someone who is very caring and am not one to give up or do the old, *'I don't care.'* But I do envy some people who are able to just switch off at any stage. This is something even I haven't achieved yet. Your resilience is based on where you want it to be. Do you want to be someone that just doesn't care? And right now, you do, well, you've got to change a lot of things in both your life and career. You cannot achieve things without either changing the way you approach situations or being flexible to other solutions.

Sometimes making a change, not so drastic as my situation, but it is all relative and is an important individual decision to make. You need to decide if you need to change things in order to achieve your personal and professional goals. Don't just think you have to do something. Nothing in your life is. You decide what you do. If it all becomes too much, you can even jump on a plane. The world is so large you could disappear and never be found again.

When you think of the size of our world—our galaxy—we are so small, so the choices in your life, when you put them into perspective, just doesn't mean that much. That's not to say that we should just stop caring or give up, but when you think about the small things in life that people make out to be such an issue, if you really put it into perspective, you get over it. And as a leader, you must help your people to understand that their *'big problems'* might be easier solved by taking a moment to size up the problem from the perspective of what really matters.

You Decide What

If you defy the odds by your mindset, you can achieve and feel amazing for what you have done. Malala Yousafzai, a young girl, defied the Taliban in Pakistan and demanded that girls be allowed to receive an education after she was thrown out of her class. Malala was shot in the head by a Taliban gunman in 2012 when they were looking for her on a bus, yet she defied the odds and survived. In 2014, she became the youngest person to receive the Nobel Peace Prize, and in 2013, she gave a speech at the United Nations and published her first book, *I Am Malala*. Don't give up. Think about your circumstances and find a way to do what it is that makes you happy. Malala is an advocate for the education of those that are denied their right to learn equally. Do what makes you proud to live and breathe each moment of your life.

In contrast, it is you who decides what affects you. It's easier in hindsight, I must say. But it is important to realize that what is happening in your situation, by comparison, could be nothing compared to another person's situation. It's not to downplay what you have going on, but it's more of an appreciation for your situation, that you can overcome anything, because many times, even before your life, someone has already done it themselves. There are many great examples of people who have defied the world and overcome great things, to have been resilient and undertaken tasks that defied logic. If you put your mind and body into a situation, you are bound to overcome grand tasks. But It is to be on your terms.

What makes you happy? When you achieve something, what makes you feel fulfilled? Grab your diary or a pen and paper and write out what makes you happy. Write a time when you have been doing something or finish a task that makes you feel fulfilled? Go no further till you have done this. It's important.

Now having this greater understanding of yourself, think of a situation where you are not feeling your best or that you are not enjoying the task. Is there any way you can include parts of what makes you happy in it? Can you add parts of what makes you feel fulfilled so that each time you do make some progress on the task, it also ticks the boxes of your personal goals? I have a personal habit that I now tick a box next to each task I have completed or delegated. I write a follow-up note in my diary, but I love the feeling of ticking the box. I even look back at yesterday and see the number of crosses and ticks. This is a small thing that gives me some sense of fulfillment that I am achieving my goals.

I would break down large projects I was working on by turning the task into many hundreds of lines that required me to confirm if they were in progress, on hold, doing, or done, and they were color-coded, so once the problem was coming to a good point, there would be more green than red on the graph. By breaking down the project into small pieces, it made it easier to complete each section in isolation, but also, each time I achieve one small feat, I gathered momentum. I would even look to tomorrow's goals and start working on them. I am driven to keep achieving these little milestones. I can turn a project that is challenging into a greater sense of fulfillment, and I am happy when I completed an individual task. I have taught myself to find fulfillment in work tasks that I previously didn't seem to find great enjoyment in completing. Everyone is different.

I even use football, and I would organize my teams into similar positions of a squad I would watch on television. I earmark certain people for 'key' positions because I enjoyed it, was passionate about it, I didn't want it to fail, and I worked harder and enjoyed it even more, when it was successful. When you have a situation where you must do something, try and model your interests and what fulfills you and integrate it into your task. What is important is enjoying the journey. If you are someone who only enjoys something when it is done, then you will set yourself up to fail. If you set yourself a goal to make three million dollars in ten years, and you won't be fulfilled until then. You will not be as happy as you can be. Enjoy the milestones. Each time you get an extra ten thousand, enjoy the moment. It's each step of a stairwell that gets you there. Each step is getting you closer, and that should be celebrated.

If you get stuck in a position where you only want to feel happy when you finally get to your final destination, by the time you reach two million, your goals have changed. You now need to get another one million because of inflation. You will never be happy if you set goals that you think you must achieve to be happy. You need to change and include your happiness and moments that fulfill you in everything you do. No easy task, of course, but throughout this book, we will continue to work on the concept of resilience, dogmatism, and finding meaning in everything that we do. Don't just be happy when you get there, be happy where you are now and each step you take toward your dreams, visions, and missions.

Emotionally you can only feel happy in the present, so find a reason to be happy right now, don't wait till later when you have achieved something. Enjoy each moment of the journey at this moment.

Section Two – Our Journey And The Ecosystem We Must Rely On

We don't do everything in isolation, nor should we. Most of our decisions or reactions are influenced by those around us. We can consider this as the circle of safety. But really, what is a circle of safety? A good example of our circle and its importance can be explained by the following: *"A lion used to prowl about a field in which Four Oxen used to dwell. Many a time, he tried to attack them; but whenever he came near, they turned their tails to one another so that whichever way he approached them, he was met by the horns of one of them. At last, however, they fell a-quarreling among themselves, and each went off to pasture alone in a separate corner of the field. Then the lion attacked them one by one and soon made an end of all four."* (Aesop, 6th Century B.C)

The reliance on other people within your circle of safety is a two-way street. In relationships where someone continues to take but doesn't contribute to the benefit of others will find that this circle of safety will either outgrow them or begin to give advice that is not in the best interest of the parties. It is important to know that, as we continue to talk about leadership, that even when we are seeking advice from others, that we keep our leadership hat on. It is important that we know, no-one has all the answers, certainly not all the right answers. Guidance is discretionary. I mean, how often do you see a manual or work procedure explaining the flow chart of how you must guide or respond to a person. There is none, so if you think the information provided to you is incorrect, revert to the point I make about taking stock of the good, the bad and learning from both aspects.

An added benefit of developing a circle of safety is that each member of the group serves a different function. Much that is referred to in team-building activities is Team Roles. There is Belbin, who developed a system for identifying the members of a team and the ways in which each member can focus on their role whilst also learning parts of each other's role. How is this important? Because for a leader to be successful, we must understand where we sit in the mix of things. Much like the saying goes: Too many cooks spoil the broth—the same goes for leadership. We must understand our alignment in the group.

"For just as each of us has one body with many members, and these members do not all have the same function." (Romans 12:4, B.C)

It is impossible to have no friction in a group. As humans, we are generally trying to achieve the best results in a society where the best applicant is the chosen one. It is not hard to see why we fight amongst ourselves. I have always worked by this saying in this case: Conflict brings about resolution. A good example is this when I was a site manager and had two employees—one which was a truck driver, and the other a forklift driver. On most occasions, each day, the driver would arrive on-site and wait for the forklift driver to unload his truck. The forklift driver would leave the warehouse and drive to the back of the site. He didn't unload the driver's truck and continued on to another task.

I recall the driver coming into my office exclaiming that the forklift driver was racist (the driver was Indian, and the other man was Irish). I shook this accusation off as irrational. I explained that he was given a task and that he was going to complete it. At this moment, the driver was not worried about rationality. After some time, he calmed down, for now at least, and continued his day onwards. At this point, another forklift driver conducted the unloading of the truck. I remember that at that point, I realized that something was building, but I let it play its course.

Conflict Was Brewing

Weeks later, I walked into the warehouse and saw the two of them in each other's faces. At this stage, they were very close to physical action against each other. The whole site at a distance surrounded them. The entire operation ceased to see the display between these two. I walked over to the two of them and stood there whilst they continued to defame each other. I said nothing. I just stood and listened. When the right moment came, I separated them. Luckily at this point, they hadn't thrown any punches yet! I told them both separately to come to my office right away. I escorted them, creating a distance between each of them. They entered the room, and I asked each one of them to sit at opposite ends of each other. This was to allow separation, but there was a tactic to it, long term.

I closed the door behind me, but the office staff watched in awe. They both had their arms crossed, red faces, and very near to pouncing on each other in a fit of rage. With a calm demeanor, I spoke slowly and quietly. They both had to lean forward to hear what I had to say. I pointed to a ball on the table and said that whoever has the ball has the power to talk. I passed the ball over to one of them and allowed them to start. Lucky, I had their respect as this wouldn't work for just anyone. As the first one had the ball and explained his side with exclamation marks, the other without the ball began to defend himself. The one with the ball looked to me to enforce the rule. All I did was nod and acknowledge that there was a breach of process. Then the arguing continued.

After a little bit of time and much yelling, the ball was passed over reluctantly. The other man began his side, and in quick succession, the other man responded without the ball. The man with the ball looked at me, and I followed the same process, nodded, and acknowledged. As the conversation continued, the volume of arguing began to decrease, each of the members started to struggle to yell anymore.

I had a chance now to speak, in that I expressed that they both were right and wrong. What I found was that outside of work, they both had pressures and that they found a tunnel to throw everything into. That tunnel was this one little issue they could direct all their problems at. What I found was that they were now listening to me in a way that they were now part of a group. The three of us had somehow developed a relationship stronger than the moments before we entered the room. What they both did, was be honest with each other, at last. They had vented. In each other, they found they could vent their frustrations.

At the end of the discussion, both men stood and shook hands. they laughed. In their eyes, I could see that they knew that none of what just happened really mattered. What was created was a bond beyond a standard professional cohort. From this day onward, both men continued to argue with each other but with smiles on their faces. They embraced something that I find amazing about Australia, which is the mateship spirit that we have here. It's not a culture that is just made up. It is something that each of us learns from each other. These two men, from two entirely different parts of the world, learned what it means to be mates, to really dig into each other, and be comfortable that their differences are what makes them stronger.

What Makes Things Better

Does yelling at each other really work? Not for most scenarios, and sometimes conflict can cause considerable issues between two parties. In this case, I was lucky as well as aware of the best way to direct these two to find a resolution. I find that people with whom I haven't had conflict are awkward. We haven't really tested our boundaries, and there are feelings that might get hurt if we don't keep within our boundaries. But what are they if we haven't tested them?

It is important for leaders to understand the boundaries of their peers, teams, and those above us in authority. An effective leader is one who is aware—able to guide the team on their path within the boundaries. Doesn't it seem strange that sometimes you talk to someone and you don't get the result you want? But another person can tell you not to worry about it. Moments later, they have made a call, and they tell you that it's been taken care of. It's not always the words that people use, but the relationships they have formed. Every conversation is different, and the way in which we interact with people and the way we come across can change the outcome of that conversation.

To elaborate further, not only can a leader be aware, but peers and employees also, based on respect, will assist the leader to the best of their own abilities. I have had times in the past where I was frustrated as I knew I had to follow something up with my employee, but when I grilled them, they then passed it over to me and said, "Oh, you mean this?" Then they have a smirk, knowing that what I had said was all in vain. Then I smiled and realized that I should have had more faith in them, and that is part of my own learning too. We need to understand that people in our circle are also aware of us. I think they are more attuned to our emotions sometimes than we are. You don't need to study emotions to understand them. Some people have this ability without training, so don't underestimate people's potential.

I think that a good leader is one who continues to question themselves. When we become comfortable, within reason, we tend to let things slide. At a certain point, our perceptions continue to slide, and before we have realized what is going on, it's sometimes too little too late.

"The real world teaches very different lessons, and it takes willful and dedicated ignorance to fail to perceive them." (Chomsky, 2001)

It is so important that as a leader we continue to assess ourselves. Now it is rarely easy to look at the way in which we acted in a situation and tell ourselves that we did a bad job or that we should have done better. But these are the hard thinking decisions great leaders make. But, that's not to say that this is the only way a great leader operates. It is a side of a perspective that I am presenting.

A Mentor or Not

A leader's journey is not explored in isolation. It would be against what a leader is defined as. Although I haven't had a set mentor in my life, what I have is multiple mentor sources. I look at people and think, *What makes them this way?* If I see something I like or something they have achieved because of a characteristic or skill. I seek it out myself and emulate it. I have copied the mannerisms of people I found to be prolific in society, there are certain ways they express themselves using their hands, and so I position myself to do the same. This is not to say that you should just copy everyone, as we ourselves have certain characteristics that people might consciously or unconsciously mirror. What I am saying is if you see someone doing something that is working, and there are good results you can get out of it, well if the way is already paved for you, then why not? Yes, we should aspire to take the road less traveled, but to do this, we must first take the path that leads us to that road. How would we find this road without it either being pointed out to us, or we open our eyes and seek it out?

To give my own perspective on how you can find mentors in the things that you aspire toward:

1. Bernard Montgomery: For always backing himself against unrelenting odds, with a good understanding of what leadership is, and his strength to overcome external enemies whilst maneuvering to get the lead in one of the largest world wars over other competent and aspiring commanders.

2. Winston Churchill: Overcoming great odds, remaining calm in a time of uncertainty of survival, and unrelenting determination in times of great uncertainty.

3. Erwin Rommel: Even when losing, he was a figure of power and strategic mindset, aware of his circumstances and honorable. Use

of the Blitzkrieg for the German army against superior defenses yet found a way around the problem, inventive and determined.

4. Tony Robbins: An aura of energy and excitement, strength & determination.

5. Henry Cavill: Body transformation, charismatic, and brimming with confidence.

A most effective leader is one that draws information from as many sources as possible. You don't need a single source. I have set myself a strict reading goal of reading more than one book per month and grasp the concept of as many different perspectives on leadership. The difference between a book and a movie is that there is so much more time available in a book to explore the depth of characters or the concept of the book. I also use movies and documentaries as sources to draw from, which give a more instantaneous reference. I also read magazines and other publications that interest me. Even subscriptions that don't relate directly to my career or life. I have found gold mines in publications where innovation is sought in a totally different way, and I have flipped this concept into things I do in my life. For example, I was reading a book on the Civil War of America and the tactics used by some of the former generals. Some of these tactics were about the rush and fallback marching. To hit the enemy hard and then retreat, therefore galvanizing the enemy to think that the retreat needs to be chased so that their armies rear can be broken, turning it into a trap where the enemy is caught.

Much the same as in negotiations where I have come in hard with my point, then quickly dropped my numbers to a point where the client has anticipated a great win for themselves. What I had done in this circumstance was to set my target number at the retreat value, showing a deck of cards that were not true. They then quickly rushed to agree at the lower level expecting that they had won, but in fact, I had placed them right where I wanted them. I wouldn't say it is deceptive, but what I would say is I have used a completely different reference to model my own tactics. I used a source from war and included it in my negotiation strategy. Everything can be used as a learning experience, so make sure you seek out every opportunity.

I had the opportunity of interviewing another senior military leader.

Question: Single most challenging leadership or management decision you have made?

Answer: *"Tough question. In general terms, trying to keep the team focused on border protection activities, which was the government's highest priority. When you don't necessarily agree with that direction, it's a challenge, particularly when you have been at sea for an excess of forty days. You still have to maintain the focus of everyone and ensure that you remain genuine, even though you might question some of the intension of the core objective."*

The Constant Development Cycles

If I am learning from other people, then maybe they are learning from me. As a leader, it is important to continue to grow and develop ourselves, and especially those around us. If we don't grow, then we stunt the growth of everyone within our inner circle. Jealousy is also a great tool, with the right mix of self-awareness to push people to become better or have things similar to people we are jealous of. If you see someone start a new job and are boasting about how good it is to be on so much money, you might, in return, look at how they achieved the new role, you may ask them questions and try and see if you can do the same. There is a potential there to mirror some of their strategies and acquire a better outcome for yourself. Much the same as people in your circle will rise up around you, unconsciously we lift or lower with the people we associate with.

"Friends that don't help you climb will want you to crawl. Your friends will stretch your vision or choke your dream." (Colin Powell, 2017)

Whom we associate with determines who we are, or at least categorizes what or who we stand for. You will hear throughout your career that when you are wearing a company uniform that you represent that brand. If you work for yourself, you also represent either your own company or personal brand. Essentially the company is paying money to market its brand on you, so you are a walking banner for the company. The media continues to find sources of people having brawls in bars and tagging it as *such and such company* abusing someone. It makes headlines, but we are associated, and the company then has to make a statement to rescind their actions and call for legal action. But the damage is done the perception is portrayed. Don't join a company or a group that has conflicting values because it will either grind you or bend you to change your values for your association.

Do you think you will get on with someone who is a liar when you believe that honesty and transparency are some of the most important aspects of a leader? Our ecosystem, or our associations, will create conflict, no one is completely the same, and it's our differences that make us better, but our differences, if too extravagant, can also cause conflict, disagreement, and dissolution of our group. A good leader understands, though, the strengths and weaknesses of each member of the group. Sometimes the issues we have with people we associate can be channeled or taught to be used or identified differently. For example, I had in a previous business one of the members of the group who was grumpy, had a short fuse, and didn't value add as much as we wanted him to. I also had a member who was quite junior. What I did was present to the older gentleman that I would need his guidance and experience to assist the newer member in a project that would benefit them both. I put them both in the same office, got them to work together on some projects, and I continued to remind the older gentleman that he was directly supporting the improvement of the junior.

In this case, it worked quite well. He took this well, feeling invited to be a mentor and giving him the opportunity to give more tasks to the junior team member, therefore giving him more time to do less. It was a win for us both, and I got to have the junior learn so much in a short period of time by having the older man focus his time on the junior. His normal attitude wasn't noticed as much. I had other employees come to me and say, "He's been really good, lately, hasn't he?" *and, "Wow, hasn't John been different?"* Sometimes when we are channeled down a different path, without even realizing it, we slowly meld into each other's styles.

I remember a situation where I was with the team, but the junior member wasn't there. I was notified of something he had to follow up to which I responded that I would follow it up with him. The older man said to me, "Greg, leave it with me. I'll go have a chat with him. I've got this." I was very impressed, to say the least. The man had taken the responsibility of the junior in the part of his development and identified that there were things that he could do to divert his path, even when it was something I would normally pull up the older man for. While teaching the junior, he was also teaching himself some valuable habits along the way.

Now that is not to say that it's all a great end to the story. Of course, there are still frustrations in this case. There were still bad habits and styles that needed continual realignment to the expectations of both of their roles. But what I learned in this situation was that if you give someone a focus where they can have a direct impact on another person, you will be surprised by the level that some people will rise to. It's on the same level as, when a new person starts, people try to guide them, as we are able to relate to when we first started, whether we know it consciously or not, this is part of the reason why we show people the things we didn't know before.

Our society and family generally set to what standards we hold ourselves. During your career, your journey reinforces your standards, and you improve upon them. As we reach a certain income, we set that as a benchmark and continue to raise up till it either fulfills us or we are unhappy with what we have. A big part that plays in on this is our values. What are our values, and do they have any real effect on our lives?

If our values are not in alignment with what we are doing, we don't do it with the same passion. We pull our rigor back, and we feel uneasy doing certain things. If I were to say to you that your number one value was honesty, and you worked with a boss who was dishonest. It would affect you if they asked you to do something dishonest. We might end up doing the function, but it would hurt us more than a physical wound because what is inside of us affects us the most. It is what is in our minds that decide whether we will get out of bed each and every day. If we bypass our values and do something contrary to what we believe in, this will create a great deal of pain within ourselves. What are your values? Can you list the top five? What do you think you stand by and which five best represents who you are?

What is the importance of your values? What do they really mean?

Section Three: Fall For What We Stand For

If you don't know your own values, how can you expect as a leader to guide your people? Your values are the core of who you are. You don't have to write them down to know what they are, they are your foundations, but it helps. Everything that you do in your life is some way or another, directed by your core values. Your values are mainly the parts of you that you gain at a young age, and they set up who you are later in your life. That said, you can change yourself, but it is a hard thing to do, even with the realization, sometimes we are hardwired a certain way. But that's not to say that if you were in a bad situation that you can't stop. You just have to have enough willpower to make it eventuate. But there is a lot of truth in studies conducted about predetermination from adolescence into your adult life, ones that have some formation with countless decades of empirical data. But you are a leader. You guide the pack. You decide your future, not your past.

Living in the past is not an easy thing to get away from. We always refer back to our past experiences. We look at prior experiences and mold them to the current situation. This would be a part of our survival mechanisms. If we didn't learn from our past experiences, the next time a lion ran at us, we might not know that it is a ravenous land creature that is looking at us for its next meal. Our ability to see the past and react using hindsight from our experiences is something we cannot throw away. But it is important that we understand that our experiences can be perceived as different from what they actually are. In this case, the saying means to look at an experience more favorably than it was. But the point is that our past is our past, and it is just that. It is not our future. The crucial thing here is to be aware of our past and how future situations might call from our experiences, and as such, we might be more well prepared. But we must also embrace the future, and at times allow similar events to unfold differently.

We are rewarded for our consistency when we react to a situation in which the result is favorable, but what happens when the next time we follow this same consistent approach and we fail. You will be judged for not being prepared, for expecting that what we have always done will always work. Even if the nine times before the tenth it worked, we have now gone bust and wasted it all. If, for example, each time the housing market crashes during and after an election in your country or town, and you decide to buy as the prices have significantly fallen. What happens if they continue to fall? You must be adaptive and responsive to the trends of the present and future. The past has many lessons to teach us, but it's how we approach future situations that our past is best at teaching us.

It is important to draw exposure from as many sources around us. If we draw from everything, we will have a more robust future experience because we are taking into consideration the retrospectives. Just relying on our past, we are only drawing from our own experiences. To draw from the past, present, and the soon-to-be future, we factor in a whole lot more, and our risk of failure continues to decline. It's not to say that you won't fail, but you have more opportunities to succeed.

What should you take out of this? Your values can change, and it depends on you and your awareness. If you have your top value as honesty, but you are dishonest, you need to understand what in your life needs to change to fix it. Before you blame others, look at yourself. What in your life, right now, is causing you to be dishonest? There is no one job out there that will help you live. You can move away and find another job. Sometimes you just have to take a dive into the deep and reach for the next opportunity. Values also change over time. Something you see as the most important thing in your life can change over time. From being a child to an adult, our experiences and our basic building blocks are what change the values that we hold dear.

It is easier to change yourself than it is to change others.

Things Change

You might have loved being with your family, and you didn't want anything else but the comfort of your mother and father. But as you grow older, you see the items that your friends possess, and you decide that you want them too because they look fulfilled by them. Maybe you'll get the same level of enjoyment out of it as they do. You then start to value achieving great sums of money. You get so involved in your role that ten years pass, and you look at what you have now. You're in a mansion, and you have all of the worldly possessions you could have. Your values of love and family will still remain, but on the list out of ten, you've moved success or achievement up that list. You have shuffled your deck of cards and evolved around the circumstances that you have put yourself into.

Our values are not impossible to change. By putting your mind to a task or being channeled down a certain path, you can also change the way in which you see things without even having to decide upon it happening. Values are ingrained and are not easy to change, but they can be changed through awareness and seeking direction to change them, and that we assimilate our values to a certain degree to achieve the things we want in life. Sometimes extreme associations with others can embody a radical change in ourselves much quicker than by doing it individually, and this is normally because of changing to align with the groupthink.

I am sure you have heard of stories in the papers or via groups you have associated with that might have mentioned someone who came from a great family and turned out to be a radical who ends up in prison or hurts someone: shock and horror. Sometimes we want to rebel against our current situation, and our family is the enemy. So, we look to something entirely different. In this, our values change. We disassociate from our normal systems and move to a new one. This is the want, the need to change our systems and values. The group that we associate with also determines what our outcomes will be. In a group, like wolves, we operate as components, and each has its part to play. Although we see radicals in our outer level of society, it is also admirable that they will stand for what they believe in, regardless of whether it is of their own volition or a form of brainwashing. If we don't stand for our values, how can we lead others?

"Those who stand for nothing fall for anything." (Alex Hamilton, 1978)

Accountability and Your Choices

As leaders, we are held to account for all that we do. We cannot hide from our expectations, and the same goes for our values. If we value honesty, and yet we lie, we will be called out for it. People seek out the best and worst out of their leaders. We mirror them as well as look for their defects. This is observational learning—when the people around us observe how we act in situations, and to a certain degree, copy how we react. They will use you as a benchmark of what is acceptable or not. I have seen it before, and when the leader pulls up the person for what they did, the person is confused and reacts poorly, saying that they only did what they thought was right. Sometimes without even realizing that they actually did what they saw, they followed the observational way of their leader in the situation. If a leader isn't aware of themselves, then we have problems.

If we value transparency, yet we hide information that is either pertinent or just general information that will be found out in the wash, then expect that people will either challenge you or shut down. You need to live and breathe your values if you expect them to be reflected back toward you. I am sure you have been annoyed by someone who doesn't seem to accept you for who you are, but on the weekend, you point someone out and judge them. You probably don't even realize it. But in this situation, you are setting a double standard, which is a big no of leadership. And I will come out and say that there definitely are some great benefits to be a leader that you wouldn't necessarily get if you didn't take the opportunity to lead, but with that comes great responsibility.

There is a fine line for me between confidence and arrogance. Self-awareness is key. I value respect, yet I have disrespected people with sheer confidence, to a point where it is just exuberance, and I say something without realizing it has caused distress. If I expect something, then I have to do so in return to the person I expect it from. As a leader, we must continue to show our values are being held to account, if we don't, we will surely fall for anything.

I know I asked you in the last section to write down your values, but what I would ask you to do is find someone whom you can trust and see if the values you have written down that they would agree they think of you. You would find that people and especially people close to you will be able to go, "Ah, yeah, that does seem to be like you," or, "Hmm, yeah, I think I agree with some of this." They will think about you and their experiences observing you and link your worded values to your actions in certain situations. It is a validation check for yourself. You might also find they will use a different word for the same type of value—one that is more suited to who you are.

Are there any values that you actually want but aren't on your top five list? Is there something in your current leadership role that is holding you back, and if you had it, you would progress further forward? What you need to do is to identify what it is you want, and secondly, why? What will it change in your life if you have it? What will you achieve that this requires you to have it?

You Decide What Success Is

Do not limit yourself to other people's definitions of success. Set your values at the expectation of what you want out of life, not the benchmark of society or what other people set up. Of course, apply this within reason. Consider what you think success is. If there is a value you want, and it's based on your definition of success, then you need to understand how to include it in your life. Sometimes doing an activity can also bring this value into your life.

I found that one day I became very grateful for the people and things in my life. I didn't have to lose everything to realize it either. I didn't fall into a terrible circumstance either. I made a conscious decision to be grateful for what I have, to be gracious, and to understand just how lucky I am. How did I do this? I did it day by day. Nothing worth having is easy, nor is it possible for it to just appear. I made a conscious effort to review the successes of each week in my life. Each review starts with my mind, spirit, heart, and body. I look at goals I have set the week prior and whether I've achieved these goals. Reviewing your actions either daily, weekly, or monthly is important because it gives you the truth about what you have actually achieved. I put my pen to paper, and I run out of pages to write the things that I have achieved. I even track the small things in life, such as how many pages per week I want to write in my book to achieve a publishing date.

When I looked back and reviewed what I did, I saw a lot of crosses, there were many times I didn't achieve what I had set out for myself, but the ticks outweighed the crosses. On days when I initially felt like I hadn't achieved anything, I took stock of the day. What phone calls did I receive? What problems did I solve? Although I hadn't achieved the goals I set for myself, I did end up accomplishing many other things. I learned from this, and I realized that I had to prioritize my time more effectively, that I had to schedule my day and put my phone and email away at certain times. I set the structure for my success. This gave me more time to focus on my long-term goals. I am not able to achieve these goals in an instant, which, when I first started working on big projects I struggled with, but through time, and experience I learned to chip away at them bit by bit. I still like to take big bites out of things, but on certain days where I lack complete motivation, I just do the minimum that I had set for myself to achieve because forward progress is still progress.

I learned that to be grateful meant understanding the achievements in my life—that included time with my wife and family. I set myself goals to go out for dinner on a Friday night with my wife, to spend the afternoon with my family, and to throw a ball around with my friends. I ticked those boxes, and little amounts of endorphins would drive me more. I realized each time I reviewed my week that I had spent some fulfilling time with my wife and family. I look at my values, and my family is high on my list, and therefore I have killed two birds with one stone, that the multiplicity of values is almost like compounded elements. If love is on the list, it's another thing to be grateful for. By writing out or drawing up our values, it sears them into our mind, and we can visualize them. We then have a clear graph of what we stand for. Therefore, it is easier to abide by them but also to reinforce them.

I pushed myself to be more grateful, and I looked at the situations I had experienced when traveling overseas and realized just how good I have it. That my life is a miracle, that all that I have, there is always someone worse off than me. And that what I have now, I should be grateful for because I will find more enjoyment in what I have now and what I don't have yet. Being grateful, though, is not only about what you have, but what you have had and what situations you will come to be within.

What do you stand for? Does it align with your values? If it does, then this exercise will hopefully give you a better appreciation of your core, of who you are, or at least what you stand for. If it doesn't, it gives you something to reflect and look further into. What are you doing now that you can change to better your situation so that you are better aligned with your values? Your values determine who you are, what you will aspire to. As a leader, we want to impress upon the people around us our structure and try and get them to align in part with our values. In this circumstance, it is assumed that you stand for the right things in life and that you are forward-thinking. As you can understand, we have the potential to influence people in our lives. These people could go on to lead the country. You just don't know, so your influence, your values could influence decisions made on a global scale. What you do today can impact the world tomorrow.

"Find out who you are and do it on purpose." (Parton, 2015)

Stand For Something

It is important to understand what you stand for. What do you want out of life? It will change in part or completely, but it is good to have a guide on your journey. That guide is the decision you made and what you want to achieve. What you need to understand is that your level of success should be based on what gives you enjoyment and fulfillment. It is easy to say, hard to do. If you work toward other people's expectations, even if you have all of the money in the world, if it isn't what you want that is captured in your heart, then you will never find that level of enjoyment or fulfillment until you realize what you truly want in your life.

Have you ever been so convinced of something that you went out against all odds and either succeeded or failed, yet you still felt quiet confidence? Have you ever been proven so right by something that everyone doubted you in? This is the feeling you will get when you stick by your values, and in the troubled times, you stand by what you believe, and when it comes through the wash, you feel enlightened by your convictions.

I ran a business where we were losing about forty thousand dollars per month. After the second month, we lost fifty thousand dollars. I worked near to seven days per week, worked as many hours as there was in a day, and didn't stop there. After a solid year of consistent loss, my managing director informed me that the failure of the site will mean the loss of everyone's jobs and that it was caused by the failure of my management. This wasn't motivation, by the way. It just added to my stress levels. I worked with everyone to turn it around, I consulted with the operation team members and was transparent about our losses, but they didn't fear for their jobs because they could see my conviction. They could see that I wasn't going to let them down and that I felt a sense of purpose and duty to course-correct while my leadership shone through the darker times.

I encountered many problems along the way, with roof collapses, audits that resulted in additional upfront costs, broken pumps, past employees stealing from the business, and the loss of the leadership team through dodgy financial practices. All the while, I continued with my resolve, and I defied the odds. I turned the business around by around three hundred thousand dollars in the second financial year of operating. My support was lacking from the outside of the operation, it came down to the dedication of firstly myself, and by my team who supported me along the way, and even my family would come on weekends to help me work. We had achieved the unbelievable. After it all, I still felt like I had more to do—that I hadn't finished. Now don't get me wrong, I was extremely proud, bragged as much to my family and friends as I could, but there was something missing.

It took me about another six years later to understand why. That even though I had achieved a massive result, I didn't feel the fulfillment that I had thought I should feel. And that was the problem. That I thought I should feel something because I hadn't set out to turn around another person's business as one of my values or life goals. When I was younger, my original goal was to fund my music career and sit in a studio producing music. I didn't have the desire to be a manager or leader turning around businesses. It just wasn't what I wanted, plus there were other things I wanted to achieve that were higher on my list than this goal. Yes, I am grateful for the great thing that I did, but it wasn't my conviction, and therefore no matter how amazing the feat was, if it isn't what I want down to my core, then it's not going to give me the satisfaction that I so desire to fulfill me.

The Fulfillment Bar

If giving back to the community is part of your values, you will find incredible fulfillment in yourself as you do this, but if earning a large sum of money isn't, it won't interest you as much. Now that is not to say that things won't change in your life like my previous example, but generally speaking, we are predisposed through our childhood to act in a certain way in our adulthood. Being successful and wealthy doesn't mean I will find fulfillment in my life. It is quite the opposite if my values don't align. If I find value in living in a small apartment with a flexible job and more time for my family, this could be the greatest fulfillment of my life. I have met many people who, when I discuss with them about traveling, tell me they haven't left Australia. It surprises me, but when I get to the bottom of it, they are content with where they are, and they find great fulfillment in being close to home. They care more for being at home than abroad. My brother is a homebody, and that suits him just fine. Don't judge what you don't understand unless you put in the time to learn about another person's version of fulfillment.

I travel with friends and family as I believe I get the best of both worlds. But I find enjoyment in experiencing other cultures and taking back home with me parts of this experience that I can use further in my life. Some of it is part of being grateful as I truly begin to understand how lucky I am. Also, I get perspectives from other cultures, and I can bring them back to my own personal development. I believe that I am very aware, and by being aware, I can see what I want to include in my life and what I want to remove from my life. I can come to a realization without having a major breakdown. As a leader, this is important. The last thing you want to do is realize in hindsight that the task you were conducting has caused you disheartenment, and with that, your leadership on the task has been less than you would expect of yourself. If your heart is not in it, people will find it out.

It was the same for me when I resigned when I was running a business in a senior position. I hadn't formally advised my team or colleagues, and when we would talk, they could sense something was up. They would ask me if there was something wrong or if there was a problem between us. Of course, we all have the ability to sense things, even if we don't know just yet what they are. But there is always that moment when the cat is let out of the bag, and we go, "Ah, that's what it was," or, "I knew there was something going on." We all have emotions, and we are all perceptive to each other. It just depends on how aware we are of ourselves and the people around us, and this is part of emotional intelligence.

Now don't get me wrong, I don't mean to say that when things get hard that we just simply walk away. What I am saying is that if what you are doing doesn't align with your values, you will not be happy until you make the necessary change to align with your values. Your values are the core of who you are, and without your values, you would lose the sense of who you are. You can see in a group of people when someone doesn't belong, they try their hardest, but they just don't fit. We can all see from the outside that this person struggles to see it themselves. As a leader, we need to be aware of ourselves in the first instance. But how do I just become aware? It's not easy to look at yourself from the outside.

The first step is to understand our values. If you did the task earlier, you would have them written down somewhere. You can visualize what you believe represents you. Now, look at something you are doing now. Which of your values does it align with? It's not an exact science. It's more of a feeling or a sense of what belongs and where. Is there something in your life right now that is causing you angst? Does it align with your values? With this, are you finding that you are losing interest in it? Simon Sinek created the 'Golden Circle' concept, which is used to understand the layers of the what, how, and why. You need to understand why you are doing what you are doing. It is easy to understand what you are doing, and it is the task or activity that you are completing. You can then understand how you do it because it is the steps you take to complete the task or activity. But the real motivation, the values, are attributed to 'why' you do it?

"If you want to be successful, it's just this simple. Know what you are doing. Love what you are doing. And believe in what you are doing." (Will Rogers, n.d.).

And that is important because for me, if it doesn't align with my values, then just because I know what I am doing and how doesn't mean it gives me fulfillment. And part of that is to understand what motivates you, and as a leader, what motivates your team? Once you understand the gravity that your values have on your decision making you can then begin to assist the people around you to also find their focus. This is not to say that you have to know what you want because it continues to change, but once you believe you have a fair grasp of what fibers make you, another part to help yourself is to help others. I have found answers from helping other people with their problems, which in turn has made me a better person for it.

But it's important that you demonstrate commitment to your values because people will see through your façade. If you don't have passion for what you do, you cannot hide it. As a leader, people will mirror you and how you come across,

"If a child sees his parents' day in and day out living without self-restraint or self-discipline, then he will come in the deepest fibers of being to believe that this is the way to live." (Peck, 1978, p. 10).

Make sure that you live by your values, as they are the core of who you are. It is hard to do so, and we slip up from time to time. There is no exact structure to it. But being aware of your values and by what you stand for, you will be more inclined to fall for what you stand for than to fall for that which you do not believe in. Because there are people and things in our lives that we would do anything for, and there are things in life we wouldn't do anything for. But then why do other people do that when you wouldn't? Because we are all different. And as a leader, it is important to understand these differences and why people do what they do.

Our values are what determines what we will be passionate about, what we will strive toward, and how much we will put in to get there. Putting the right person in the right position is critical because you can develop someone with the right skills and experience, but it's their attitude that matters most. And that is directly linked to their values. If doing what they are doing right now is what they love most in life, you will be hard-pressed to find someone from somewhere else with the same level of personal connection to the role. The enthusiasm that comes with alignment to our values is because of the fulfillment we attain from doing what connects us to our core fibers.

Look at what you are doing. Does it make you happy? Does it draw you close to what you hold in your heart?

Section Four – The Wrap-Up

A leader is taught by doing, in most instances. Summarily it is the hard yards that make the leader who he or she is in the short and long term. What is important is that the leader of your journey is open to change. This is a time when so much will come our way, and we must show our determination and resilience to adapt and overcome. A leader is also not someone who is alone. Some people see a leader as the person standing in front or behind a group. In a workplace, someone who is not technically a manager or a senior leader can sometimes be a leader without the position or title. There are countless examples where junior employees will revert to an older colleague who is senior in knowledge, not necessarily senior in their title.

Sometimes it takes hard conversations or yelling at each other to break down the boundaries that separate each one of us. As I like to use in many heated conversations, conflict brings about resolution. In the end, people just want to be heard in their own way. We all just want to feel fulfilled in what we do, even if we don't know it. That is the reason. It doesn't always mean finding a solution, and sometimes the solution is to just listen and then walk away once the other person has been heard.

Sometimes the way in which a problem is resolved is just by hearing it out, not actually solving it as such. Sometimes situations solve themselves, and most of the time, we solve our own problems.

You will find in your travels that there are people out there who are jealous or are insidious. Sometimes they work against you and those around you. I am sure you have found an experience where someone has been spreading rumors and tried to create tension between you and your colleagues? This sounds like a torment, but it's a good training environment. What you will find is that these people are a good training tool for you. A good leader needs to learn the good and the bad from those around them. These people you can sometimes consider are influencers. A great leader is not one who is known for specifically what they do. They are known for what they stand for. This is attributed to their values, who they are. People don't follow someone because of the specifics that they do. They follow the person because of their aura. These are people we consider to be powerful and inspiring.

When a colleague is insidious, they try to make us turn on each other, and like the example of the lion, they will strike when you each turn on each other, then their job is done. A great leader is one who learns from these people and understands their every step. Just being aware of their ideas or actions ensures that we are ready for them at every turn.

"If you hope for peace, prepare for war." (Renatus, 4th Century)

A leader must plan, and review, and continue to plan and review. The importance of awareness is quintessential to success. Not only awareness of ourselves but of those around us. Much can be learned from those around us. A leader must also be ready to confront those who proceed to create dissension. This comes down to timing. We cannot always resolve things front-on. It takes the right leader to understand the right opportunity.

Leadership takes ownership, period. A leader shouldn't be a know-it-all. No one wants a leader to know more about what they do than they do themselves. What people seek from a leader is direction. Sometimes people get lost in the thought that they must know everything. Otherwise, their position is fraught. But the truth is, people, need to know that their leader believes in them, and sometimes without knowing the exact details, the leader will plan based on trust. Respect goes a long way, and in an industry like my own where our reputations precede us. I sometimes know about a potential interview candidate even before they walk in the door. I have floated potential candidates' names around my office with some of the more experienced employees who flicker their eyes and recount the name until they remember an experience where they have heard of them before. And so, as the saying goes, 'don't burn your bridges' because a reputation definitely has the potential to precede you.

What you stand for is part of what defines you as a person, as a leader. Not all people will understand what you actually stand for, but they will have a feeling of who you are. You are also defined by your actions. People respect and dislike people who stand for what they want. They also understand that if something isn't part of who they are, they are content with walking away. You need to be aware of what you are willing to sacrifice for what matters most. As a leader, you need to understand what motivates them because their lack of engagement could be the direct result of being somewhere that doesn't align with what they want. And identifying where they fit and where their passion will come from is critical to the successful career of a leader.

The next time you have a meeting or a conversation with one of your team members about a task or project that they are working on. If they start to pull at the seam and seem frustrated in the way in which things are progressing. Ask them:

1. What do you think are the main issues?

2. And once they have spoken their mind, ask them how they believe we can overcome them?

3. What can we do as a team?

It depends on the level of ownership that the person has with the task that determines how much work they will put in to find legitimate resolutions or just stick with the current process being followed.

Exercise: What motivates you? When you start a project or task, inside or outside of work, what is it most that excites you? Where do you think your strengths assist you? List out the task or duty and write down what interests you the most. Understanding what motivates you helps you to understand your values better. And understanding your values sooner rather than later will help you to find fulfillment as a leader in what you are doing. Without this, you could go for many years without understanding why you don't enjoy what you do.

Chapter <IV> - Throw You a Bone

> "If you want to discover just what there is in a man—give him power."
>
> (Miller, 2016)

Introduction

You've been let to wander. You've made your assumptions and made decisions that have brought about some great victory and some deplorable defeats. But the purpose of this section is for you and those whom you seek guidance from—to pull in the reigns. You've had your chance to explore, but now it's time to consolidate and realize your true potential and capabilities, pulled back onto the correct course.

It takes some real isolation from the path of leadership to truly understand how far you have gone. Sometimes your leadership takes you into a different situation based on the industry or business that you operate within. But perspective comes from being allowed the opportunity to learn from your own mistakes and be led down the garden path. Because only then will you have learned on your own, and you will appreciate the support to get back onto the freeway.

The purpose of this section is to explain why you sometimes feel as though you are in control, you have a safety net, and at some strange unforeseen point in time, your legs get swept out from beneath you. You begin to fall downwards, and it's spiraling. The only way to stop it, or at least slow the stem, is to do something about it. Think on your feet (pun intended) and make decisions to get back to where you were before. But what you find is you can't really get back to this point. Somehow you overcome it, and the place from whence you were, is now very different from where you are now.

When you look at a situation in different time periods, your perspective changes significantly. What I might say, though, is that hindsight is a great tool for reflection. Time changes the way in which we perceive things. And that is part of what being a leader is, to reflect and understand what we have done, and learn from it, so that in our next dealings or tasks, we use a more concerted approach, as compared to the original approach without reflection on the situation.

Who do you think of when you are in a bad situation? Who has your back and is willing to stake their reputation, time, and effort just to get you out of trouble?

Section One – It's Not Always Because We Are Sinking

It is rare to find a large business owner with copious amounts of humility. I guess as part of a large owner's ethos is their confidence. Their job becomes less about the actual physical work and more about their levels of influence in their industry. It took me years to understand this delineation between physical work and influence levels. In the room with a group captain and many senior members of the ADF (Australian Defense Force), everyone was well on time. They sat in accordance and with professionalism in their quiet chattering. Once the group captain started to speak, everyone in the room turned to listen with all their focus, stopping mid-sentence. During the forum, I had the opportunity to speak on behalf of my company on our plan to overcome some recent challenges that were being faced.

During the conversation, I had stated a key point of the discussion, then the group captain asked me a question, which was what I had provided an overview of. I explained the point again in a very similar way that I had just explained it. The rest of the audience didn't correct him or say anything but continued to listen to the main point again. After some discussion, once the group captain had finished talking, he opened the discussion up with the other members of his team. They inquired on our plan, but that aside, but the lesson for me was he had a position that inspired this level of respect. Though in the same respect, the people in the room could sense his level of confidence in his position and knew that they were to wait their turn until they could take up their line of questioning.

With so many people on the other side of the table, I wasn't at my most confident, some of the questions got me offside and made some of my responses vulnerable to follow up questions, going down the rabbit hole. This was a tactic, the number of people and the format in which they did the discussion was a way of getting me offside to give up more information than that of a smaller team discussion. Though at that moment I asked a question back to the group that no one was able to answer, the Group Captain sided with me and questioned his own team that with their line of questioning and my knowledge of the operation, that I was still able to answer everything in good detail. Though when I sent one back their way, they couldn't give me a tangible response.

Upon reflection, it really took me a while to understand this conversation, and I think in each time period of my life, I will grasp it in a different light each time. But in this time period right now, what I got out of that was a man who knew his level of power and ability to read the room. By my sheer poor body language and presentation, he had the upper hand. You know when you are in a situation, and everyone is looking up to you, when you've been there, you can understand this in its entirety. We've all been there, and we just might not have realized it at the time. The Group Captain was in complete control of this conversation. He got from me my desire to understand, in essence, his level of power & influence.

I think what he saw at that moment in me was that I wasn't afraid to ask a question that would throw the entire group off their track. I have been lucky that in some tight situations, I have asked a question or made an evaluation that has caught the attention of someone who was listening, because just my luck, I captured the curiosity of someone with a deeper or most precise-level of understanding of what it is to have influence. Not everyone gets these opportunities, and they cannot be taken lightly.

Although I was getting an incentive amount of praise, at the same time, there was an eye-to-eye understanding that this would boost my output. And it did expand my output, and it has helped me to use this experience to improve myself and others in future scenarios.

"You can learn expertise and gain experience, but attitude is inherent." (Branson, 2014).

The Learning Curve

What did I really get out of this discussion overall and learning experience from my experiences? I got to see into the eyes of a man who was in a critical military position who is sure of himself, has a façade of humility (which works on the surface), confident, to the point of boiling over into arrogance, and has a great deal of influence. Is this something that I want? Yes, it is. Did he know that? To an extent, in this conversation, he had the upper hand because, in turn, he had something that I wanted. And that's what I take out of a leader's role as they progress away from physical activities and move into the influence on others.

It is not specifically what I had said, nor what he had said. It is what he is, and it is what he is comprised of, the substance of a leader is what people value, it is how the leader performs under pressure. And this is what people see him as. My wife reminds me (normally when I ask her) what my leadership style is. She tells me, *"You are firm, but fair. When I first met you, I thought you were arrogant but I now realize that it's a lot of confidence. At the same time, you need a little bit of arrogance. It shows people your thick skin, and that you're not afraid of them. You care and are passionate."* Not in any of that was a mention to what I have physically done. Nothing mentions my level of physical strength. But what my leadership is defined as is what I am, not what I do.

Attitude is inherent, to be inherent, it is who you are, in a way, you can akin it to your soul, what you are made of. I'll be honest when I say that I am highly qualified, but I am qualified in more things than I can remember. If I can be like that, what do you think you see when you see a resume or page that shows someone has too many qualifications to count on their hand? An abundance of exposure; experienced in a lot and master of little.

That can be taken in two ways, don't let me be one-sided, it might show that the person is striving for exposure and a thirst for learning, which in turn could show exceptional attitude, but at the same time, someone who is highly qualified doesn't mean that they are willing or able to overcome situations with their attitude. Most people stay in their comfort zone and refer most things they do back to their job or their studies.

What We Would Like Over What Happens

I am a firm believer in quality over quantity. I have been an example of this. I would work from five a.m. to six or seven p.m. every day, and I even worked most Saturdays to get the job done. But I never was able to produce a result without mistakes. I would do extra hours just to check what I had done to ensure that there were no errors, yet I would glaze over the most obvious errors.

It's funny when I say this. I have seen emails in the past where I have forgotten to sign something, or I have made the most dubious errors when talking with a customer or friend. I say I focus on quality, but sometimes I am so excited to get something out that when I say the words, they are all jumbled, and I end up sounding like I have just said two words together. When I talk of quality, I am at the realization that we are all specialists in certain things. I am not oblivious to think that I am amazing at everything, nor should anyone in this world think that way. I will admit that I am very talented and capable of a lot of things. But far from perfect.

As part of being a leader, our emotions are critical to our success. It all depends on the situation but think on situations where you have seen your boss or peers passionately conduct an activity because they are all or nothing in the situation. Or when you see a war movie, and the leader takes the first step at the front of the battle line. Although, in some cases, this is just the movie's aura, it makes sense that people are driven by their emotions. Something critical to a leader is the ability to switch their emotions on or off depending on the situation at hand. I've never met a leader who isn't affected personally by decisions they or someone else has made in the past or future. We all react differently, and it's how we react at times that defines our leadership. People may not study human behavior, but if they see the grimace in your face when you hear something or something happens, they can see what you are feeling. And their reactions will be affected by you.

The best leaders I have ever seen are the ones that remain calm in all situations. Although inside, they might have a heart rate that would start a plane engine, they don't necessarily show this outwardly. Internalization is part of who we are when we react to hard circumstances. And the way in which we internalize events shows the people around us how much something has affected us.

Take this scenario, you have just started a new job, and your boss ran into your office and started to yell at one of your co-workers for something they did wrong. Now granted, you may at some point intervene, but I reckon you might close down into a shell. You will double-check your work and ensure that you don't make those same mistakes. But in that case, you have closed yourself off. You are more focused on your own quality and will take more time to ensure you have covered yourself. You won't go beyond the boundaries of your role as you would fear the same reprisal as your co-worker.

Now consider this second scenario, your boss walks into your office and has a conversation with the employee about how they made the error, but fairly enough, it is an error that has been picked up by the boss, and they just wanted to make the employee aware. Arguably this is why the boss checks over the work to make sure that it is right. We need to be mindful and diligent. No one wants to make minor errors. I reckon you would think that this manager would have your back if you made an error, that you would feel as though you could be a little more creative in what you do because if you did make a mistake, it wouldn't be read as a personal attack or error by your boss.

Now, what if I told you that both of these situations were the same manager, just on different days, and to two different people? Emotion and consistency have a lot to do with a leader. As I have stated, a good leader is firm but fair, and that goes hand in hand with emotion and consistency. It's how the leader reacts and in what situations that defines who and what they are.

A Good Leader

"Mission-Team-Me." A similar approach to the United States Marines, the Australian way is the description of the priority that a leader must demonstrate.

"At the top is the mission (or the broader needs of the organization), after which you should look after the needs of the team. Only then may you attend to 'me.'" (Jans, 2018, p. 51)

Prioritization is key because we could all be doing an amazing job, but if we are all working in different areas and going in different directions, our ability to do great things together is diminished.

Leadership is about being a realist while also showing those around you that there is more honor or ability for us to achieve great things. It would be silly to think that a leader in a bad situation would be honest to the point of people hearing the words of defeat and giving up. But all conversation needs to be determined in each case and the best possible solution founded. What I mean to say is that a leader is someone who must be able to grasp the situation that surrounds them and apply the best leadership practice that is needed, based on their discretion. That said, there is no rule book that determines the best leadership practice for each situation. There is no grand concept that applies to all situations.

Positioning is important as a leader. Where we are seen by our peers, customers and employees make a difference. A leader must position themselves at the right place and right time. When there is an important photo with a new client or contractor, the leaders stand toward the front, smiling, shaking hands while cutting a banner or opening a door. Much the same as when prime ministers and overseas correspondents meet, they gesture to each other as if they had known each other for many years. It is a perception of their position and their position toward each other. If a leader in your organization is continually standing over your shoulder, you will feel a lack of confidence, and as such, you will feel micromanaged and potentially lack confidence equally in your abilities.

Much as a good leader will rely on his or her people and allow their people to make errors but give the person the ability to rectify their mistakes personally empowers a person to take ownership. As a leader, it is important to position yourself in the right place and at the right time. Suppose a minister had the opportunity to help at a homeless shelter with two people watching, or another one with many people watching. It's a no-brainer. This is not to say they are bad people, as the end result might entail additional support or funding due to more air time and, as such, more following. But in retrospect, in a workplace, it is important to understand the value of your positioning. It won't always be about the big-time TV shots. It also comes down to the hard yards and the parts that haven't been shined before.

We must be selective in what we focus our time and effort on. It is impossible to be focused on so many different things, and if we do, and when we have, we fail to achieve everything with quality. What is important for a leader to focus on is the quality of their leadership and the way in which they present themselves to their peers or direct reports. It's not always the physical activities that a leader undertakes and the things that are in writing. The quality of a leader is in their grounding and stability. People can see someone who is a leader. Sometimes people are empowered by their position or title that they have a walk or a way that they talk in a conversation. Sometimes 'you just know' who is the leader in a situation.

A leader must understand that they must be firm but fair. People generally don't respect a pushover, but they don't respect a tyrant either. There is a fine balance between the two, with more weighing toward being a pushover. People respect flexibility and empathy. I have found that in the past, just by allowing an employee some grace in regards to a personal issue, their ethos change considerably, not just in the way they work but also in the way in which they interact. It comes down to a sense of belonging and pride. I don't pick a job. I try my best to pick a boss. We have all had that one manager who made our lives hell. And when we finally gave up, or they left, there is such a relief. But it's short-lived. There will always be someone to distort our status quo.

Along with a leader being flexible with their people and peers, a leader must also be flexible in their leadership. Just because your style of leadership worked somewhere else doesn't mean it will work everywhere. The industry sets the tone for how you need to operate. You can evolve the place you are at so that you can transform it into your leadership, but to drop a lead balloon is a sure-fire way to cause damage. We've all heard it before when a new manager comes into a business, and you hear people say, "He won't last long," or "Ah, another one," as indicating that it's a revolving door of people. To be flexible in our leadership, we have to be self-aware. If we cannot look inward, we won't know what we are projecting outward.

Our Influence as a Leader

"A wise leader takes every communication situation as an opportunity to influence and inform" (Jans, 2018, p. 81).

Managing how we are perceived is very important. Part of this comes down to who you use to portray yourself. Influence, once understood, is a creative skill. With influence, you are able to communicate who you are way before you ever meet people face to face. Your associations give away what you represent. Have you ever looked at a presidential candidate (as it gets more airplay in Australia than our own elections) and seen that the media would pull out things they had done in the past? The candidates that were favored, their reputable charities were placed on display, 'we are guilty by association.'

When you were young, you would use your friends to find out if a certain girl had an interest in you—even getting them to talk about you in a favorable way. I have done the same thing in business, knowing that someone that I spoke to had a good relationship with someone I was trying to get a message to. I would speak with this person, and I would tell them all of the things I am trying to improve. I would impress upon them that if I had someone who was interested in assisting, I would be more than able to bring them on board. And then, like a miracle, this person would just bump into me and would start to make small talk. From there, they bridged the gap, and we spoke more in-depth about what they can bring to the table. I influenced them by association to do something I wanted them to do.

Much the same as our perceptions, we can influence things and have people assist us in how we are portrayed. Sometimes though, we cannot help the way we are portrayed, much like the media when it comes to people in the limelight. Sometimes a story is more fitting if there is more drama involved. Sometimes the way someone is portrayed is incorrect, so we need to be able to understand whose perspective is trustworthy and who is subject to scrutiny.

Do you know how you are perceived? What characteristics do people think you emit the most? Do you have a reputation in your area? If you don't know, why don't you ask someone that you trust or are close with? Ask them what you would think people think of you. You might be surprised by what reputation you have.

You can change your reputation, but that takes time. What is most important is that you are who you say you are, easy to say, hard to do. But as they say, you have to 'walk the talk.' It is easy to say something, but to follow it up with action is where the merit comes. If you don't follow up, you will get a reputation for failing to follow through. What we do describes who we are. Word of mouth still goes a long way.

I employed a site manager, and I made the standard request of asking for their top three references. I got through to the first two who praised their work ethic, the third though didn't answer, and I left a message. I then called a contact of mine that was in a contract that the incumbent was from. I found out further information about the applicant. Days later, I got a return call from the third reference, but I didn't answer. Over the course of three days, I missed phone calls from this person, continually trying to get through to me to be a reference for the incumbent. A couple of days after this, I called the person back as a courtesy and advised them that I had already hired the manager. They said they were calling as they wanted to be a good reference for their previous colleague. They could have done what most people do and leave a message and leave it at that. But the reputation of the manager was great, and he had a very good reputation in the industry.

People will go beyond what is expected if they believe in you and that they know what you are capable of. In this case, the reference was proud to be a point of call for the future success and career of the manager. If you treat people well, they will return the favor. It doesn't just come down to the tangible. Sometimes it's just who you are that matters. If he were a rude person with a small pocket of friends, do you think that this reference would go out of their way to make sure I heard the best qualities of his character? We are who we say we are, but only by doing what we say we will do.

Seeing Something We Don't

Sometimes people want to reach out and lift us up, not because we are falling, but because they can see our potential. Maybe not consciously, but we all have a sense of our place in the world. We all have some sort of clarity on what we can do and how we can produce things. Not only do we have people around us that help us because we are falling, but because they see a mutual benefit in lifting us up. If you were given an opportunity to be in a team of high performers, and you, in this instance, were the outcast who performed the worst. Don't you think that you would try harder? Naturally, we lift our game. I would say that nine out of ten people would rise above and reach new heights.

In school, I was in the lowest English learning class. I had no real care for it. One day, I completed a creative story on a war scenario. I recall it being like a Tom Clancy-esque story. I got a really good mark, and with it, I actually placed in the advanced English class. I was way out of my depth, to say the least. I didn't even know what a noun was. When

I started getting involved in the class, I realized I had to because everyone knew the answers, and I had felt so dumb. I went home and looked in the dictionary at what all these keywords meant. Our pop-quizzes were the definitions of these terms. Learning all of these new words, I actually started to find an interest in poetry and lyrics. I dived further into the meaning behind words.

I find that the more I seek, the more I read, the more I learn. Or, as it can be put simply, the less I see, the more I know, the more I see, the less I know. By broadening your horizons, you will grasp so much more depth to your mind, your heart, and your soul. It will enter into your mind many more questions of life and where we fit, but it will also put you into a better location, physically and emotionally. I think the reason I am such a calm person is that I am able to phrase things into a better perspective. Having seen so many of the world's wisest people and their struggles puts into perspective the small issues that I face in my life. Giving me the ability to frame the struggles I have overcome, and you can do the same.

Opportunities present themselves at certain times in our lives. It could be that someone leaves a business, leaves a space to fill, and there you are, available and ready to start. It can come in a number of weird and wonderful ways, but we must also seek them out. Opportunities present themselves to us, but we must be readily available to approach them. Sometimes people don't even know there is an opportunity, and when it passes them by, they wonder why they didn't get it. Being aware of our current situation and understanding the greater situation, you will be more equipped to shape yourself for new opportunities. Luck is when opportunity meets preparation and awareness.

Experience gives you photographs or stills where a similar situation fits the description of a past event that you may have experienced. Being open to different things gives you more capacity to understand and deal with future scenarios as you have experienced them before. What is critical is being open to change, to being open to opportunities that will come your way, because we are all given chances. Whether we see them or not, they are there. It's our awareness of this that will allow us to fall or slide into them prepared than if we weren't.

How do we prepare? We study. It doesn't just mean reading books. Studying can be done in many forms. I am sure you have sat in a shopping center and just watched everyone as they pass you by, right? That is a form of study. Human behavior is fascinating, and I could watch it all day. So be open to learning, don't shut any doors, and be ready for opportunities because they could come at any point in your life, good or bad times, they are coming your way.

Section Two – Flexibility and a Step Back

A leader doesn't have to be great at everything. A good leader is able to realize the talents of their surrounding team members. If you have ever been to a board meeting or tender discussion, the leader will generally provide the summary, sit back, and let the rest of the team fulfill their parts of the story. A good leader not only leads the team but provides a basis for a discussion or plan and values the team by giving it the freedom to express ideas. I am enlightened when one of my supervisors or team members comes to me with an idea for something that they think would work in operations. I take their idea and tell them to run with it and let me know how they went. At that moment, they feel supported, and they are given the space to make an impact. It gives them the feeling of togetherness, not only with me but with the setting they are performing this activity. They become empowered, and the ownership of this activity transcends into other parts of their role.

Not all ideas are fantastic, but it's a leader's ability to realize that it takes small steps in decision making to learn the best possible steps that separate successful leaders from the ones that just maintain the status quo. Granted, people don't always make the best decisions in innovation, but when you give someone the opportunity to realize their own mistakes or misleading's, they learn from the event much more than if you shut down their idea before, and you will produce a better concept for the next time. We never learn to run before we crawl, and the same goes for mentors, innovators, leaders, and entrepreneurs, we need to ensure that we are flexible and able to take a step back, grasp where a person is in the organization, and give them your value in time, and flexibility to innovate, to provide value add, and learn from their own success or failure. Much the same as when you have been taught along the way, we all make mistakes. The biggest mistakes in life are the best lessons.

It's hard sometimes to take a step back. Even as a leader we think that the best way to help someone is to crowd them and throw a safety net over them. But that's just it. It's a net that we throw over them. I recall a time when one of my managers was away, and the supervisor stepped into the role for a couple of weeks. I came down from my upstairs office every couple of hours and asked how things were going and if there was anything I could help with. It only took me a couple of times doing this that the supervisor bit back and said, "if I need your help, I know where you are, but you have got to trust me."

I realized then that I was micromanaging this supervisor. Even though this wasn't the way I was approaching the situation, it's how I was coming across.

Our persona, our public face, is the way in which we are perceived. We've all heard the line "but... I didn't mean it like that." As a leader, there is much scrutiny in the things that we say. If we hold a hard line with our people, they won't forget, and they won't be flexible in return. It's important to have latitude with our people so that they realize when you make a mistake, they address you with the same respect that you addressed them previously.

If you have come down on them like a ton of bricks, you won't necessarily have them do the same, depending on your position in the organization of the social ladder. But people don't tend to forget moments in time and where they can use the circumstances as a point of leverage in a future discussion or negotiation.

"Do to others as you would have them do to you." (Matthew 7:12)

Flexibility is not just about you giving, and your people getting, and vice versa. It's about give-and-take and understanding when you are in someone's way. It's a hard realization at times that you are the problem. And that to get forward, you need to get out of the way. A leader at times needs to be absent to allow their people to make decisions without their direct involvement and to refer to you when they need it. For someone to learn independence from you and those around them, they need you to learn interdependence and be there when needed most.

Planning Is Everything

A leader is not someone who does it all or doesn't do anything at all. A leader is part of the process, the guide, the person who groups the team together. As I have mentioned earlier, there is a major difference between a manager and a leader. And it is up to a leader to really understand the required levels of flexibility and to understand when you need to be out of the picture to let people learn and evolve. We feel the greatest satisfaction when we achieve something on our own merits. Our self-pride and confidence come into play. This is an evolving thing. We don't have a chemical composition that stipulates one-part flexibility and three-parts free space. A scary thought that so much of leadership is, in fact, discretionary. It's really what makes us human. Look at the great leaders of the past. They are doer-people who have made decisions and lead for what they see as the best outcome. But no great general can be everywhere at all times. A great general puts the right people into places that will be most effective. And those that are most effective are empowered to make decisions and given the flexibility to strive.

The latitude that a leader or manager gives to someone is discretionary. Sometimes the latitude is due to other pressing matters, and the amount given isn't actually what is intended. I have found that other leaders at times have thought that if they aren't giving you daily directions, that you are losing a sense of 'their purpose' or 'their direction.' What I have found, and am learning to become better at, is to give people a sense of the end goal. What is it that we are setting out to achieve? And then provide milestone updates. I have found this to be an effective way of creating purposeful direction. I don't know many people, if any, that prefer to be micromanaged. People like to be given direction and the ability to get there via their own methods.

"Give me six hours to chop down a tree, and I will spend the first four hours sharpening the ax." (Abraham Lincoln, N/A)

METT-TC (Mission, Enemy, Terrain, Troops, Timeframe and Civil Considerations) is a planning tool developed by the United States Army. The Australian Army learned from their experiences, and the way in which they operated in the Gulf War was different from how they operated in Afghanistan. What would happen previously is that the leaders in command would plan everything down to the minute, and they found that when something didn't go according to the plan, that the entire operation plan gave way. What they had learned through multiple conflicts is latitude. An example is, they would provide the team leaders with the METT-TC method. But they wouldn't tell them how to do their jobs. So, they would advise the teams that they had to get from point A to point B. They had intel on the number of enemies in the area, but it wasn't exact but near reliable. They advised that they would be going through multiple breaches and clears of buildings on their way to the area. They had their team and an adjunct team in support on either shoulder. They had three hours and advisement that there were civilians in the area and to only engage when fired upon following rules of engagement.

What this gives the teams is clear guidance as to what is expected of them. But the situation would be different if they were told that they would enter the front door only, and if the plan changed, they had to go through the side door. But what if only the back door was available, they would have to call back to base and get clarification. This would mean wasted time and the potential for mistakes to be made along the way. That is why it is so important that the leaders of teams in any environment understand the way in which they provide guidance. It is discretionary, but in these two situations, it is obvious that nothing goes according to a strict plan. But a plan that provides latitude and allows those who are doing the task enough structure and support to achieve the mission (objective) will still achieve the same result, but even better than one that is rigid and unwavering with fluctuations in the situation at hand.

Planning is fundamental to achieving great results. There is no doubting that a solid plan can assist a leader or team to achieve great things. But a plan is only as effective as the people who enact it. And a plan needs to be flexible. A plan is a structure and the guardrails.

Something that epitomizes the cause of an effective plan can be seen in *The Ass and the Sick Lion*.

"The ass told the jackal to offer his sincerest reverence to his master and to say that he had more than once been on the point of coming to see him (the lion). "But the truth of the matter" he observed dryly "is that all the footprints I see go into the cave, but none come out again. So, for the present, my health demands that I stay away" it is wise to see one's way out before one ventures in." (Aesop, 2014, p. 77)

I have looked back at plans I have drafted, and the ones that are fluid and able to fluctuate naturally are still relevant to the current situation that I am in later down the track. At the same time, plans that have been too detailed are only relevant to the time and exact situation at hand. It is not to say that planning for everything is a bad idea. A leader needs to be flexible in his or her own approach to a situation or desired outcome. You might have a team that requires a lot of attention and may need to be given bulky structures, but there comes a time when a leader needs to distinguish between hyper-care and the need to then work on the amount of latitude they give.

Finding the Right Fit

Control can also be a perception. For a leader, it is important to know what needs to be taken control of and what can be left to others to manage. Leaders positioning and timing are important for a leader to propel their careers. These are things that a leader must look to and understand.

It is important as a leader to be as unbiased as possible. But again, it depends on the circumstance in which the leader is present. You might be wanting to succeed in an industry that is quite biased and to make waves would be counterproductive to your ability to ascend the ranks. But let's take a normal situation, for example, people would prefer a fair and just leader, over one that helps his mates out only. Maybe the mates would love him, but it would only last for so long. We have all seen leaders of our past (or managers) rise and fall due to the same predicaments.

"We see the world, not as it is, but as we are, or, as we are conditioned to see it... when people disagree with us, we immediately think something is wrong with them. But...sincere, clearheaded people see things differently, not looking through the unique lens of experience." (Covey, 1989, p. 36)

An experienced leader doesn't necessarily mean the best applicant for the situation. As alluded to in the above phrase, sometimes experience tarnishes or directs our perceptions before we have allowed the exposure or event to unfold, and we make our assumptions. New leaders, in this case, are more open to change or differing situations, as they haven't experienced them before and are not as easily able to make a presumption about the situation. What matters is perspective, the leader's ability to differentiate previous situations and to measure what is adaptable to the circumstance. And if it doesn't fit, throw it out, don't force the point. Because that is when the leader gets into the area of the old ways and can be tagged as backward thinking or set in their ways. A leader shouldn't be afraid of making changes or testing the boundaries of preordained methods. Sometimes it is best to take some risks because, without risks, there are no rewards.

How do we take a step back? Easy to say, very hard to do. If you are invested in something, personally, you will always claw back at the seams to get involved again. When you hear of a business owner micromanaging everyone, it's because not only is their career on the line, but so is their personal success or failure. That is a hard place to separate the two. But it is all the more reason for someone in this position to take a step away because they are emotionally charged. Their decision-making is based on their personal circumstances, not what is the best position for the business or department. If people see a step back at this level, it will cascade into great levels of appreciation because to be able to step back at that level means a great deal of trust in your people.

If you can prove to your people that you are taking a step back, and they can see it, you will have your people's respect. Of course, unmeasured or unstructured flexibility will create loopholes for people to act out or test their boundaries. Autonomy requires structure, and allowing someone in your team or group to have flexibility in their structured space will get you more desirable results. No one likes to be micromanaged. We all like to do it our way, and even if we use the structure we have been provided, we like to find solutions using our methodologies. And there is nothing wrong with that, I have worked with control freaks before, and it's a hard place to be. I can tell you that I haven't lasted long enough with them, though. It makes people move away from them. We all want the space to grow and learn, even at our own pace. Good leadership sets a structure that we work within, and great leadership allows autonomy within the structure.

Even when things go wrong, if you have the back of your group or team, ask them to help resolve the issue, you will firstly be teaching them how to fix their own issues, but also commanding in them, that you trust them to pick up the pieces and continue on. No one is perfect at this, but in my past are many occurrences where I could have just jumped in and resolved the issue. But instead, I reverted to the manager in charge and let them fix it themselves. I was even asked by them on some occasions, "You could have just sent it through to him. Why didn't you just fix it then? I reminded them, "This is your operation. I am your support, but my expectation is that it's for you to resolve." It is reminding them of their position description but also reminding them that the result would be the same if either of us did it. It's the point of who is in command and control of the activity that is occurring. And that is important to understand who does what in these situations.

The Best Way to Learn

It is hard, but sometimes we need to let people fail to understand what they have done wrong and how they can fix it. I have dropped a previous employee without support in a situation where I wanted them to learn the hard way. I ignored their calls and emails and let them face the challenge alone. At one point, they caught up to me, and I could see the frustration. They wanted to know if there was a personal problem between the two of us. Did they do something wrong to cause this issue?

I replied quite coldly with, "Nope, it's all good. You just need to get this fixed."

When they asked how, I said, "What do you think needs to be done?"

He said, "Well, I think I should do it this way."

I bit my tongue, knowing there was a more effective way. But I let it go and said, "Let's try it that way. Let me know how it goes."

I have found that I have intervened similar prior events with the same issue, and I knew the way to resolve it, but what I found is that each time I gave the answer, it was fixed, and there was no great deal of learning. In this scenario, I let it play out, the desired action wasn't going to take place, and a disaster was about to come, but you know what, if the times before didn't teach him anything. Maybe this one would, because this time, the result will be one that is not desirable. In this scenario, after it all blew up, he knew that there was another way and that this was a strange learning curve I threw at him. I am sure he will not forget for the next time.

We cannot always be carried. Sometimes we need flexibility, autonomy to be forged in fire. Sometimes we need to learn the hard way to appreciate just how much can go wrong and how painful the experience can be. When you were a child and you touched something sharp and it hurt. I am sure you were hesitant the next time, right? Think about a situation where you had a horrible time. It was a nightmare, and you didn't think you would get through it. But of course, you're here, and that means you did, right? What did you learn from this experience? I can take a guess and point out that you learned you are more resilient than you give yourself credit for—that you will approach this type of situation with more experience next time, and that you will be able to guide or teach some of the people involved in the task next time so that they can support you and the whole activity better. And lastly, I can assume that you will take it, just a little bit less personal next time it happens.

If any of the above can apply to your situation, that is the greatest part of what has happened. Learning from your experiences is a critical component to your survival and your ability to evolve with the future. I did a project through my company which was on behalf of the Australian Defense Force, which was to roll out a forward operating warehouse on a Naval base. The task was to involve the customer in the activity for support. During the start-up of the project, I realized that there wasn't much information on what was actually required, nor was there much guidance on our structure or parameters.

Because of my passion and my want to succeed, I took charge. I set the structure and direction of the project, presented it to the commander in charge as a collaborative approach. I set the framework, budget, and expected outcomes. I developed a project tracker and rolled the project out. Our timeframes continued to change, and we went from three months to six weeks in having it all completed. This included recruitment, relocation, infrastructure, and equipment, which was no easy feat. In the end, we were successful in completing the project and were rewarded accordingly. I am someone who makes decisions in quick succession. I had been involved in other tasks similar to this one in private industry, and I was used to making decisions on the spot. Very different in comparison to the public sector.

Unfortunately, and fortunately, after six months, the operation had to move, so I had to do the same project but transferring what we had into another location on the naval base. The problem was there was no internet connectivity, we had to share our operating space with public workers, and we only had four weeks. Well, this was a great start, to say the least. We were again faced with multiple challenges. I was lucky I had all of the formats and project trackers. I also knew how to get traction from the last time I conducted the project. And so, in this instance, being lucky it was similar, I was able to use similar tools to achieve the end result. I also was on a project to close a twelve thousand pallet warehouse down and consolidate it into another location: different business, different environment, similar principles.

And so, I used what I had previously used, but in the meantime, I had studied more about operational management and applied some other practices. I sourced from many areas and put together a project, and rolled it out. Did I roll it out great? No, from the customer's perspective. There were too many disruptions and errors along the way. The actual project rolled out well, and I completed it to the planned completion date. But I also learned some valuable lessons while doing this project. Number one, time of year is very important, and you cannot keep everyone happy.

We moved the warehouse and closed the other one on the last day of December, what was the problem with that? Our employees were on leave, we had to get in unfamiliar contractors, and the issues that came along with that were many. In hindsight, yes, we completed the project within the allotted timeframe and budget. From that perspective, it was a success. But I learned a lot more about planning from this. And three months later, the problems were forgotten about, but my experience and what I learned will last me throughout my career.

That is the important part of failing, hardship, and problems is to learn from them. For when the next instance occurs, you are more readily prepared. You are able to relate your prior experiences and develop a strong framework to deal with changes outside of your initial planning.

When things don't go to plan, be flexible, be resilient, and able to change the way you approach things to suit. If you are rigid and stuck in your ways, you are just that. You won't be able to change with the times, and in the world, we are in today, nothing stays the same for very long. Being adaptable to change will open up new opportunities to you that you were either waiting for or unexpectedly fell into your lap. Luck is when preparation meets opportunity and awareness.

Section Three – Planning And Enacting Our Goals

Time management is essential for a leader. The ability to manage our time, which is a timer that will end one day, is the difference between achieving great things or some great things in the time we have. Which would you prefer? To experience all that life has for you to experience or get to the end and wonder if you wanted more. The only way to test that theory is to get out there and experience, be part of it, and when you do look back, you will probably still have things on your list you wanted to knock over, but if you've had a crack, you might feel a bit better knowing you gave it your all surround by your family and the memories of what you did, rather than surrounded by what you could have had.

How do we achieve so much in such a small amount of time? *'I just don't have the free time.'* Our time is what we decide it is. If you were to sit in a room and count the seconds up to ten minutes, it would feel like an eternity, right? But in the blink of an eye, when you are having fun, ten minutes is just not long enough. Time is a metric that we have created to measure distances. How we perceive time is how time is translated into what we do. A lot can happen in a matter of days and even seconds. It is up to you to decide how you will use your time when you will have time and what you want to sacrifice to enjoy your time, doing the things that you will think most benefit you and your progression.

I also think one of the most important things you can give someone is your time. Not everyone wants a handout. They might just want to be around you or hear what you have to say about them. It isn't just tangible objects. In essence, it is the sands of your hourglass. It is parts of you that you give away to people around you, and to understand that puts the value of time into perspective.

But how do we achieve what we want? Firstly, we need to know what we want. Easy right? Not so because what we want changes all of the time. But similar to our values, we can see a blurry shape of what things we want in life. Our core values give us a sense of direction to what we would do, what is within our boundaries, and what we can perceive ourselves doing. So yes, we can determine what we want. But to do that, we need to set ourselves some goals. We need to identify what we want to achieve to be able to reach what we want.

"Never put off until tomorrow, what you can do today" (Twain, 1870).

It's this easy, ready? The package to achieve everything in your life consists of setting your goals, monitoring your goals, aligning yourself and refocusing on your goals, reviewing your progress, adjusting your milestones, and rewarding yourself for the goals you complete. Simple as yeah? It is easy to say, hard to do, and still harder to enact. But that is not to say that it is impossible. You can achieve anything you set your mind to. If you look in your workplace, you would see managers or leaders who fly by the seat of their pants, that live day to day and react to everything around them, somewhat in a state of chaos. If it was easy, everyone would be doing it, and something worth doing is worth the hard work.

Organization Of Yourself

Do you see other leaders who bring a diary to meetings, follow up on things, and generally do what they say they will? If you asked them if they planned, they might not consciously realize it, but yes, that is what they do, and I am sure if you ask them, you will find out in greater detail the specifics of how they do it. But how do they do it? I find that starting with a diary is critical. I have the tendency to forget things, even a lot of things. And by having my diary, I can recount conversations or activities by the flick of a page.

When I first started out in the workplace, I was told by my manager to buy a book and use it. So, I did, I overused it, I used it for everything, I even started to take it to personal events and wrote notes. I overreacted and used it in excess. Then I stopped using it completely. I did this on and off for a couple of years, using the diary, then getting rid of it. I found that when I had the diary, I was planning and could remove things from my list. Without a diary, my list continued to grow, but I wasn't really aware of what it was. I could just feel there were a lot of loose ends that were building.

It took me many years, but I finally found the correct balance, a daily journal that gives me just the right amount of structure but also the freedom to make changes and be flexible. This works for me. It may not necessarily work for you, but finding what does is important. To achieve your goals, you need to work on them every day. Daily progress is what will get you close to your goals. Breaking down your goals into smaller milestones will help you to gain traction each day. Each time you complete something, you gain a level of attainment. Taking big bites is not as effective as the small pieces to fill in the gaps. Because by setting daily expectations of yourself, you set yourself smaller, more manageable targets, and if you are unable to fulfill them on that said day, the disappointment is much less than a huge bite.

That is not to say that it might not work for you, but it's a consideration. Now you don't have to be someone who writes down every conversation and ticks every box. It comes down to a compromise with yourself. You decide your balance. When you have kids and a family, you will be torn, and you need to commit yourself to a level of review that works. Having none doesn't work and having too much just makes you give it up, and then you start again, much like I did.

Our Own Discipline

How do we set out goals? Well, as I have noted before, it comes down to discipline. You need to set yourself some metrics for your goals. You need to have enough achievable small goals that will keep you focused daily on your long-term goals. You need to hold yourself to account. As a leader, no one is going to remind you to use your diary or set your goals. Not even if you have a great mentor, this part is of your own volition. Not an easy task, I assure you. But the benefits are whatever you want them to be.

A part of your discipline is what I describe in the basic building blocks, conditioning. You are conditioned to respond based on certain outcomes or decisions you have made. How you approach these situations is dependent on your conditioning. We obviously seek reward over punishment. If you set yourself a goal, and after you complete a milestone or get somewhere that you think, *I've done a good thing here*, then reward yourself. You then develop a pattern of rewards for your work. When you don't achieve it, and you don't reward yourself, you're going to try harder next time, right?

"A man is a product of his thoughts. What he thinks, he becomes."
(Gandhi, 1936)

The same happens in the workplace. Managers will sometimes pick an employee of the month, give them gift cards, a special mention at a function, an end-of-year raffle, and the list goes on. Don't get me wrong. Sometimes these aren't the best practices because they become a dependency for some, and if they go away, the bad side of people can come out too. It all comes to each workplace and scenario as to what works best. But we are conditioned to respond based on the reward and punishment of each situation. I know my parents did, but I knew when I was in trouble that the stick was coming out, it's funny to look back now, but I remember the feeling, I was in flight mode, I had to get to my room and barricade that doorway.

The same went when I begrudgingly ate all of my greens to get access to my favorite toy. That is a conditioned response. We can condition ourselves or others through some simple rules which determine the reward or punishments for our tasks. Discipline is our code of behavior, using systems to realign or determine what is right and wrong in the situation and how we are either rewarded or punished to redirect our actions for the next time this is to occur.

"If you fall down. The way to correct your progress requires you to work on 80% realization of what you have done well. And 20% focusing on what you haven't done. It's normally in reverse. But focus needs to be put into focusing more on the wins you did achieve. And not what you haven't yet achieved." (Mylett, 2018)

As a leader, it is important that we set a structure for our peers or employees so that they also achieve their goals. A good leader will bring those around them up with them. Bad leaders will stand on you and ensure they stay in their position. Great leaders remove themselves and make more leaders. But to be a leader, you must understand the why of what you do. Why do you do what you do? Our purpose, our values are what structure our why—our compass. Understanding why you do what you do, your goals, the things that achieve why you are a leader, or working to achieve things is why people see you. It might not be right in front of them, but seeing you, they will see you with a sense of purpose. It is part of who you are. When you speak, you exude what you are all about. How you stand, your body language, depending on the topic, is how you react.

Everyone can see this, and you can see this in other people. You know when someone has a purpose, when they have a vision. It comes in many ways. Even your pace, how you walk—depending on where you are, all compliments your vision, your why. As a leader, it is important to understand your vision and how it is a part of your everyday life because your daily steps are what gets you to the mile—what gets you to the final phases of your goals.

Setting yourself structure, however flexible, is very important. If you do not set yourself some life expectations, some goals, and milestones, you will not be grateful for what you have achieved in so much as part of your reflection on what you do. Everyone is different, and our measurement of success is varied. You need to identify your success and how you will value it. With your structure, the amount of latitude or flexibility you put into it is discretionary. You decide your levels of success and failure, and you decide the criteria. You will be your toughest judge. We don't go into a bad state because of everyone else. We go into a bad state because something inside of us has made that decision. It's not that simple but understand that our circumstances are a product of our environment. Our mind is a product of our own devices.

Don't Set Yourself Up to Fail

I used to focus on the negative things in life, so I kept getting called a negative person, which annoyed me. Through some self-realization, I changed my approach, and I think over eight years, I saw the most change. I still look at possible outcomes, but I look at what I can learn from the bad. I set my criteria for gauging things while also looking at the positives of the negative circumstances and taking the lessons out of everything.

We decide our plan, that is the best part, our vision is our own, some people might want us to do it their way, but in the end, it's our choice. We were born with a set of cards. It's our decision how we play them and at what point we lay them out. When kids break away from their parents, they go through a rebellious stage because they are deciding their fate. I was one of those rebellious kids. In these instances, we gather new sources from different people, we try different things, much the same as a leader, we must learn from different sources and gather intel. Our childhood is similar to our adulthood, and it just depends on the similarities you see.

Let's use an example. If you want to finish a project plan and you have the next three months to prepare it, please don't cram it. I did it so often in a prior life, and it always ended up with problems. Plan to start from Wednesday and complete just a fraction of the tasks you could do on that day in the time you set yourself. Don't fall for the standard: "I'll start Monday." Be different and start at a point in the week where you are not tired or compounded by the Monday workload. Tuesday is catch-up, and Wednesday, you are planning the weekend out. In this time, you will be more effective because you are setting yourself up for the weekend, and you want to get things out of the way to do as such. You will knock this task out rapidly, and you will realize how achievable the work was. This will assist in building momentum.

Don't set yourself up to fail. Starting fresh on a Monday is just a way to say to yourself, I can pig out until then, which will just extend the process. The same as planning for later, do it now, and it gets easier. I've conditioned myself to enjoy planning, writing out my goals, and setting milestones. I like ticking that box. My conditioning has taken time. It started off on rocky edges. There is no easy start to the process. But what you need to keep in your mind is what you will achieve if you do this? Your conditioning will set you up like an electrical diagram, you will follow the chain where there are connectors until you reach the start again, and you repeat.

It's much like being fit—there is no easy solution, it comes down to doing the hard yards, putting in the time and effort, and when you finally get the result, you are appreciative because of the struggle to get there. In leadership, we have to show our people that the hard times will bring about good times. It is easy to lose sight of this, and as a leader, we must project beyond the now, into the ideal or the will-be. We have to be definite in our resolve so that people believe us—believe what we are doing, how we are doing it, and why we are doing it.

You must understand that to set goals, you must think about what you want. Most people have new year's resolutions, which is, in essence, a goal, to lose weight, it's sometimes a throwaway goal at the end of January. If this is a goal you set yourself, write it down, put it in a place where you will continue to see it each and every day for the rest of the year. If you create pain in not achieving your milestones, you will create pleasure or happiness in achieving it and then not receiving the pain.

Displaying Our Goals

Your goals need to be visual, and you need to be able to see them. When you walk into a safety-conscious operation, you see the signs that say, "Safety is our number one priority," or, "Safety first." This is a display of values, ethics, goals, their structure that they will work to. For it to be on display, you would believe that it is what they or you live by. The same as your goals cannot be stored in a box underneath your bed. They need to be prominent, and they need to be a part of what you see each and every day. To keep you focused. Do you think it is easy to forget your phone pin code? I would hope not because every time you touch your phone, you have to type it in. It's seared in your memory because you see it and do it so often. The same theory applies to your goals. See it, and you will be it. Much like we mirror other people, we mirror our goals, and we will become what we have set out to become.

If you already have your goals set, how do you display them? Does anyone know what you are trying to achieve? There is a part of you that will exude what you want, it's part of what you are passionate about, and people will pick up on this. Even without realizing it, you will talk about the things you love in life, and people will get the inkling that you are working toward it. But if you don't put it in front of people, they won't always realize what can be done to make it easier. I had a group of managers in one of my teams, there were three of them working on the same task, yet they were all doing it in isolation.

I pulled them all into the office after I had written down each of their goals on the whiteboard and asked whose goals each of them was. Each of the team members said, "Yeah, that is mine," then I turned, and they looked at each other. It was realizing that they were all working on the same goals yet working toward them in their own silos. Now, this is not to say to stamp it on your forehead, but something close is not a bad idea because you might have commonality with people in your organization or community that you would never even have known. And the commonality that you have can work toward sharing and developing yourselves equally, or as in most relationships, someone will benefit more than the other. Generally, the weaker is brought up to the level of the stronger in the relationship. It allows for collaboration.

When I put together organizational goals, I break them down into small pieces. I start with what I visualize when I think about the goal. I give it a short, one-line description, then give it the metrics. This takes a lot of time, people look at it, and some don't, but it is important to get them involved in the process. If you don't, it only causes them to say they never had the chance to review it. The goals also need to be talked about often by the leaders, if it isn't, but it is expected that everyone abides by it. Make sure that if you want something to happen consistently, then you must do just that. It must be spoken, shown, and measured consistently.

Sharing Our Goals

There is a social stigma that sharing your ideas will lead to someone stealing them. But if you look at it from another perspective: what if they did steal it and failed, and you were able to understand why it failed? Then you could take it over and add that last ingredient to make it stronger and more resilient. Or maybe they are thieves, and they take your idea. Who cares? Do you know what that means? That your idea was great because someone saw it had value and therefore wanted it as their own. Jealousy means you've got something good going on. Embrace it.

In most cases, people are collaborative and want to work together. We are a society, which is made up of all of us. We don't call it the human individuals. We call it the human race because we are a community, amongst communities, within communities. Yes, we secularize, but for the most part, we like to be a part of something. By making your goals or ambitions known, you are transparent, and if you share, people will share with you. The commonality is what makes us friends or co-workers.

Our commonality is what helps to bring us together. Have you ever had a problem, and someone came to you with a different approach? At first, you thought, *Hmm, okay, I don't think it will work, but whatever*, and then it worked? A different approach sometimes is what gets us unstuck from a situation we are in. It's our differences that make our projects so much more effective because we can add value with different approaches. Look at your goals, make sure that you talk about them, make sure that people know where you want.

In a leadership position, I interviewed some good people for a role. I only had two spots to fill, and a day after the two people had accepted, a colleague of mine asked me if I could interview one of his previous employees who he believed in. I took him for the interview, and I was impressed, but I told him I had no roles available. A month went by, and I still had nothing available, but I knew his connection and worth. So, I called my brother and asked him if he was looking for any employees.

If people believe in you, or you can impress upon people your goals or value, then people will invest their time in you. I didn't have to make this connection, nor did I have to follow up on it, but I was invested because I knew what he wanted and could find him a match where I had the connection. Leaders are meant to bridge those gaps, to find people for the right spots.

If people understand your goals and an opportunity comes by, they might throw it your way. Don't be afraid to tell people what you want. When you go for an interview, we have the tendency to say what we think people will want to hear. I have changed my approach. I ask them what they want from the role, and then I tell them what I am after. If it aligns, then great. If it doesn't, then I'll gladly move on. Fulfillment comes from what aligns with your values and goals. If the role looks great and is great, but it isn't part of who you are or where you are going, you will soon see the shine disappear, and you will start to reassess where you are. Being upfront with your goals in life and being transparent means people will generally show you the same in return.

The mirrors around you

Much like the basic building blocks, observational learning is demonstrated in this area. If you do not show your goals, your direction, and your cards, don't expect to know where your people are at. Have you had someone in your business put in their resignation, and you were taken by surprise? You shouldn't be. You can see people lining themselves up for it, they take an early day, they have an "appointment," or they've loosened up a bit more. They start talking to you about future-proofing their role in some cases. As I said before, we exude our goals. If you are aware of it, you can see it happening. If you are transparent and people know your direction, I can guarantee you that the majority of people around you will do the same. It's not an exact science, it's human behavior, and I can guarantee you there are more books on this than there are stars in the sky (well, maybe not, but you get the point).

Be forthcoming with what you're about, don't expect that people need to tell you what is going on if you don't do it in return. The same as prior managers I have seen that tell their team to involve them in what is going on, they do so, but then they get in trouble for every decision they make. Or they get told that 'you should have done it this way.' Then they do it that way, but it should have been this way. Then they ask the employee to stop including them as it is a matter that they shouldn't be included on—getting the picture? We have all had this in our career, or at least seen it unfold on one of our colleagues. It is the micro-managers book on how to really annoy your employees.

The below is a table I have attributed my value and timely contribution to certain parts of my life. They can be considered in most people's lives as The Big Three. If you look at this table and relate, something needs to be reassessed. It could be, like in my case, that my work has little value to my mental state, but it contributes to my family and health. I have many goals, which I will come to later in the book about how it is important to set short-term and long-term goals. There is no easy way out, and there is no reward without the risk of failure.

"The competitor to be feared is one who never bothers about you at all but goes on making his own business better all the time." (Henry T Ford, 1923).

It's not about what works for other people. It's about what works for you and your team.

Item	Value %	Time Contribution %
Work	20	60
Family	40	20
Health	40	20

Figure 1 Weighing of Values against Time Contribution

Control sometimes means giving up on things or reducing the amount of time you give to a certain task so that your circle of control can remain in check. Retrospectively you may also enjoy taking on more and having less control. It depends on the person, the leader, and what they want to achieve in their lives. What matters most is that we attribute the most time to the things that mean the most to us, not the other way around.

"He who wants to keep his garden tidy doesn't reserve a plot for weeds." (hammarskjold, 1963, p. 22)

Reviewing Your Progress

On a whiteboard, piece of paper, or somewhere you look at often, list the top three most important items in your life. Next to each one of them, I want you to write two different percentages. The first is for how much you think it weighs on your emotions. And secondly, how much time you put into it, what do you think your time contribution is toward it is in your time out of 100? In this activity, can you see a noticeable outweigh, is there an imbalance? Take stock of your current situation, and ponder on whether this is time you should look to change, or is it worthwhile to your goals?

Be consistent in your approach. If you want it this way, stick to it, and if you do end up changing your mind, be upfront and admit why it needs to change. If you don't give people this respect that you may have changed your mind, or the business wants a different direction, fill your team in. Don't leave them in the dark. That will only make them leave you in the dark.

If you have set up a goal that has an end destination, which I would hope you know is the goal. Then you will be able to review your progress. One giant leap is not how we achieve our goals. We achieve our goals, for the most part, by each day's activities. If you have a major project, having weekly or monthly review meetings is important. Not just to see what is left to do but also to look at what you have achieved in the timeframes. You will be able to see what you have overcome quite quickly, and what is coming up might have the same speed for completion, you can learn to adapt as you work your way through things and can apply best practices on the fly.

Reflecting on what has been done will give you that greater insight into the rest of the project you are working on. All too often, project managers or leaders just look at what is left to do, but the lessons learned are what stops you from making the same mistakes over again. Don't become a recidivist.

"Insanity is doing the same thing over and over again and expecting different results." (Narcotics Anonymous, 1981)

A team has many people with different experiences, you will not be able to master every skill yet people in your team have also learned from their experiences, and they can bring those lessons along to the group. Reviewing what you do is very important. When reviewing something you have done, consider reviewing it by the below:

- Greatest milestone and the success that came with it
- The greatest challenge that was overcome
- What would you do differently next time?

Reviewing your progress allows you to adjust your milestones or even tweak them so that they are encompassing some of the new tools you are either using or have created to make your activity more achievable at each interval. You don't have to put a large amount of writing into the above criteria, just a one-liner that you and your team agree on which were the most relevant to answer the question in short. I have looked back at a previous project I did when starting another one that was similar and looked at these criteria. By having just a short revision for each section, I was able to draw the top three considerations for my future-proofing. At that moment, what I considered being a different approach might work, it may not now, but it gives me a perspective of my mindset during that time period. Which in itself is interesting to see my own development and you can do the same.

The Last Piece Of Good Goals

You need to set your disciplines, and you need to condition yourself for the long haul. You will need to ensure that you reward or punish your efforts, decisions, and progress. Now your forms of reward and punishment are based on how you will realign and continue your progress, and it is different for everyone. You may find that rewarding yourself with a nice meal after a solid week of eating well is a good reward, or ticking a box and feeling fulfilled is enough. You might also make yourself do an extra two hundred push-ups for eating poorly for the week. However, you decide to do it, it has to work for you.

The same for your teams. You need to establish what works when rewarding them and set the bar for them when it comes to rewards and punishment. I had a time where I would give out movie vouchers to the employees for doing a great job, they would raise the bar, and it was so consistent that when I started to raise the bar again, they would then expect the vouchers. On a Friday afternoon coming to my office asking for an appraisal as they were hoping they would get the voucher and take their family out. The disappointment came when I didn't hand it out, and it didn't just affect them. It affected their family as they had spoken about it for the week. The build-up makes it even worse. If we set a structure, it must be consistent, and if circumstances change, then be transparent.

Sometimes a stretch target is also good. I have learned from this and set more realistic and intangible benefits that have a greater reward than physical items. But that doesn't mean that is the only way, and it depends where you are and working with that you have to factor into your decision making. The same goes for punishment if you set up a system of punishment.

Some more intangible benefits we used were a car space for the highest performer, rotating the best employee each month, so it was fair but still performance-based. Called out in front of the whole group as a vote of recognition and inviting the employee to a meeting with the customer to get awareness but also some senior FaceTime and perspective on the grand scheme of what they do.

I once used a board in which each employee was listed on the wall, and their pick rates were on display, so visually everyone could see their own numbers, but the team could also see each other's numbers. Wow, you might be thinking. Yes, it was a good learning experience, but it was a poor system, and it created angst amongst the team. It actually punished me, but what I have learned, again this is my experience, is that if you give someone the metric, and if they care enough, they will be annoyed more at themselves than you can be at them. We decide what affects us, and if we do it from the inside, the punishment is much greater. Consider before you put it up on a wall. For me, I have worked out better systems. But what I can say is that I learned from this experience, it will not happen again. In that format, it will be in a different way than it can be presented. As a leader, knowing your people and what makes them tick will help you to make your reward and punishment system, your disciplines to help the conditioning of yourself and your people. It has to be fair as a group exercise. Without reward, without punishment, we lose our sense of discipline, and our conditioning lacks the resolve that it requires.

It is critical, but it is one piece of the puzzle. The package is what is important, and that is setting your goals, monitoring your goals, aligning yourself and refocusing your goals, reviewing your progress, adjusting your milestones, and rewarding yourself for the goals you complete.

Section Four – The Wrap-Up

As a leader, people look to you to provide direction. Sometimes they look to the leader to find comfort or a person they can blame for their dangers or suffering. We are the same as they are. We look to someone or something to give us guidance and support to get through each struggle or challenge that we face. There are layers or cascades of leadership, and that is why all business has levels of responsibility and an organization or hierarchy. It is not only for the accountability factor, but a clear structure that cascades information and direction at the levels that they are required.

We must be able to understand the perspective of those around us. It is not fair or reasonable for a leader to assume that everyone must understand them. It's the other way around. A leader must be able to put the shoe on the other foot and take stock of other people's situations. An effective leader is aware of his or her surroundings and adjusts based on the circumstances. As I discussed previously, a leader is part of the process, not solely responsible, and not totally in control. If a leader were in complete control of everything, he or she would be out of control within moments. As humans, we are unable to be at every point all at once. People, in my experience, have trouble understanding that, at times, we cannot control everything that happens in our lives. It can be quite frustrating when there are circumstances outside of your control that are impacting parts of your life, yet we have little or no control over them.

Even when we are in control, in some situations, we feel the same anxiousness, as though the risk we are taking will cause an impact on our stress levels. But in most cases, we undertake additional risk or anxiousness due to different circumstances or the increased ability for something to pay dividends.

Being anxious means you are taking a risk. Success and fear are not separated, nor is there a time where you are staring down the barrel of the gun with little to no fear in your heart and mind. When you hear of a fearless leader, this is a presentation of the self, not the actual soul of the leader. Fear is natural, and with risk comes reward, but with risk comes uncertainty. At times, clarity is lost as you find yourself in a state of confusion, you assign yourself to too many tasks to keep your mind from losing its place, but in the end, this is part of the reason you lose your place. What is your current biggest challenge that makes you feel you lack control? Where is your risk, and what steps are you taking to make the best of the current situation?

It is human to want to control your destiny, the things that you do, the people that are around you, who you associate with and how you come across. Control is what you are able to mold. But where you lack control is where most people struggle. When we are not in control, most people feel uncomfortable and lose where they stand.

"The greatest battles of life are fought out daily in the silent chambers of the soul." (David O. Mckay, 2004, p. 294)

You can learn to improve a situation through other methods. You might not have total control from start to finish, but by including other perspectives, tools, and systems, you might be able to allow the flexibility of other people's theories into your analysis.

When you set a goal, as we discussed, there are a lot of factors to consider. There are so many tools out there that can give you a good basis from which to start if you haven't already done so. Don't start from scratch, using other people's previous success. In essence, their ideas are a show that something they have done works or is relevant to what you are doing. When someone copies me, it is a show of success. Jealousy comes from the want for what other people have. Setting goals requires structure and consistency, as a leader we must present a structure, determine it, review it, reward it, punish it, condition it, but still allow flexibility within that structure. It is a determinant of your situation and the people that you form yourself with or within.

What I hope most that you get from this chapter is to learn from everyone around you, but to throw your own ideas out there and see how people react. If you put your ideas and practices out there and people react badly, you have an indication of how you could do it next time with some feedback. Learning takes being patient, resilient, and disciplined. If you want to succeed at anything and everything, you have to try everything and anything. Be open to change, be flexible to the situation, because the leader that lasts is the one that keeps on going about his or her business regardless of the situations at hand, don't falter. Just continue to work away at what you are doing. Success comes from taking all the rejections and searching for the right yes to get you where you want to be. Act as who you want to be, and you will become.

Exercise: Although I am not endorsing marketing, I use a system called Trello. I have categorized it into a software Kanban board, which you can list your goals in *To Do*, *Doing*, *Completed*, and *On-Hold*. I have used this system via the application and in my daily diary. Find something that is visual that you will see every day. Don't let your goals be written down, and close the book. You need it somewhere that reminds you every day of what you are trying to achieve. If you already have something good, if you don't, the exercise is to write out your goals. They can be daily, weekly, monthly, or annually. It is up to you. But make sure that at the least you have three goals for the next couple of months. No matter how busy you are. Even if you already have goals, add some. What is something you haven't done before that you might learn from? I booked for my friends to go to the Sydney Orchestra, not something I do every day, but why not? Explore things that you wouldn't necessarily do every day. I didn't think I would like to read books until I did it one day, now I cannot stop. Maybe you can do the same?

Break it down into parts so you can visually see your progress toward your final goals. Here is my example, I want to read a book that is three hundred pages long, and I want to complete it within one month. I have given myself a target that I will need to read forty pages each day. This will mean that it will take eight days or eight sessions to complete the book. Each time I read the forty pages, I tick next to the line. Now that I am at fifty percent, I can see how far I have come. I am just under halfway through the month. I feel like I am building my own momentum and driving myself to complete this goal. Now think of some of your goals and what you need to do in pieces to complete them.

Chapter <V> - You're on Your Own Now

> "The knife's edge that separates failure from success in life, that edge is your attitude, which has the power to help shape your reality."
>
> (Greene & 50 Cent, 2016, p. 6)

Introduction

You are on your own. The accountability of your choices and your role lie with you. You had your safety net, and that comfort is now, no longer. If you have a mentor, that is good, but you need to find a point in your life where you make your own decisions and start to elevate yourself to the next level.

I want to take you through my exposure to learning on my own and what it means to really grasp that concept. There is no longer a safety blanket. Failure is when I am left alone. Success means that everyone who contributed to your development comes out and reminds you that it was them who got you there. But nonetheless, it was all you. If you have made it on your own in a role or in a personal situation in life, it's you and you alone.

This is a great deal a part of the experience. That one person can know when they are going to either be outbid or unable to provide a select service to a customer. My previous director at the time said in a meeting with a customer, *"Don't need the practice. Don't need to fail"* (Bardell, 2018). This was an example that showed his time in the business, understanding that he is at a point where there is no longer a requirement for himself or the business to practice a task, because ultimately, in certain circumstances, it just results in a failure that is experience.

What I will explore in greater detail is the changing leadership styles in the workplace, very simply stated as the old and the new. At some point, the new will become the old, and there will dawn a new 'new.' As I have stated previously, leadership is about being flexible, being diverse, and adaptable to different situations when required. There is no leadership style that works in every situation, and to read a book that states specific leadership styles should be taken on board but amalgamated with your style. There is no point in changing who you are or how you operate unless there is a need for it. In some circumstances, it comes down to your willingness to change the situation at hand. I stress that it is important to understand that no person has all of the answers and that the best source of information is from everywhere.

You might think that the way I talk describes leadership which requires you to only read books on business or management. And there you would be right and also wrong. As I have spoken about in my history, experiences come from everywhere. Our history in literature helps to explain situations that continue to happen even though they have been happening for many centuries. I read in a book about property prices in 50bc rising and falling. Much the same as now, so not everything changes, and sometimes everything changes. My main point is that you need to grasp many concepts, look at many different things in life, and be willing to be diverse because what I truly believe are the great leaders of now, are emotionally intelligent and progressively aware.

Section One – The Old and the New

In my previous industry, if there is a task that you don't do, and it is not part of your core competencies unless you're willing to invest large amounts of capital into the venture, it's not worth the risk. Because subcontracting work out means more touchpoints and less control. If you are contracted with the customer to provide the service, and the subcontractor lets you down, in the eyes of the customer, you have let them down. Turning down work or opportunities comes with experience, and it is not to be misunderstood as arrogance. It can appear from a customer's perspective on the border between these two areas, but it takes experience to understand the risk of taking on activities outside the spectrum of the business's core competencies and knowing what ventures can be taken on with nominal risk to high reward.

This is part of operating on your own. Taking on risk without fully understanding the level of detail or attention required can be a big mistake. And these are the mistakes that you learn the most from. Because these are the decisions that you make that stop you from having a peaceful night's sleep. These are the experiences that help to remind you of the consequences of making mistakes in judgment. It is very important to understand the risk that is associated with making decisions. There is no possibility for us to know all of the risks, but if we put pen to paper and work collaboratively with other team members to gain a greater perspective (experience of others) in the mix, we will have a far greater catchment of what can and will go wrong in any situation. Even when you are operating without a safety net, don't be so innocent to think that you have to make all of your decisions in isolation.

Mens rea in common law is the definition of the conscious decision to commit an act. This is the actual mindset that needs to be proven in the court of law for a crime that has been committed. There is also the separation by *actus reus,* which is the physical action made that constituted the crime. Now, what does the law have to do with leadership? Well, in this case, you may make a decision, but it's the thought process behind it that also is a contributor to your action. If you do something intentionally, with awareness and purpose, you have committed the act or activity using both the mindset and physical action. There are many leaders or managers out there that do something, which is the act but doesn't necessarily understand or make a conscious effort as to why they do something.

That is important to understand that for every action or activity, there are two parts to this, that you must make the decision to commit the act, and then you must physically conduct the act. I am sure you have dealt with a manager previously who made a decision and had no idea why the decision was made. If you have seen a manager get in trouble for what he or she did or didn't do, you will find that you can prove the action they did, it is physical and the easiest to prove. But the hardest part is the *mens rea* which is the conscious decision to make this choice. Sometimes when you discuss with someone their motivation to do something, it is hard to pin the physical activity to their mindset.

Being consciously aware of the decisions that you make should make you more accountable for your decisions. If you are well aware of the consequences of your actions, you are more likely to take a moment to think about your actions prior to physically committing to something. If you give your team enough warning about something, and they still do the activity, they will make a conscious or unconscious effort to keep away from the warnings and work around the boundaries. If you give them no knowledge, and they make a mistake, it proves the mindset is still hard. We are unable to read minds unless you are a mentalist. Same in leadership, you could plan for everything and yet still be unraveled by things that you weren't aware of. Yes, you might have committed the act, but you might not have known what the repercussions or the follow-on effect would be.

When you next look at a team member or leader, look to see if they understand what they are doing fully and whether they are doing something out of instinct or want, as compared to a comprehensive understanding of the pros and cons of their actions. It is a hard thing to understand, but I am sure you have also done something without fully grasping the consequences of your actions—understanding that sometimes decisions are made without an understanding of everything which is important. Because if you question your leaders for making decisions sometimes, maybe think on this. That we don't always know every part of what we decide, and there is a level of 'gut feeling' involved in our decision-making processes, even though we might think our leaders are or should be infallible.

The Difference Between The Two

A manager manages. And a leader leads. To be a leader, we must lead, and by example too.

"Leadership is the capacity and will to rally men and women to a common purpose and the character which inspires confidence." (Bernard Montgomery, 1942)

It's no easy feat. And it's an evolving activity. This doesn't mean that to be a leader we have to stand at the front of the team when we go somewhere or that we are in front visually. Different situations call for different compositions. What it does mean, though, is that we lead, and the most characteristic way is by example. Have you ever made a decision and not involved anyone in your team in the process? When you rolled it out, people either became submissive or fought you at every step, right?

Now when one of your team makes a decision without your awareness, it affects you. It's not right, is it? Because you are their manager or leader, and they need to get your approval. This is the problem with the classical theory of management that the manager is in their position and must approve every decision. But in the modern idea of leadership, the leader is in the business of serving all parties. There is no aristocracy. And what I am finding in business today is the young and old dynamic is fantastic when it works collaboratively, but when the two leadership & management styles conflict, the work struggles to get completed effectively due to inter-company personalities.

The new leadership style is about collaboration, sharing information, being transparent, and reducing the borders of privacy. Whereas the old school method is to keep decisions with the upper echelon, provide only the applicable information, and maintaining complete privacy. Both styles have their benefits, and they both have their problems. I am part of the new methods of leadership, and I can see the conflict that comes when I deal with the old school operators. I have been told countless times that I am giving too much away, that I need to slow it down as I am going too fast. But in my experience, I have created loyal relationships with customers, peers, and employees as I don't have anything to hide.

Even touchy decisions that require a greater level of secrecy, I generally find a way to approach the subject well in advance of it happening and explain the pros and cons of the situation. By being transparent, I have found that people know where they stand—along with what we say and what we do, which can be two completely different things. Sometimes it is just best to come out and be honest with what is going on with your people. If you have witnessed a difficult time at work, you have seen management having behind-closed-door discussions—you just sense something is wrong. Some people become paranoid that they start looking for new roles, and by the time the decision is made, you have people leaving the business.

Leadership is getting people to the point where they do what you want them to do, to achieve an objective, but as if it was by their own initiative or a shared understanding. Management is the law, the parameters, and the structures that keep the team in the right lane.

It is important to understand that learning from old-school leadership is no disadvantage. It gives the learner perspective and a greater appreciation of how people lead and manage in different situations. People also have a tendency to change how they come across different situations. When your manager or leader is away, and you begin to reign down your rules on the team or people in his or her absence.

"Dangerous is the lion's lair. Even when the lion's not there." (Plutarch, 1958, p. 53)

This is not to say that this will happen in every case. I am realistic in the understanding that no one has all of the right ideas. What is most important, and I have stressed this before, is to take your inspiration from many sources.

If the leader or manager that you report to or are affiliated with is absent, consider that there is a lot of practical reasons why a leader should also consider the slow and steady process. People don't always react to change at the coal face as though it is the best thing to do. People become complacent and like to stay with the consistency of their daily lives. Change can be great, but it depends on the environment in which you are operating within. Some people are aware of their situations and want change, *"Some people get wet in the rain. Others feel the rain"* (Miller, 1972). Leadership, as I have mentioned, is about flexibility and application. Leadership must be fluid and interchangeable through time and take exposure to different techniques.

There are plenty of old leadership styles that will continue to work today and, in the future, as every industry has its own composition of people. And ultimately, people together, molded together, are what makes the culture of a business. There is the expression that you would have heard in the workplace, where people say, 'he won't fit into that business' or 'she will get a real wake-up call when she starts working there.' People can sense the type or style of person that you are, and each business has its own makeup. The same as a family, where reality television pits the outcasts against the polar opposites, and the clash begins. I am a firm believer that conflict brings about resolution, but that is only if both parties are willing to come together and mold with one another.

The Mortar of Leadership

Culture consists of shared beliefs, practices, and attitudes that exist in an organization which is the product of individual and group values, attitudes, perceptions, competencies, and patterns of behavior.

I think that the newer styles of leadership also come from a place of anticipation, the expectation that certain things are certain. The old leadership sees the new generation as entitled and unaware of the struggles that must be faced to achieve what the new generation feels entitled to. But times have changed, and the expectations of both leadership styles must come together and evolve. There is no one solution that will work as it is a collective. I have found the most conducive team environments to be a mix of old and new school methods. There are many different perspectives that also force people to move beyond their individual biases. Because in a group scenario, it will flesh out, and the majority (in most cases) will come up with the best solution.

It is important that people come together with a solution focus in every challenging circumstance. You could have all of the greatest individuals in a room together, but if the team is about ego and only focused on who achieves the greatest results first, the team will fall to pieces. Whereas a team of people that come together, that works together and finds synergy in working as a group and the possibilities are endless.

In 1892 two brothers opened a bike shop, fixing bicycles and selling their own designs. They had a passion for the mechanics of aviation, and with no tertiary or college education, they had to work out the designs by observing birds and how their wings spans could manage their weight in flight. They were in a race, but without their awareness, another competitor had a grant from the War Department in 1898. Approximately fifty thousand USD, when you convert from 1890 to 2021, it's approximately one million dollars. Why were these two brothers able to beat someone else who had an abundance of funding?

These two men had a vision, and they wanted to achieve something so grand that they put every moment of their life into it. Consider the competition. They employed engineers, surveyors, administrators, and managers. They had a goal, but at the same time, they worked their hours, they had a job so long as the project continued, and they were paid a set wage. A vision trumps funding. Why do you see so many people rise from nothing to become something amazing? It isn't just wealth that helps to achieve great things, it certainly helps, but it is attitude and determination that are the secrets of success. In this case, it was the Wright brothers who, on December 17, 1903, succeeded in flying the first free controlled flight of a power-driven plane.

This example shows that a vision can overcome anything, and you can achieve unbelievable results. The difference between a day job and a passion is substantial. Absorb every setback and take it as an opportunity to learn. In the case of the Wright brothers, they had many setbacks.

To be honest, it is hard to imagine their success. They started out opening a newspaper of their own volition and then opened a bike shop. Going from a bike shop to creating the first power-driven plane is hard to comprehend.

What you must take out of this is to feel the rain, don't just get wet. Be aware of what you are being showered with because every moment of hostility, peace, conflict, and cohesion are the experiences you need so that you can grasp many different concepts of leadership.

Being open and aware puts you well beyond those that just 'get wet.' By being aware of all styles, old, new, organic, progressive, and whatever additional buzz word you can think of, is that you can read every situation. And you will get better each time you do so. When you are in a bad situation, take stock. Do you think that you might approach the situation differently with what you now know?

This is something you need to continue to ask yourself, don't just believe that if it worked in the past that it will work the same again in the future. As a good leader, you need to question your checks and balances and approach the situation each time with a renewed perspective. I have to look myself in the mirror sometimes and remind myself that I am a great leader, regardless of whether other people think it or not. Because I am the successor of my errors and achievements, so be aware of what you do because not everything that worked in the past will continue to work in the future. What would you do differently?

There is no reason why an old mindset won't work, but having a mindset is a focus, nothing wrong with a focus, but as we discussed earlier, dogmatism doesn't work. The world is more progressive. In the last thirty years, we have crossed more boundaries in technology, society, psychological, industrial and what it means to be a leader that were previously areas that would take hundreds of years, are now only taking years. Why? Because the internet has broken down all of the old boundaries of the world. If someone does something wrong in the media, we can find out within five minutes of it happening. In the 1920s, if something happened on a different continent, you wouldn't find out about it until the papers were released and it arrived in your country. It could take easily up to three months for news to come back home due to the logistical need to physically send the message. That is a huge difference in time.

I asked a senior military leader, "What are the best ways for new leaders to practice their leadership?"

He answered, "It's all about opportunity. If you are in a position to support a new leader with opportunities in a safe and supportive environment, you should take it as it will help them gain experience and confidence."

Information is Power

Information is so easily accessible to us in this age. If we see someone in a dress or uniform that we would like, we can purchase it right away. Think of it like dominos—a long chain of dominos that goes from one room to the next. Now we are able to pick that domino up and place it at the very end of the communication chain. We have invariably bypassed all of the physical separation and steps to get to the end-user with information.

As a leader, being able to change rapidly is required in the modern amphitheater. If an industry overseas gathers momentum in the hearts and minds of the people in our country, people will then relate and expect the same or similar conditions. Much as the expectations of leaders, if you look at the difference between a president and a prime minister, they are presented in two different ways. And therefore, we expect what is of the higher quality level. We don't settle for the least. We want the best.

If you look back at past leadership, there are a plethora of inventive practices that were used. This section is not to say that the new model is the only way to go forward. What I am trying to portray is that learning from both will create a leader who is versatile. Based on our values and disciplines, some people actually are more efficient and considerate of older style leadership. And what do I mean when I say an older style of leadership? I mean to say that it was a leadership utilized in different times, where there were no mobile phones, emails, and other electronic delivery systems. The people of the 1940s relied on different systems. It was a time after a war where people felt security in the leadership that overthrew a harmful dictator—that the leadership prevailed with a resilient system of people who worked for society and future prosperity.

In our current situation, at least in western society, we have had a lasting peace that has shaped how we perceive our situations. Our way of life has become an expectation and a reality. It is hard to get people to knuckle down at times because there is no harsh punishment in our system where we are able to support people should they fall into financial or emotional hardship. The motivation of people has changed. In the 1940s, leadership styles used perseverance over evil and unwavering support of the free world. In our situations, if the going gets tough, we have the ability to walk away. We don't have to put up with the harsh realities because global war hasn't existed in over seventy-five years.

Momentum Shifts: The Domino Effect

When you make a decision, have you realized that by doing so, you have unexpectedly set in motion a range of changes that you didn't initially antiquate? We need to be mindful of the decisions we make, but don't fear that making decisions will be a bad thing. Sometimes bad things happen because of what we do, but it all depends on our thought processes. Do you think that the difference between a company executive deciding and knowing the consequences and another that doesn't know the consequences is better or worse? That's a moral dilemma for yourself. But knowing the ramifications is important, and it is not the only factor to consider. There is a lot that goes into making choices. And with one decision comes many more choices that come along with it. Leaders would be out of their jobs if things didn't continue to pop up.

Consider how war not only changed when women were in the workforce but what it did do was start a movement that no one at the time could have anticipated. It was needed as men were on the battlefield, and women were required to work in the factories where the men were predominately operating. It created a movement for women to move into the workplace and become part of the professional environment. Men couldn't stand alone in the offices. It was becoming a shared environment. What is notable for a leader to understand is the ramifications of decision-making. Whether it is good or bad is not the point. What is the point is that our decisions can create domino effects, so we must consider all aspects of a situation before making decisions?

The Vietnam War, amongst other things, had the involvement of the west because of the thought that if communism got into the Cong (Vietnam), it would create a domino effect. That if the country came under the influence of communism, then the surrounding countries would follow suit and become communists. This was just after the Cold War where America and Russia were in a crisis that our mass weapons were so powerful that we could annihilate the entire planet. It was all about leverage, that if smaller countries could be turned to 'the way' that eventually the whole order of things would cascade along with it. I won't spoil the end of the war, but let's just say that the decisions made as part of this event had many things that came from it. That the decisions made from start to finish have changed the way in which western society operates even to this day.

Understanding the contrast in time periods is interesting, and leadership attributes a lot of its style from the time period. I couldn't imagine what it was like to live in England or even Europe whilst the German Empire strolled across the land turning entire cities into rubble. What it did do, though, was create some very strong and hardened, and resilient people. It also polarized the people of that time, either to join the Axis or Allies. It was a very simple choice, and there wasn't an opportunity to join another side. But in the modern-day scenario, there are many different banners. We do like to put each into its two categories, right and wrong. But a lot of the scenarios create sides of selection. They side with someone based on their leverage, what they can get out of the situation and what they have been promised.

A lot like leadership today, people will side with the majority of the two sides, but there are people who sit in the middle and swing based on the favor or leverage that they can get in different circumstances. Depending on the promises, they might even swing their vote or side and go with the latter. Unfortunately, the moral code of our modern-day society would not be in alignment with the older post-war system because there was a clear sense as to what is right and wrong. But now, in the modern scene, with a constantly changing front of the house, the sense is now a gray area. What was once seen as wrong is now right, and acceptance is expected.

It is quite interesting to see the many sides of each argument. With the change to the laws and the introduction of more fair practices that ensure, in the most part, that discrimination cannot occur, it's interesting to see the polar opposites and selective sides of the discussions. Because there is merit in most discussions that people have about the policy change and the societal changes that are sweeping, especially in the past ten years, and understanding both sides is important to leaders as the decisions you make. It's good to see how people react to societal changes, as you can learn how people think. There are even certain socioeconomic groups that have similar opinions on matters. Understanding someone's background will give you a greater perspective of their mindset.

How Our Pasts Make Up Who We Are

People are predetermined by their past. People who have their parents present a consistent message are conditioned to be the same way. That is a generalized comment, yes, but there is truth in the masses to this statement. I am sure you have heard the expression when someone calls another person a sheep. It's not because they are all fluffy and white. It's because they follow suit. When you see a pack of men together, they become partly animalistic. We revert, sometimes, to our more primal conditioning. If the group makes a decision, people in that group will generally go along with the masses and follow suit. This all depends on our moral compass, too, or our values. They play a big part, but if we go headlong into some circumstances, our values tend to take a backseat. And this is where people regret the night before or the choices that they made. Some people could take decades to realize what they had done was against their values. Some people's values change, and then this event is highlighted for them as a reminder of what they could do or shouldn't do.

If you develop your emotional intelligence, which we will speak about in great detail in the final chapter, you will be aware of yourself and others. Your awareness of people around you gives you scope and gives you an understanding of what you have to work with. Understanding as a leader as to where you work, who you work with, and the general socioeconomic make-up of your employees and peers will determine your leadership style. There is no hiding the fact that kids who have wealthy parents have greater education or opportunities to achieve more education, sometimes though they are neglected, and as such lash out in various ways. The same as kids with poor parents generally have lower education, and sometimes though, they are spoiled with attention and lash out in various ways.

Now that was just the same sentence reversed. Because there are so many variables to our circumstances, don't fall for the fact that someone is poor that they act in a certain way. The same goes for someone with a wealthy background. You need to learn more about someone, scratch beneath the surface to find who they really are. I come from a lower-middle-class background, and when I was given the opportunity, I was and still scratch at every possibility. I know what it is like to have very little, but now that I have a taste for a bit of everything, I cannot stop myself from wanting more. My experience, while not terrible, was dire enough to instill in my mind a certain sense of instinct that drives me to continue to get more.

A wealthy person's background won't necessarily drive someone to want for more unless it is a passion or personal desire, our past doesn't predetermine who we are, don't judge any book by its cover until you have got to know someone. The need for more might not necessarily come from a place of financial difficulty, but it might come from a drive to be like a parent or be better than someone. It is important to understand that which drives us. It may look like the same desires on the surface, but your motivations are entirely different. It is our past that predetermines our future. Even if we don't want to admit it, there is so much evidence that leans toward this factor. Now I don't say this as a polarized person. It is best to understand a person and where they are headed before you judge who they are. It is important to know that in so many ways we are all very similar with just some alternations in how we interact with circumstances in our lives.

What We Do That Counts

You don't truly know someone, and it would be an error to think that you know someone for certain. To assume someone will act in a certain way every time is a mistake. What your awareness should do is teach you to understand someone, but in each situation, be prepared for flexibility. Be prepared that the way in which you present something will need to be tweaked for each and every event. Someone who you would think would grow up to be a terrible leader might end up being the very best there is.

I remember doing an internet survey that pointed out the worst traits of three famous leaders, and all of the good qualities were that the leader was a clean eater, didn't drink, was physically fit, and a vegan. I thought, *Well, this must be someone who had it all going for himself.* But it was Hitler, and the two men that were heavy smokers and drinkers were Roosevelt and Churchill: two prolific leaders who with their nations overcame a great evil that plagued the whole world. I thought to myself, *Well, maybe I've been looking at things the wrong way.*

The way in which we present ourselves doesn't make us who we are. It's our decisions, the choices that we make that affect people define you as a leader. Whether it be new or old leadership styles, it's the decisions you make today and the ones that you don't make today that make the most impact on who you are as a leader in your environment. The decision to act could have the very same consequences as the decision not to act.

I am stressing that you need to be open to all things, great and small. You need to look at how people were in different time periods because you hear people say, "How could they be like that," or, "What a terrible time to live in." We don't understand them if we make this decision. This is closing the door to their experiences. You will find that some people loved it the way it was, that they don't understand today's environment. A great leader will be flexible, adept at looking at yourself, the world around you, pertaining heavily to your emotional intelligence, and that which encompasses all of these character traits.

We need to be aware that the decisions we make are what define who or what we represent. The expression 'gave himself enough rope to tie his own noose' is the thought that sometimes if you say or do too much that you are building a repertoire of events that get you later on. This is not to say that you should be minimalistic. Certain areas of leadership require decision-makers to think on their feet. But where possible, if you are armed as best as possible, you will make better decisions as you will hopefully have an arsenal of knowledge and skills to prepare you for most situations.

It is interesting to see new leaders coming into the industry and how they stunt when certain decisions need to be made. I know instantly what course of action we need to take, but it is interesting to see how they hold up and need time to consider all of the possibilities. This comes back to our earlier guidance and our experiences in life. With too many experiences, we can get lost in our past and forget that the future needs adaption. But it also gives us a template for future scenarios that we know will play out a certain way if we make the decision to do as such. Much the same as when we see new leaders coming into the ranks, we need to guide them in hyper-care but let them make their mistakes because the greatest lessons in life are the ones we make for ourselves.

Section Two – What Is Your Motivation To Be You?

Why do you do what you do? Is there any reason why you want to be a leader or that you want to make yourself better, or that you are genuinely a good organizer of people? I don't think there is anyone point where you know who and what you are, and who and what you are to become. It's all the small ticks in the boxes that develop the final plan. It's the milestones along the way that make the most of who you are. Have you ever found your motivation out of necessity?

People stand up tall when they believe in something. Sometimes it's when they have no alternative, and people have a great deal of ability to question the status quo. People are also easily able to become complacent when things don't seem dire when there is a way out that is easier than going head-on with the problem. Conflict brings resolution, but it's not an easy road in the short term. What about the long term? Where do you see yourself? Who are you, and what do you think it will take to become who you so desire to be? And why?

Life is about what you do when you hit the ground, and people will look to you as the leader to hit the ground running. If you show signs of despair, you damage the entire leadership structure. There is no problem with showing transparency, but it needs to be managed effectively, or you will end up causing cracks in your team's capacities.

Nature and Nurture

What determines who we are and what we will become? Is it our DNA, our birthright, or is it our experiences that shape who and what we are? There is reason to side with both individuality and then the collective.

Nature refers to our birth and that we are predetermined to be a certain way based on who we are. Sometimes you hear people use a surname to define someone. Could it be that we are born a certain way and are unable or unwilling to change based on who we are?

Nurture refers to our experiences—our lives and our interactions that have set up who we are forged by the fires of life, and that who we are and what we will become is based on our circumstances.

So, which is it? Nature or nurture? It is a mixture of both categories. We are born a certain way, and there are parts of us that we are unable to change without physical modification or psychological changes occurring, which you could then relate to nurturing. I know I was born a man, but if I so chose to become a woman, I could in the present. Who I am inside might stay the same, but the outside might change? Or maybe I choose to be different, and now you wouldn't know me from a bar of soap. Is that really possible?

I think there is evidence of both, respectively. Psychoanalysts in the past have conducted exercises where twins have been removed at birth and later in their life reunited. The test was to determine whether it was nature or nurture that was predominant in who we are. There are conflicting parts to each experiment in which some resounded a swing in either way. To be fair, there are also opinions that work as an equal to both sides. There is still a conflict on the theory, a good discussion point.

Does our leadership, our dreams, our goals comply with a genetic predisposition whereby we are already determined to be a certain way? Or are our dreams developed throughout our experiences, from the mortar that makes up who we are and what we are to become?

It is a combination of the two, and if we do not consciously decide who we want to become or what we want to stand for, then our nature takes the lead. I think that we are born a certain way; if we don't make a conscious decision to take action and become what we decide, then we will follow a pathway that could certainly be predetermined by our genetics. The conscious decision to make a change and become who we dream of being is part of the nurture in our lives. If we see something someone else has, and we want it, we can achieve what we put our minds to.

I have lead projects that I had dreamt would be completed in full and on the required date, yet I had a great level of doubt in the back of my mind. Yet, I continued to fight the doubt and put up solutions at each turn. I recall being in meetings, and the majority would let me know it was going to fail, and we wouldn't meet the date. Some staunch supporters, though, kept me grounded. We persevered regardless of the noise, and we got so close to the point of breaking. Yet, after all of the chaos, and it was a success. We achieved a victory. We made a date and completed the project. Against all odds, we achieved what most would say was impossible to achieve. What you believe is what you will achieve.

There are countless success stories riddled throughout the world of people who started with nothing and got everything they desired, and you can do the same. Sometimes we feel defeated because we reach a point where nothing good has happened, but it is in the same respect as weight loss. When we get to a point where we feel nothing has happened, the very next couple of days is when the actual progress begins to take place. It is at the point where we are just about to give up that is the deciding factor. When you are so close to giving up is the real test of those who are willing to go the whole way. I have had many times in my life where I have been so close to throwing it all in, and I have persevered and realized the benefits once they have come. It is no easy answer, but by keeping your goals and aspirations somewhere visual, you will be able to revert back to them and see them. Even drawing a picture of what you have in mind will help to keep you focused.

I had the opportunity to interview a current senior military leader. Noting that this member is currently serving, so all names, dates, and operations have been changed to generic descriptions to respect the privacy of this leader.

Do you think that leadership is something you are born with or something you learn?

Answer: *"I think having EQ is probably something we are born with, i.e., some people are better with people than others, but you can learn leadership along the way through both courses but more importantly through experience. For example, while I had plenty of experience with leading a Navy team in my time at a military base, I needed to learn to provide leadership and direction to an APS (Australian Public Servants) team and, to a certain extent, to the contractors that supported us there. All three groups (Service, APS, and the contractors) have different cultures because they have different drivers. To ensure you can provide leadership to separate groups like that, you need to develop empathy for their circumstances as well as develop a key objective or value set that all can agree to. For this base, we were focused on supporting the customer safely. I felt that given I had just come from sea, I was able to provide a real-world experience of where support made a difference to my ship. This is also why, where possible, I tried to get members of all groups (particularly the non-service people) to visit military capability so they could see what their involvement meant at the end of supply."*

Writing This Down

How do we stop ourselves from becoming complacent? There is no pill or special treatment that causes this. It takes time and focus on the short-term and long-term objectives. Have you set yourself goals? Have you written them down? If you have, you will have found that your entire ethos shifts you toward them, that in some way or another, your goals are achieved.

By writing things down, we are much more able to retain the information contrary to when it is just heard. Also, by the simple fact that it is visually there, and we are able to return back to it for clarification when we need to. Many times, I have had a conversation with someone, and many months later misinterpreted what was once said, but when I review what I had written down, it helps me recall the message more effectively. There is so much information that enters your mind that things get jumbled up together, and a similar situation to another can get lost together.

"Your brain echoes with messages that can inspire victory or defeat, even when they don't come out in words." (Lewis, 2011, p. 305)

You cannot honestly say that you can remember everything that was said to you, nor by writing can you, but you can paraphrase and hold onto what matters most to you with the time you have to write it. This is one of the fundamental language skills along with listening, speaking, reading, and of course, writing. Human communication is brilliant because it is formally structured. They say that math is the most basic form of communication as it is either right or wrong. There is no middle ground, so the way in which math works is there are two possibilities. With the human language, there are a plethora of possibilities. A sentence written can have a completely different outcome to a sentence spoken. Tonality and the passion that comes along with verbal communication takes a whole other turn.

If I were to hear a speech that was dry and had no form of tonality, I would most likely fall asleep. I have been close in the past to falling asleep during a lecture. The way in which something is presented makes you remember or forget it in the same instance. How information appeals to us depends on the way in which we are wired or what we want to get out of a situation. Someone who is presenting must also appeal to the room, depending on many considerations. If the room is read wrong, the presentation could fall entirely on deaf ears.

How we become memorable and how we retain information is dependent on how we interpret the information. Engagement is a big part of discussion and retention. If you are not engaged and personally involved, you will be less likely to recall or have the feeling as to what is presented. Passion comes into play also in this instance, so when we write things down, or we are trying to remember something in our own way, we can use pictures to give us tone. That is just it, do it in your own way. If you write in a diary, don't write it so that someone else can read what you have written, write what works for you. Our personal touch to the things we want to remember is what will link closer to ourselves than a message written for someone else.

Everyone retains information in their own way. For me, I write everything down, I also get a sense of achievement out of seeing in front of me every day what I have to do, and as I tick my boxes, I see what I have done. By seeing everything in front of me, I am also able to prioritize, I can see on my board everything that I have to do for that day, week, or month, and I can consciously decide what takes priority over which tasks.

Your Mission Statement

Have you ever considered what your mission statement is? Have you identified your mission, and what steps will you take to achieve it?

"History will be kind to me for I intend to write it." (Churchill, 1948)

I think that it is important to write down your goals, where you see yourself, and to write down milestone achievements that will get you where you want to be. There is no easy solution to achieve great results. It is the burden of hard work and backed up by long hours. Not just in the position of doing, but also by thinking, and thinking, and contemplating and visualizing the end in mind.

"I see, know, hear and feel that the purpose of my life is..." (Robbins, 2013)

Tony Robbins is a master curator of empowering people's lives to be what they have always wanted them to be. A great example of creating a sense of vision and, ultimately, your life's mission statement. A mission statement is a powerful depiction of who you are and what you are trying to achieve. But it's not a simple task to just write it on the spot. You have to know what you stand for or what you want to stand for. To hear in your heart what you desire to be. Your values and purpose in life are determined by your end goal in mind. What is your target?

I want you to write down your mission statement. You can use my mission statement as a template which is listed below. Note that my statement might change in the coming years, or it might not change, so be open, don't think that what you write down now is the final product. It takes several drafts to make a final.

"It is not the strongest of the species that survive, nor the most intelligent, but the one most responsive to change" (Megginson, 1963). It doesn't matter what they say you can or can't do. They can't see your heart in your chest. Only you know the size of your heart. It's not the size of the man in the fight. But the fight in the man. The great thing in this world is not so much where we stand. But in which direction we are moving.

Strategy: I will adapt and overcome any obstacle in my path. PERAO – Plan, Enact, Review, Adapt & Overcome.

Vision: I am standing in my home, tall, in a position of strength. I am free, watching my children run around the house. I am smiling because of how proud I am of my life, past, and present. Nothing will ever stop me. I am coaching people and helping them to be better, I am giving to others, and my family is happy and free.

Values: Strength. Determination. Service. Awareness.

Priorities: I will be involved and encourage my family, friends, and colleagues.

What I will do: I will be powerful & courageous every moment that I am alive.

Stop reading, finish your mission statement. It can be a draft. It doesn't need to be finished and then moves forward.

....

In order to understand yourself, you must understand what it is in life that you want to achieve. Do you know what you really want in life? Consider this, are you in the right place to achieve what you want in life? Read your mission statement again.

Are you in the right place to achieve what you really want in life?

There are many people in this world that are unaware of what they want in life. And all too often, it's never too late to make a change. It's just a state of mind and where you are in life. At any time in your life, you can determine your future. It is directed in every day that you walk this path. Don't look to tomorrow to start doing differently. Start in small steps today.

"What can you do today to move toward your dream?" (Hyatt, 2018, p. 195)

It is easier said than done, and I am understating the point. But a leader, someone who wants to aspire to inspire others, must grasp the hardship, take on the problems, and work out a way forward. A diamond isn't found in the ground the way you see it in a shop front. It is a leader's role to take on the hardship that becomes the object of beauty when it's on display.

Overcoming the Great Challenges

Think of one of the greatest challenges you have faced in your life. How did you feel when it was over? Relieved right? It is through these struggles and hardships that we become the best of who we will become. But what is lost in this entire sequence of life is the importance of reflection. Think now about one of your greatest challenges or struggles in life, and it doesn't have to be work-related. It can be anything you have encountered in life. Let me guess, you were stressing, uncomfortable, even felt like you needed to consult someone. No matter how much you complained about it, it just wouldn't go away. But somewhere along the way, you started to see the light at the end of the tunnel, right? You had been working on the problem, and it felt like you would never get through it, but you did.

"Our greatest glory is not in never falling but in rising every time we fall." (Goldsmith, 1760).

But if we just keep going, we always make it out on the other end stronger. No matter the circumstance, we always make it out on the other side stronger. Each and every day of this struggle, of our struggle, makes us stronger, wiser, smarter, more resilient, and more able to overcome the next challenge. It is because of the hard times that we respect and appreciate the good times. Without the hard times, there are no good times. It is the roller coaster of life. And through the reflection of how we adapt and overcome is what makes us better each and every time we come to the next challenge.

Motivation is linked to our passions. We need to understand what it is that interests us. If we know what aligns with our values, we are also in a better place to make decisions and overcome great obstacles.

When you look back at a hard moment in time, you get a smile on your face, don't you? That you're not there anymore, and you're here. It's much easier to laugh about something now than when it was occurring. But think about what you did to overcome that situation. When you were backed into a corner, or you had to perform, you did, right? And you made mistakes along the way, but you continued to do your best until you got to a point where you overcame it. When you look back at these moments, you'll realize that if you have this same situation occur again, you will act with more experience. With past performances, you will be better equipped to deal with the situation.

Be considerate of the situation and determine the steps you need to take to complete your project or desires. Write down the steps required to complete the activity. Once done, add a step on each page of your diary for the next couple of weeks. Tick them off each day, it shows steady progress, a measured approach, and it gives you the space to determine if there are additional things you need to include. If you rush your tasks, you will end up missing things, and without giving it the space required, you won't consider all of the outlying effects. Pace out everything that you do, don't rush because then you end up making the same mistakes you did last time.

Changing the Way We Feel

We all need a break. When you are young, you can go on for a long time without a break but taking time away from the day-to-day is important to your future. Whenever my wife and I go away on holiday, we put our entire lives into perspective. We ponder, *Is it worth it, what we are doing now for what we have?* Reflection is important so that you can tune up your life and determine if what you are doing right now is worth all the work.

Try this activity, smile right now, give yourself a big smile. And I mean a real big genuine smile. Now think of your loved ones, the ones you would do anything for. You do what you do now for them, right? But don't stop smiling. Do you feel a warmth in your heart? Take a few moments to think about the best moments in your life. When you have overcome something, and it made you feel so good. If you don't have this right now, just think about your family.

Now think of someone that is giving you grief or a challenge you are currently facing. Don't stop smiling. The situations in your life will undoubtedly affect you. But remember that the only person that can truly make you feel the way you are feeling is you. Just by smiling, you have changed the way you feel. No one did that but yourself. You can stop smiling now if you want. So, consider the challenges in your life—your current stress points. When you think about them, your heart rate starts to elevate.

What are your principles that you listed above in your mission statement? These feelings you have right now, are they listed there? I don't think so. What you say your priorities are and what you are feeling right now are not one and the same. That's a problem. To achieve your mission statement, you must live by your principles. Your principles are your priorities. You will always feel stress and heartache in life, but you cannot let them overcome what you want to achieve in life. People will always try to bring you down, we are competitive by nature, and people continue to find a way of bettering themselves, even if that means lowering you, so they stand tall.

We all carry things on us that remind us of either a loved one or a time where we found significant happiness in our lives.

"I carry the things that remind me of you." (Bridge, 2004)

I carry sentimental items: a ring from my brothers, a ring for my wife (and tattoos of the things that best represent who I am. We all carry in some way, shape, or form the things that either define us or by what we want to be defined. These are things that no one can take from us, and the memories that you cherish should remind you of when things get hard.

A leader's mindset is important. If we are down and out, people will mirror our behavior. If you are a good leader, people will see something is up and try to help you to get back on track because if you raise your team up, they will want you to get back to the standard. It is beneficial to the whole community to ensure that the leader is correctly placed so that everyone can thrive in the environment. There is no easy way to change the way you feel, but there are many exercises, such as smiling, that can instantly change your feeling, even if it is just for an instant or within that moment.

The best way to get past an issue is to go through it. The hardships that you overcome today are the memories and lessons you have from tomorrow. Trust me. There have been some very trying times in my personal and professional life in which I have reached the verge and thought I could go no longer. But I rose above it and became greater than yesterday, and so can you. We get better and better at this with time and our experiences.

What Experiences Bring to the Table

You can be better than anyone, be the competitor that goes about your day without considering the opposition. By solely focusing on yourself, with an end goal in mind, you will achieve what you set your mind to. But you have to live and breathe it every day. There is no break from progression.

"You attain happiness by making significant progress toward meaningful goals." (Hyatt, 2018, p. 201)

Now, this is not to say it is easy. There will continually be roadblocks and obstacles that will challenge you and try to halt your progress. But adapting and overcoming these obstacles is part of progress, and there is no easy way to the finish line. There is no finite answer to all problems, nor a solution to every problem by means of one source. Your personal leadership enthralls you to be better every day, to be flexible and adaptable to an ever-changing environment.

What comes from experience is to measure twice, cut once, which is an expression used by carpenters. A colleague of mine asked me, *"What is the difference between the smart man and the wise man?"*

I threw at him a couple of thoughts off the top of my head, but I was far off the right answer. And what he said changed the way in which I thought about situations in my life.

"The difference is, the smart man learns from his own mistakes. Whereas the wise man learns from the mistakes of the smart man." (Tucic, 2016)

In most situations in my life, I am the smart man, maybe even the dumb man, because I make decisions based on my gut feel at the time, and without checking, I have stepped into a mess of things. But the value of this insight I was given is something I will continue to keep in mind for a long time in my life. If I can become a wise man, I can learn from the mistakes of others and before I make the mistakes myself.

It is important to be true to what you are made of. Who are you, and where do you want to be? If you can have at least a close understanding of these points, your most of the way there. If you set your mind to something nine times out of ten, it will come true. Because if you live and breathe it, it becomes you. It motivates you and to be what you aspire to be. And if you live by this method, nothing will stop you, unless you allow it, the way you feel is controlled by you, and you alone, no one has the power to best you, you will best all, by way of your focus, your flexibility and adaptability.

Ask yourself, are you where you need to be to achieve your aspirations in life? And if not, why not? In which situations today do you need to be courageous. You know the questions you want to ask, but you chose not to. Ask them.

……………………………..

If you look at your mission statement, it is what motivates you, yet somehow what you are doing right now doesn't align, then you need to look at this further. It could be that you are doing something for the money that will get you the item that you desire and that it will align with your goals. But consider what you are doing. It can be a stepping stone toward your future goals. That isn't an issue, but just look at the path you are on, and if it doesn't help you to achieve your goals, whether they be short or long term, it needs to align. If it doesn't, somethings got to give, and you need to decide what is most important in your life.

You hear of some people that say, "I wasted the last six years at that place," or "What a waste of my time." Now, take this with a grain of salt because sometimes people don't review their time effectively, and they may have learned a lot of things from these experiences. But on the flip side, it could be true that what they did was for the money or because someone did it before them. Everyone is different, but you need to be open to the review of your own goals and where you are situated. It is a fearful experience because you might actually realize that you need to make rapid changes in your life. But what I drawback is a leader is seen right through, and if you are not passionate about what you are doing, this could be the very reason you don't find that self-fulfillment in what you are doing.

Don't be afraid to take action. You can see some people who have a lot of experience will say it how it is, that they are not afraid of 'the management.' This is because they have been around and learned from their past failures. You talk with some people in life, and they say that if they aren't happy, they are more than willing to move on. You can't believe their resolve, can you? But it comes from a place of prior experience. I don't want to harp on about it too much, but if you have written out your mission statement, own it. Be an example of what you set out to do in life if you want to do something and it seems impossible. Find a way to make it impossible not to do it because you don't want to look back on life in twenty years and regret anything you have done. You want to be an example of the best version of yourself.

The same expectation that you have for your people in your teams, you want them to be the best versions of themselves. Making them better makes your job and your life easier. Help your team find what is best for them. It could be that you offer someone a suitable alternative to what they are currently doing. I have had in the past employees come to me and say they are no longer happy doing the same job every day. So, I work to understand what it is in the now that is the problem. And if I am unable to find a solution to this, I find an alternative, I pair them up in another area and give them the opportunity to try a new role.

What is important to get out of this is that your experiences help you to decide in advance or in hindsight what actions you should take based on your experience. As such, experience cannot be read in textbooks or studied. Experience is doing the hard yards, getting out there, and making decisions that will result in either good or bad leadership. What you need to do is to determine and review your decisions and be experienced so that you can either mitigate or resolve challenges for the next time a similar situation comes across your table.

Section Three – Reading the Room

Leadership comes down to awareness, and then we start to step into the influence section. If you are already there, you will have an appreciation for this, and if you aren't aware, good, I hope you will learn from it because influence, for the most part, is about what you represent and what you can see in others that you can either shift or gain backing from other sources to propel your ideas or the ideas of others forwards.

Your ability to read the room—to see what is going on right before you is critical to your success as a leader. If you are unaware of situations that are occurring around you, you will have great difficulty overcoming the many challenges that you will face within your career and personal life. What is reading the room? It is the ability to understand the agendas of each person that you are nearby, to understand what motivates them, and what will be the deciding factor in their vote or choices. If you can read the room, and understand what is actually going on, then you will be able to influence the decisions being made by people.

Why do you want to read the room? It could be that you are going for a new role, trying to pitch a new project, or you are trying to make a sale in a meeting room, and you're not sure what they actually want. Being able to understand the dynamic of 'the room' is the difference between making the deal and hoping for it to come your way.

But how do we read the room? It actually comes from a lot of the subjects we have already spoken about. We will delve further into emotional intelligence in the last chapter, but what we will go through is observation. The basic building blocks summarize how you will read a room. Simply, if you can see people's body language actively and that you understand their conditioning, how they come to a decision based on the reward or punishment of their decision making, you can view them and see patterns in their methods, and you can either draw on their desire or see their level of empathy in the room. It sounds easy, though, right?

How We Physically Present Ourselves

It's not only looking the part. It's also doing and being the part that matters. Wear the uniform. But do it without needing the world to see it. Do it and fulfill the responsibility of the past men and women who wore that uniform too before cameras existed. The honor was what equaled the accolades. Not the likes on your photos. Remember this.

Body language, as we have discussed, can give away how someone is and without them even realizing it. Simple signs can show if someone isn't interested in the conversation, they won't ask questions that bring about detailed explanations. They will keep at a surface level, and they may cross their arms or point their feet to the door, ready to move. They might close their diary or slide their seat back, ready to move away. These are just a couple of simple views of some people's body language.

I have even done the same when I have spoken with someone, I have turned my feet and turned my neck, and it was uncomfortable. I was even nodding my head impatiently, and they continued to talk slowly and with a lot of detail. I realized my body language was one that was aggressively trying to get away, yet they continued on as if I were there to stay. Even if we are aware of our own body language, some people cannot see ours. This is a powerful trait to have—to be aware of yourself and others, and you will be able to understand when you have either made the sale or lost it. The same with your teams. If you are presenting something and the majority of the people listening are nodding their heads and trying to get you to hurry up, consider changing how you are presenting.

You need to also understand the environment before you make an assumption on someone's body language. You might find that one person in the room has their arms crossed because they are cold, and the other is because they are closed in and sick of your sales pitch. Or they could be in reverse, and you need to understand the person before you can throw your assumptions against them. If you do this, you will read them wrong, and you will label them with something incorrectly. So be careful thinking that after a couple of hours of studying people's body language that you are an expert because that in itself is a big error of judgment.

What it will do, though, is give you a good grounding to then do further research on people to understand their body language. People who are also consciously or unconsciously aware of their own body language will also be able to either attempt to fake or present themselves differently. So, reading their body language could be very difficult as they could shift how they sit or physically react. Don't put all of your eggs of awareness into one basket, because as I said, it would be a big error to do so.

Our Group Ethics And Decision Pathways

It comes down to the patterns of behavior that will be the tell-tale for each individual. If you understand the group dynamic, you will understand the conditioning of the group. We operate differently by ourselves, and certain groups have different group think. You may be a fence-sitter in your personal life, but when you are in a group, you might harness your influence over how the group comes to its decisions. Understanding how a group works and decides is important. Each group or organization has a set of ethics, these are generally set by the majority of senior leadership, but each operation in isolation can also run by its own set of rules. These rules determine what is right and wrong.

Understanding these rules is critical to understanding how a group or individual works within that group. If you can understand the conditioning that the reward and punishment system has an influence on the decisions of the party, you can direct the group to the decision you want, based on their set of rules. Generally, they are unwritten, so understanding them either takes time to be around and understand or someone in the organization that is aware of how they work and will spill the beans on how it operates.

You will have seen before that some groups won't make a decision unless the autocratic boss makes the first move. People will look at the corner of their eyes to see if the boss is either disapproving or approving the conversation to continue. If you can see how they are conditioned, it would look to be that it comes down to an approval process by key members. You can direct your focus to that person. This is a tell which you can jump straight onto. If you can work with the person who makes the decisions, the group will side with the autocrat. This comes back to body language because you will see how people sit or stand and where their flow goes. And by flow, I mean their eyes, their legs, their arms, all parts of them. You can see their stance, and it could be very subtle or very obvious.

I have been in meetings at the defense department. The commander sits at the front of the room, and depending on the rank or level of the other participants in the room, they will sit on either side of the commander, and by rank, it cascades down to the end of the room. I can see straight away that the decision-makers are all in one solid location, that if one disagrees, they will tend to all disagree, which brings us back to the groupthink. You may even focus your attention, in part, on someone on either end of the boss who might favor your decision and work on the other person, who then might also side with you. It is important to have people who will support your ideas, the more agreeable people are in the room to your ideas, the more likely you can also win the agreeance of the decision maker in the room.

The conditioning of the boss or group decision-makers depends on their limitations. If the scope of what you are presenting is outside of their means, you will fall on deaf ears. The good idea is to present multiple scenarios in which your presentation or activity can work—be flexible so that you have options. Take for example that if you were to present three options to a customer and weigh them up so that the one option you want to go with is more appealing, it will make their decision as if it were their own choice as you have provided them with three options. If they see that the other two options would result in failure or not align with their scope, they will favor the option that does. This is somewhat deceptive, but it is a part of directing groupthink. This is conditioning—the receivers using failure or punishment and is not the first option people go with. Find a result that follows Occam's razor, which means to present the solution with the least path to resistance. In other words, what gives the greatest benefit for the least amount of resource or time to achieve.

When we are in a group ourselves, we change how we operate unless we are neurotic, but we won't go down the psychoanalysis pathway just yet. You might not notice the change, but in every social or professional group, you change how you associate and disassociate with who you are when you are alone—your persona or mask changes. You pull one off and fit another one on. In some groups, you might enjoy your experiences, and in others, you might have your guard up the whole time.

Knowing how you impact a group is interesting. If you use your awareness and look at the group, try analyzing it for a second. Look at who the leader is, whether it is affirmed or just assumed. Look at who makes the decisions, who is the influencer, who is the person who finds middle group or sorts out conflicts between each other, who is reserved but normally is a loudmouth, who is going out of their way to get along, but everyone can see that they are trying too hard. Which one are you? Where do you fit into the group? Take stock of where you fit and how you are different outside of the group.

Look at a group you are trying to get into or that you are trying to pitch to. Look at these dynamics the same way you looked at your own group. You will find commonality, and if you can understand them, then you already have a personal understanding of this group, and you don't need years of getting to know them. Humans are very similar, and our group formations, whether they are professional or social, are somewhat animalistic. We have hierarchies in businesses to set in stone the formations, but there are always people in the group who influence decisions, and therefore they are not listed. They might be in a key position, or they might not be.

Use your group and try and set it as a template of the team that you are presenting to. Maybe it's a new football team you want to join, look at how they interact, the main characters of each group have similarities. Your template can be used, within reason, to identify consistencies that you can take hold of, and when you want to influence the groupthink, you can use past ideas and experiences to support you. It's not an exact science.

You need to understand the dynamic of the group to understand what responses come with a green light and which comes with an ejector seat. It is a fine line, of course, but using past exposure will support you. Along with experience either dealing with this group or speaking to people who know the group, you will gather additional insight.

I have gone for an interview and researched my interviewer. During the conversation, I had brought up subjects that relate to their own extracurricular activities they listed on their bio. I fit it slightly into the conversation to create unity or some form of awareness of who I am. This is a way to slightly influence the decider in the group, and then they will bring up commonalities or personal experiences that relate to the topic. It isn't a strategy that works in its entirety, but the point is to use multiple sources to understand the conditioning of a group or individual.

Influence

This can be represented in many ways. What I will focus on, though, is your influence and the influences that are in your life. Do you think you are influential? How much influence do you think you have? Your influence depends on who you know and who knows you. Influence is when you have an effect on someone's behavior and decision-making. The ability to influence with precision is a powerful tool to a leader, and you can see it happens through association in most organizations.

It is a subject or activity that you are either born with, and it's an unconscious activity, or you will learn it through experience and getting better by using different techniques in your business and life. Influence is important when you are in a senior position because a larger part of your role is not doing physical work but more about directing the focus and influencing decisions to either assist yourself or other groups that you might have some effect on. Influencing a decision by the decision-makers can be of great benefit in which you can reap significant rewards. Without actually doing the physical work, you can influence the focus of people to do what you need them to do. This is the core of what leadership is.

"You cannot lead people who you do not influence." (Hunt, 2015)

One of my greatest examples of how effective you can be at influencing is when I was able to direct the focus of an entire region in defense. I developed a marketable slogan, goal and, in a collaborative effort, got the base Commander to roll it out throughout defense and within our organization. The agenda of this focus was One Team as there were some issues between the master and slave relationship, and this was then to accomplish our goals as well as the customers. I didn't have the same level of influence, but I had enough sense to assist in directing the focus of someone with a lot more influence than I could have imagined.

The program was rolled out as an initiative by the defense force, who were bringing my company into the fold from their own focus. What was most interesting was that the initial 'One Team' strategy came from a campaign I was working on in my company called 'One Fox' which was an initiative to share resources internally.

The same applies when you are in a group. Much like the sections before, you have a social influence in the group you reside within. Each member of the group has a certain position, and your level of influence depends on your position within the group. It is not to say that if you have a great idea, people won't take it on board, but even a small phrase or idea from the 'top dog' will be resounded based on their corporate or social position in the group.

What is your influence? As a leader, you can easily influence the decisions of your team members by placing 'seeds' in their thoughts. If you think that we should operate in a certain way, if you are able to have conversations with the people in your team, you have started the process.

If I say to you, "Don't think of a storm," I've won at influencing you because I can guarantee that in your mind, you have already visualized a storm. Maybe I inadvertently wanted you to think about today's weather and not the direct idea of the storm. Influencing can be indirect, and because you think of today's weather in some more subtle direction, the idea is your own.

Step1: You should talk around the subject, let the person come to the conclusion of what you are, in fact, looking at. If they draw the dots together, it is them putting the pieces together and, as such, reinforcing that they came up with the idea.

Step 2: Use reverse psychology, paint a picture that maybe their idea or the idea depicted is what you are after, that maybe it isn't the best option. If you play it well enough, the person will either defend it or take ownership of the idea. You need to be subtle in your approach to reverse psychology because if you hit it too hard, the person will either side with you or catch onto your ploy.

Step 3: Undersell the idea, lead them to the water, but let them know that the idea couldn't be capable of certain things, although there is a solution, and that is part of the upsell. You might find that the idea they came to is on the border of something you want them to get into. And as such, it is an easier transfer from their current idea to something that is closer to what you were thinking. If you can undersell their idea or transfer their idea over to something that is comparable, you are most of the way forward.

From here, the person will talk with friends and colleagues about the idea and your idea that they are empowered with, which will build momentum for you or your group's idea. The person will enact the same process you took, and they will use a similar technique and build followers. If you do this with enough people, everyone will be beating the same drum, and the shift that you want or the idea you want to present will already be in the back of everyone's minds. Therefore, your presentation will be easier to get across the line as people are either for, partly, or against it, in part.

Influence is not an instantaneous activity. It takes time to come to fruition. If you want instantaneous change, you must have a very high level of influence over the people that you are with. But in my experience, to influence something or to get your way, you have to take this in steps. You have to take your time and be conscious of the direction you want to head with your idea. Don't be foolish to think that you can entirely manipulate people if your idea is earnestly against their values. If that's the case, cut ties and move onto the next person. Once the group is following, it would be easier to turn or assume the people who are harder to get on board once you have the group in order.

Trying to turn someone into an Individual is harder than if they are in a group. And the same can be said in reverse. So be conscious of who you are trying to influence and at what point, either individually or in a group. Because the two can have entirely different outcomes. You must first understand who you are dealing with, and doing this, you need to build your ability to read the room. A lot of this comes from experience, but that also requires conscious experience. You need to be aware of yourself and how you are presenting yourself to the group or individuals.

Inception is the movie about planting an idea so that the ownership of that idea is taken without fear that the idea is not actually that person, and therefore the person considers the idea as completely their own. This is the best version of influencing, getting someone to do something with so much zeal because they are empowered by their own motor, but the original spark was lit by you without their awareness—the ultimate idea of leadership.

Negotiation

Think: win-win.

Presenting something and knowing the actual result is like when a magician shows you his hand, but in the other, he does the actual trick. When you present your first option, but you know that the desired result will be the lesser of the two, but you need to make sure that they think they have made a choice, and as such, are empowered with the choice they have made. But all the while, you have led them to the decision that they have made without their awareness.

What you first must know is your audience, who you are speaking with, because presenting multiple options must be represented in a way that you can influence their conditioned choice (either reward or punishment choices). Understanding them, the people or person you want to negotiate with firstly is very important. You have most likely heard of the famous line, "Sell me this pen," by DiCaprio in 2013. The normal response is to sell the pen by describing what it actually does, and you sell that it can do functions that we already know it can do. It is a test of salespeople in some situations to sell ice to Eskimos. There are a couple of easy ways to get this across the line, but this is the example I have used.

- o You need to understand your target market and who it is that you are trying to sell the pen to. You need to counter their request by firstly and respectfully asking them if you could ask them some questions before you attempt to sell them the pen. You would need to understand the motivation for actually needing the pen, and we don't generally buy something because it appears in our minds. Sometimes we need something because it is a necessity for us to continue to do the things that we are doing in our lives. What do they use the pen for? Is it to take down notes, or to use it to fulfil other things in our lives, that gives you more understanding about their reason for the pen? Understanding the 'what' they use the pen for is important.

- o Then you need to understand how they use the pen. Do they use the pen while on the road or in board meetings? Do they have to find refills, and then the pen is interchanged between others? Do they use the pen so that it can present something about them, do they like executive ones or ones that symbolize their power and influence?

- And lastly, why. What is the purpose of this pen? Who are they, and what fulfillment does the pen bring? There is a purpose to the pen, and the reason this is such a good session is that the pen is so common, making it uncommon is a hard sale, but in doing so, you can sell or present with passion anything. This will make the item irresistible, and they won't want anything but what it represents. Also, reminding them of the core of why they want the pen will be a critical success factor. If you find that the pen is a means to an end, maybe presenting what they really desire is more important in this situation.
  - The why is what will sell the pen—it is the reason behind the sale and how it makes them feel. The feeling in a sale is what pulls the person into the deal. You don't put a car on finance because of the big price tag at the end of the contract, and you pay for it now because of how it is going to make you feel today. Otherwise, you would have saved up, right?

Now that you understand the what, how, and why of the person wanting the pen. You can now counter their other. You don't necessarily need to sell them the pen. You might find that although they want the pen, their circumstances would present them with a better option. Why not sell them a tablet? A portable electric device that they can tailor to their actual needs, they might be on the road a lot, so they can use it via voice command in the car to record notes. They might be missing information in long conferences, so they use the tablet to type out their notes in a conference just by hearing the speech and turning it into text using some simple software.

This is just one example of how you can find what someone wants but then realize through exploring them and their circumstances that you can present them with something more beneficial to them.

Understanding the person before you give them the options is critical. If you try to sell or present to someone something that they have no interest in, or their capability to use what you have is not there, they will easily turn you away. But if you know them and what they can take, you can shape your discussion to tick the boxes of the real need that they have.

"Would you like fries with that?" this is what makes McDonald's millions of dollars every year. The fries are just an addition to the main product that you are looking to purchase, and this is where the mark-up is really applied. The main product is what gets you in the door. There are many advertisements by McDonald's where they are selling a burger for two dollars. The money they make on this is either at a loss or break even. But the additive products that go with that burger are where the money is made. You may go in and get a Coca-Cola, fries, and maybe an upgrade. The mark-up and profit are made on these items. The way of effectively looking at it is by understanding what each product is used for. They have a product that is the draw or point of sale, which is getting someone to come in on an impulse to buy the product.

You can use your negotiations in the same way. If you are selling a product or providing a service, you can provide the base product at a much lower level or attractive level to get the point of sale in place. But you can add services or products around this to get your addition of mark-up. For example, in logistics, the storage of products can be dropped substantially, the actual cost of storage can be break-even, and the customer is satisfied with that price. Then you give them handling rates for moving the product, and you can increase these prices so that you offset the lost margin on the storage into the labor component.

Leadership requires a lot of negotiation. Sometimes someone will come to you and complain about what they are doing, you might then try to suffice all of their desires, and they will still feel like complaining. Maybe the real reason they are complaining is that they don't understand that what they make impacts the entire business. If you can find out why someone has an issue, you can more effectively deal with it and supply solutions rather than just band-aid the problem.

When you go speak with someone, do you go to the person who you find just tells you what you want to hear? Maybe it depends on the day, but also, I think most people will go to someone that they believe will tell them what they need to hear. We might not like it, but we grow from it. The same as a presenter or leader, you will go to the person that gives you what you need for the most part, rather than the person who gives you what you want.

Negotiation also comes down to losing sometimes. It is sometimes better to give up, walk away or let the person think they have the upper hand. It is, of course, dependent on the situation. If you see further dealings with this entity or person, it is worthwhile to take the good with the bad and let things flow. You might find that in this instance, you have had a big loss, but in the next instance, you might make up those losses. It is not the same as gambling, and you will just continue to throw money away doing this. What it is, is a calculation of events and your position within the negotiation room.

As a leader, you will negotiate for the most part of your day, even if you don't consciously realize it. You might negotiate with your senior management that if you can prove that you can guarantee them a result from what you are working on that they will extend to you certain resources of events that will support you. Within that, you might have had to make some deals with people at your level so that you can get these results whilst getting the benefit of the additional items provided.

What about when it's busy at work? If your people put in the extra time to reduce the disruption to your service, they are in turn negotiating with you, they are getting a financial benefit, or they will expect that when things get quieter that they can gain some additional flexibility. I have seen it in larger organizations where people will work the same hours every day, yet the workload hasn't changed. They are getting their extra couple of hours of pay, and the workload might have even halved. But in the times where it gets considerably busier, they seem to retain the same hours. This in itself is a form of negotiation from your people, and treading carefully on their financial system is a dangerous area to be.

Negotiations should result in both parties mutually getting what they wanted or part of what they wanted from the deal. If one side gets it all and the other is out of the deal, you will find that the next time this comes around, it will be dealt with very differently. Be careful when you negotiate. Being fair and reasonable has a big part to play with the longevity of relationships in your dealings. If you burn your bridges, the day that you need some help, you might find yourself being emptied out by the people you used to do the same thing to.

Think: win-win.

No one goes back to someone who they think has screwed them. A fair deal is critical in sales because the sale you get today could end up being a long-term partnership. A hard negotiation is fine, but it needs to be fair. For example, if a customer of yours expects you to continue to squeeze your margins until you don't make any money, at some point, you will tell the customer to either leave or will increase your rates really high to get them to move away. If you don't do a fair deal, you will end up hurting yourself in the long run. Fair trade is an iconic Australian ideology, and this style of negotiation will ensure a long-term relationship, don't burn your bridges, and always know that a deal should result in a win-win.

Section Four – The Wrap-Up

We have moved away from the concept of the support blanket and really focused on what each one of us needs to focus on to become a better version of ourselves. Although there is still a lot of information that comes into play, I have really focused this area on self-reflection because awareness of ourselves is important. Because at this point in your journey, or previously, you have come to a point where you need to take a step back and look at your own motivations. At times in life, we find ourselves delving from our long-term goals, left to wander, and unable to see the forest for the trees. Sometimes we get too involved in the minor details and forget about the big picture.

Along with self-reflection, there is also the concept of the old and new leadership styles, which are common in the workplace and society. There is the idea that certain leadership styles work for certain areas of organizations, but what is most important is the understanding from all parties that the most effective leadership style is that which works. There is no one style that fits an organization, and a culture, which sets the foundation of leadership for a business or environment, is formed by the people of the organization. To have a good grasp of leadership requires a great deal of flexibility and adaptability. A good leader will understand the people and work to the best advantage of their skills and experiences. As a leader, it is the ability to work with all other leadership styles and find the best possible solution collaboratively that wins each day.

The hardest time in my life was in a professional capacity. I was working fourteen hours a day on average, five to six days a week. And each day, my mind was getting more and more tired, along with my body. I hadn't crashed yet. I read a very powerful paragraph that filled my spirit with the understanding that, against unrelenting odds, we must continue to be courageous, hold and preserver. As hard as it is, and as it was, throughout, I continued to feel the want, the need to give in. But I continued against what my heart told me—the next paragraph encapsulates facing your fears beyond circumstances affecting yourself.

"This sight broke the spirit and paralyzed the energies of the Romans. It might have been expected to rouse in them feelings of anger and revenge but instead filled them with fear and trembling. Yet Crassus, at

this moment of his suffering, behaved more admirably than ever before in his life. He went up and down the ranks, shouting out to the men. 'Romans, this grief is a private thing of my own. But in you abide the great fortune and glory of Rome, unbroken and undefeated. And now, if you feel any pity for me, who have lost the best son that any father has ever had, show it in the fury with which you face the enemy. Take away their joy; make them suffer for their cruelty; do not be downhearted at what has happened; remember that if one aims at great things, one must expect great sufferings. Rome became great not by good fortune but by courage and endurance in the face of danger'." (Plutarch, 1958, p. 145)

In this case, it was Crassus's son who has paraded around on display, hung up, and dying. Now, in this case, it is a bit more dangerous than my scenario, but the learning can be applied. What was expected of their leader, to be down and to fall over due to a great personal loss, was turned into a motivation to be better, to turn the tide around. Sometimes, and if you have had it happen before, you know that if you suffer greatly, you come out the other end just a little bit more resilient, and each time your skin thickens. The learning in this story is don't let time control you. You control the time. Use your brain, not only your heart. Eliminate emotions by letting go of the past and thinking about the present. Steps to success and peace. Because you will always suffer in life, but if we could remove the past and focus on the now, we would get so much more done. We would be so much more effective if we could eliminate past expectations and focus on the right solution for the problem at hand.

Life is made up of many seasons—the long cold, the transitory times, and the long-awaited summer that brings vibrance, warmth, passion, and life. But the long winter should be respected for the lessons that it teaches us. Its ability to take us deep and to learn graciousness from the absence of light. Nothing stays the same. But we continue to move along life's path, side to side. Forward and backward. But all along the way, our spirit and our decisions move us forward continually. We decide on our course, just like the sun. We rise and fall. And each evening there are sunsets. And each morning. The sun rises once again. Life is a gift. And it is meant to be shared for the rest of our lives.

We need to be positive in our interactions. Misery loves company. Let's not be part of that group. Changing your emotions and the way you feel is critical to a leader. We don't get the easy job of sitting back and watching things happen, we have to face things head-on, and that brings about bad times. But being aware of what is most important and how we can shape our reality right before our eyes through our decisions, choices, and the way in which we see things will get us through the hard times and overcome the great challenges of our roles in life. Know that you are on your own, but on your own, you can shape the way forward. There are no predispositions, and it is what you decide you want.

Exercise: I want you to think of your next task. Before you even enact the work, consider who you could draw from to give you a better understanding of the task. You might think you have all of the answers but entertain the fact that you might not know everything. Ask people you haven't spoken with before and see what they think about it and how they think you could approach it. Take on board what they say, even take notes so you can think on it a bit more later. Even ask someone in a different area, immerse yourself in different ideas through other people's thinking patterns. You might learn some valuable lessons, and you might learn that you know more. What you have done also is got people thinking about your problem. You might now find that days later, one of these people will ask you about your progress, or they will have thought about it, seeking out other people how they would approach it and come back to you with another solution. Collaboration brings about surprising results from people. The evening including someone you normally wouldn't, you might even get some of their respect without that being your primary intention.

Chapter <VI> - The Wolf amongst the Sheep

"The object is to win fairly, squarely, by the rules – but to win."

(Vince Lombardi, 1970)

Introduction

When the ship sails toward the sunset. Overcome obstacles, achieve goals, be who you choose to be. Be the person that people respect. But how? We all have our own way of achieving what we want in life. But what is important is taking things face-on where it needs it and knowing when to take the indirect route. This comes from experience, study, and intuition. In this final chapter, we will go through emotional intelligence in greater detail as it is one of the fundamental resources for leaders to use and understand. It is a tool mainly focused on self-reflection, and it brings influence.

I want you to aspire to be the greatest version of yourself. If what I can get out of writing this, apart from sharing my experiences and my concepts that I believe are important, is to ensure that you develop a better understanding of yourself. Your eyes will open up when you start to understand your limitations, and from there, you can begin to push your limits because you can see the fence line, you can measure up the distances you need to jump above it. Train harder and harder to strengthen the edges of your mind and appreciation what you can bring to the table.

Emotional intelligence. What is it, and what is its importance? I want to go through what the value of emotional intelligence is, and if harnessed correctly, you can become very good at reading people and being able to flex with the situation that you are in. I got into emotional intelligence many years after I was already a manager. From what I know, it should have been the other way around. I'm not going to change it now, but I want to be able to teach people getting into leadership the benefits of learning emotional intelligence from the start of their leadership pathway.

Although, when you read this, it is also in reverse, all of the experience of this book focuses on what you bring to the table, and this last chapter is talking about emotional intelligence, right? Don't think me to be a hypocrite because what you will find is that we have been speaking over emotional intelligence throughout this entire book, and it is just given different titles and positions. Do not be fooled by headings. Emotional intelligence is everyone related to leadership and human behavior. Understanding the definition of emotional intelligence is the observation and theory, whereas the basic building blocks are the raw aspects of this concept.

How do you aspire to be the greatest version of yourself, and how do you develop the people around you? By understanding all about yourself. If you do not understand how you work first, how can you give advice or fix things in other people's lives if you do not understand what you are capable of? A hammer can be used to hit a nail, or it can be used to build an entire house. Understanding the capabilities of the tool or the user will determine what can be made out of smaller things that you have at your disposal. Now, where do we start?

Section One - Empowering You

You want to be someone that holds a good position somewhere, and I don't think anyone aspires to be the lowest rung on the rack. To get here, there, we must be the best version of ourselves. Harder still is to be focused on yourself and be who you choose to be, don't be forced to be like someone else or unless you choose this route. Become the competitor that everyone fears. They have anxiety due to your unparalleled success. My wife said to me one evening, *"you know, don't change who you are. Because even though I don't understand you or how your methods work. What I do know is that what you do is what you do best. And it's obviously working because people like and respect you, and you have achieved a lot of things so far."* It was as we were going to sleep one night. It was just a once-off comment that is engraved in my memories. It might have been a once-off comment, but it made sense to me.

I had thought that maybe I needed to be different, but this then reminded me, whether my wife knew it or not is something that helped to retain a part of who I am. My identity and how I operate, and the same goes for you. You need people in your life that will help to remind you of what you want and who you are. We might be the Wolf amongst the Sheep, but even the Wolf has a pack to return to each evening. Don't believe for one second that you need to do everything alone. Collaboration is unity, and unity is strength. It sounds ritualistic, but we have safety in numbers.

What you bring to the group is important to understand. Your position in the group, in your social status, and in your life is something we all struggle to understand throughout our lives. Because the groups are dynamic and continue to change, regardless of whether we want it to or not, along with that, in each social circumstance, we embody a different set of characteristics and emotions. I vary quite often. In some groups, I take the lead. In others, I take the back seat and let others take charge of the group. Some people have to be the boss all the time, and they will have a conflict with another person with the same personality type. What is most important in all of these situations is that either when you change or you don't change, that you are who you choose to be. Being able to be led is an important part of leadership. If you don't have followership in your brain, then find a way to learn from others and realize when you need to take the initiative and when you need to be told what to do.

1. Self-Awareness

This is the first step of emotional intelligence, and I don't mean that you have to do this to enter the realm of emotional intelligence because, as I alluded to earlier, emotional intelligence is something we all do every day, but it is just titled differently. The first step of emotional intelligence is aware of the self. Because if we can see what we have become or what we are doing, we are much more able to change our situations through our own actions and before we can change anyone else.

It is our choice to see ourselves more consciously, which is the first step toward understanding emotional intelligence and the benefits we can bring and it can bring to us. But seeing ourselves doesn't mean we will change ourselves. What it means is we are observant, and we are aware of what we are. If I know that I react in a certain way due to a circumstance or event, then I will be more observant of it because I am aware of myself, sometimes I tilt my head down and look at my shoulder, and we see everything through our own eyes. When you look into a mirror, you still see everything through your own eyes. But having the chance to watch yourself move without changing it is an interesting thing to see.

If you can see yourself and what you stand for, you will have an appreciation for a connection with yourself. You might not realize in full just who you are or what you represent. If you have ever filmed something or someone has filmed you without you consciously acting for the camera. When you have a chance, watch it and the things that you do. I have seen myself on camera and been in disbelief because the way I move and the things I have said just didn't feel like I was there.

Because the way in which I perceive myself is the same as I perceive others, our emotional connection to things that we cannot see inherently is different from the actual. Even when you run your hand through your hair and it feels like it is all slicked back, but you look in a mirror, and it's a mess. But whilst I couldn't see myself, I believed it to be something other than what it was in actual fact. Seeing ourselves is important because what we think we portray or emit could be entirely different from what people see of us, and when we see ourselves, we see what other people see.

Empathy has a part to play in this. The way we see ourselves and others will change how we view ourselves. If we have done something and the person we are interacting with is visually uncomfortable, we begin to question what we might have said. Have you ever had that moment where you are asking your friends what they think of a series of conversations you had with someone and seeing what they thought? Part of this is self-awareness because you are trying to piece something together without understanding the full picture. If you are pondering to yourself about something you could have said or done that might have been misconstrued, then you are self-aware.

Sometimes you need to think of self-awareness as being in the third person, to see yourself as a character, even like in a game where you can see yourself acting from the outside, like an out-of-body experience. Think about who you are, what do you love? Who do you love? What is your motivation? We spoke about this in the prior chapter, but again, what motivates you to be who you are? What are your fears? What do you dream about? What do you think is your greatest strength? And what do you think needs to be developed to be a better version of yourself?

If any of the above are questions you ask yourself, you are self-aware. You are asking yourself questions, and you are trying to understand more about yourself. A lot of our life is driven by our nature, and we live so therefore we exist. We don't think about every second we breathe. It just happens, there are many reasons behind why, but there is a lot of our life that in some way just happens. The moments when we question ourselves and take a minute to understand why we do the things that we do gives us a better understanding of the nature that resides inside of each one of us.

Sometimes when you are on auto-pilot, you even shudder and ask yourself, what just happened? I've been driving before and wandered off in my mind a couple of days into the future where I start to plan out the rest of my week. I pull up to a certain round-about on the way to work and then go. I don't remember driving for the past ten minutes. Then I work my mind to retrace the road I just went down.

Understanding how I operate in auto-pilot is part of self-awareness because so much of our lives, or whatever amount you think you do and is built on our nature. And this is why, when you get into looking at yourself with more awareness, you will get fascinated with how you come across to people. I've even looked into the mirror and tried to shake my own hand to see how someone would see me at that first appearance when greeting them.

We all go through moods. We might not even think that we are the problem. Even with a keen sense of self-awareness, hindsight reminds me that I was wrong. But at the moment, I will look at myself and think nothing is wrong with me. Our moods can change how we see ourselves and others.

Much the same as in leadership, we have to strip ourselves from doing what is not working. Being aware is not just looking at yourself in certain situations. It is looking at yourself in all situations.

2. **Self-Management**

It is great to see ourselves but seldom do we change who we are unless we are forced, or we make a choice. There are a lot of people out there that are aware of how they come across, yet they are content with whom they are and are unwilling to change. There are plenty of occurrences where people admit their faults, yet they do not choose to change. Only once we get to a point where it is beyond or on the verge of failed recovery that we come to the realization that our lives have become unmanageable and that we must change. That is because the nature in some people is so strong that they are aware but not managing themselves.

It is easy to tell someone else what to do and even tell yourself what to do. But actually, doing it is the hard part. We are all guilty of sitting on the couch and wanting to get the house clean, but just a couple more minutes of what you are doing now won't hurt, till the point where it's now too late, and it's a task for tomorrow. But it is never too late, and putting a timeframe in which there is a cut-off is part of the reason why people find it hard to change their situations.

I had the motivation one night at around ten o'clock, and I thought, *My car needs a good clean,* and so I went down into the garage and started to clean the car out. It was a great feeling. I had such a rush that I spent a lot more time cleaning than required. Afterward, I hit the hay pretty hard. Sometimes we just get a rush of spontaneity, and things dawn on us to just get out there and do. What I am alluding to is you set your clock by a social standard. Vacuuming the car at this time would seem strange to the common denominator. But that's just it, do you want to be common, set up by other people's standards? I wouldn't think so.

There is a requirement by social considerations that we manage our affairs in a certain regard. Society is indeed formed by the majority of our shared ideas and values. So, we need to manage ourselves at the right times, and with consideration to our social standings, I just need to throw that out there. Now more to the actual management part of this section. If you see that in a certain situation, you are moving around the room quite nervously, your ability to change your body language is important. If you can see yourself through awareness and then you can put your sweaty palms on your dry pants to dry them. You can sit with your two feet planted onto the group flat. You can take a glass of water and try to stop that shaking knee, and you will be on a starting path to changing or managing your physical appearance. Your body language, as we have spoken about previously, gives you away.

Managing our body language is important in a corporate situation. There are certain professional expectancies, and by being able to manage our nerves or absolute frustrations, the way in which we are perceived is changed. If I am a raging person in an office, people will see that I am out of control, maybe too passionate, or unable to manage myself effectively. On the flip side, if you see someone calm and speaking to people with respect, these people will generally bend the rules or go out of their way to help this person, as you are more likely to help your friends than your enemies.

Part of managing ourselves comes down to the basic building blocks of conditioning. If we understand that in society, we have certain things that condition a negative or positive response, we will act accordingly. The same goes for how we manage ourselves. If we respond negatively or positively, we will be able to condition ourselves in a certain fashion. If something we did gives us a reward, and through our awareness, we realize that it is something that presents us poorly, we need to reconfigure our conditioning. Changing the way in which we react to a set of actions is unnatural. It is not easy, but if we are aware of ourselves and we choose to act, then we can self-manage and condition ourselves for the better, or worse, depending on what we want to achieve.

As a leader, self-management is important. If you are someone who loses their temper at simple things, managing this will be difficult because we all have a natural pressure level. But being able to condition ourselves by firstly being aware of how it affects others (discussed in the next section), we will be able to slowly change this. I had a colleague who, when he got frustrated and at the point of losing his temper, would remind himself to calm down. He would make a silly joke about the situation, which was a conditioned response to the scenario. There are many ways of conditioning yourself to manage your emotions. In the past, I had used a rubber band on my wrist. If I enacted something that I shouldn't have, I would flick it. It has worked, although at some stage or another, I have broken the band.

Managing ourselves is a lot harder than we think. There are many times where I have said to myself that if I get in a situation where someone talks down to me that I will stand my ground and speak my mind. But sometimes I forget all of this motivational speaker, and I revert back to my normal *'yes sir, three bags full.'* But I started to overcome this by writing in my book a list of key things I will do when I have this conversation. Although I haven't completely fixed this, I am getting better by practicing my habits or responses daily. This is how we manage ourselves, and it's the same as managing other people. It is giving clear direction to ourselves as well as others. Practicing what you preach is easier said than done if you believe it.

The same goes for observational learning. If you see how other people handle themselves and you want to fit into that mold, by being aware of yourself, you can see the gap between you both. And the management side is actually doing the things you need to do to bridge the gap. If you can see someone who is calm, maybe your boss, you will unconsciously emulate them in part and start to learn how they deal with events, in your own way, of course. If you are conscious, this moves a lot quicker because you can practice these habits by picking parts and enacting them. We are what we do every day, and it's the small steps that make the biggest changes. If someone holds their pen a certain way, try holding it the same way. You will completely copy it, or you will emulate it and mold it to your personality style.

To manage yourself, you must make a conscious effort to calm or change yourself. If you don't want to change, you won't, and if you are forced, it won't be the same as an allowed change from yourself. To manage one's self is to determine how you will succeed because you can change the way you are perceived by being aware and bridging the gap between the two personalities or perceptions you choose to emit. Being conscious of yourself is the first step, and choosing to change what you are doing at the moment is the second step.

3. Social Awareness

We are aware of our own emotions or at least a lot more than before reading this. Although we don't view them constantly, we have a sense or feeling for how we present ourselves. Social awareness is being aware of other people. In large part, it is directly related to empathy. Our ability to empathize with people gives us a greater insight into who they are and what they stand for. Much as we have looked at seeing ourselves is how we see into others. We need to be conscious of how people operate. Most people are run by their nature and the day-to-day autonomous actions that people do. But then people act with their chosen decisions, and we need to be able to have good insight into how people operate to understand them, and in turn ourselves.

Have you sat in a shopping mall and just watched people? It's fascinating to just watch people and how they operate. I am sure people watch me and find it funny the same as I do. In respect to this situation, to fully profile or understand someone, you need to converse with them. Then you can realize who they are. But you can get a good sense of who someone is by seeing their characteristics in a social scenario. What you see is the persona in this situation, the mask that they place in this 'shopping mall.'

Along with social awareness comes the ability to treat people in a way that you will get the best out of them. If you have had in the past, or currently, a boss who is very aggressive toward you, I am sure that you hold things back in fear of being reacted to, right? Do you think, though, if you were talking to your employee and you knew they feared you, would you change the way in which you present yourself? Being aware of how other people want to be treated is critical. If you treat them how they want to be treated, they will respect you, outwardly too, they will sing your praises because we want to be treated a certain way. And if you can be aware of the way in which they want to be treated, they will gain a connection with you. You can also get things out of them they wouldn't give to the angry boss. They would even tell you information that might help you out with your standings.

If someone is now invested in you because you took the time to understand them and how they want to be treated, they will invest time into you. Therefore, creating a connection. But how do you be more aware of someone? You need to look at them and how you engage with them. Take a conversation you had with someone. What interests do they have? Who don't they like? What are they passionate about? Why do they take days off work? Who do they associate with? What do they do in their lunch breaks?

If you don't know the answer to any of the above, then ask them, or find a way in a conversation to find out these things. Knowing these parts of their life and being able to relate is your awareness of who they are. The little details of someone's personality tell you a lot about them. Could it be that without a coffee in the morning, they wouldn't be able to function? This is a connection to a sense of security (as well as caffeine) as well as a part of who they are. I have many friends that are on the borderline of addiction, yet they love the feeling it gives them. Take the coffee away from them, and you have some real problems. We find security in things that are consistent in our lives. What if one day you brought them a cup of coffee when they didn't have one? I reckon you would be their best friend, but things come around as they go around.

I believe that when you pay it forward, you invest time into other people. They will do the same in return. If not them directly, others will. Do you want to be known as a kind person? Don't just give out when on the television or in front of the camera, do it in the small areas. You will find that it will increase your integrity, even if you aren't genuine, and you can fake it well. It's the little things that count. People will see at the edges your true identity, so it will be an easy feat to embody what you want in every part of your life, great and small.

Look at people around you, and see how they operate too. They might act differently with you.

I had found in my professional career, even when I was a young manager, that I still got a lot of respect from people that didn't show respect to other people in the same position and age as me. Why, you ask? Because I treated them how they wanted to be treated, I empathized with how they were and asked about the things that they cared about. I invested my time into learning about them and talking with them so that I had skin in the game when it came to understanding them. It created an investment on both ends of the relationship that we both had put time into. Therefore, it's hard for them to pull away from this if I continue to put in. Being aware of what drives people and what they are passionate about is an 'in' to be a part of what they are all about. It's not an exact treatment, but for the most part, it works quite effectively.

When you first start dating, you pay attention to all of the little details. Later down the track, the care for this fades, but at the start of the relationship, it's overtly given. Why do we do this? Well, there is the simple benefit of a relationship and the extras that come with it. But on top of that, it is easier to invest in the beginning than it is to pull away during the course of the relationship. Once it is formed and established, it is harder to take away, and we become aware of this and how we do the same, or we give up and cut ties. Most of the time, though, we are all aware, in some way, that we invest a large amount in a new relationship and then start to mold it to our normal life, fitting it in where we can.

4. Social Skills

As a leader, you need to be able to accomplish connections with people in your network. It is a big part of your influence. Understanding where someone has an interest or is putting their time towards achieving something is an area where you capitalize. You can show a vested interest in what they are doing in the early stages, and they will bring you in too. I have had friends that long after the start of the relationship has faded, they continue to talk to me about a topic that I no longer have a real interest in, but I continue to listen as actively as possible, and it fills them with the fact that they can express themselves.

Active listening is when you truly commit to a conversation, and before you list a question to ask them from their words, you actually stop that thought and just listen. Then at the end of what they have said comes, you stop for a moment in awkward silence, but it is actually a truer version of listening than it is to have questions lined up straight after they have finished speaking.

There is another way to do this. You can structure a question for them by using referencing what they have told you. Such as, "Really, so when he shot those three goals, do you think he knew about it?" But I would say that generally, the best form of active listening is to just listen and let the person have their say.

I remember when I was first joining the workforce, and I got invited to an interview. I went to the office and wore my best suit at the time and waited in a reception area with three people. Then the receptionist requested us to go into the next office. We all stood together and headed into the office. There was a desk with three chairs in front of a man behind his desk and another chair on the side. The man was abrupt in his approach and said he would ask a question, and we would go in turn to answer it. After a short couple of questions, he then said that he would ask questions, and the first person to call out the answer would get the chance to have his say.

I remember I think I answered one question. I was so nervous I didn't even hear the question by the time one of the other guys in the room had the answer. A couple of minutes later, the man looked at me and said that I could leave. I stood up and walked out of the room, thanking him for his time. I felt so confused, to begin with, and being in an unfamiliar suit, I felt quite uncomfortable and as such hurried to the train station. I caught the train home and stayed in my head thinking over what had happened.

I got home, and I was furious. I couldn't believe that I had been treated this way. I realized that it was a trial by fire, and I just didn't have the social skills at the time to storm out of that office with my principles intact. I allowed someone to treat me as a simple number, and when I wasn't good enough, I was kicked out. What did I learn from this? I can see such a difference in who I am today as compared to that day. I walked into the office without a good level of confidence, I allowed this person to treat me poorly, and I didn't have the acumen to be in that conversation. What I won't do now is go along with something that I am not comfortable with, and it is my social skills I have built through study and experience that have taught me these lessons.

Every situation calls for a different set of skills to be used, and it depends on where you are and what is happening that will change your approach. Unconsciously this will happen, but if you are aware, you will be more attune to the scenario and be able to direct or influence your or another person's circumstances. The greatest salespeople are the ones that you think are your best friends, and then they swoop in for the kill.

When you can find common ground with someone, you are harnessing your best social skills. Finding similarities or areas where there are mutual benefits for people is where your social skills will be best developed. It is also a good idea to learn about people in your areas so that you can find common ground. A good leader expresses their interest in things that you would find most people commonly can relate to. Capitalize on these common grounds because you will create a better form of unity with your tribe.

I am a great fan of football, but when I was younger, I had no interest. It wasn't something my family was involved with, and my friends were the same as me. But when I got into the workplace, everyone continued to talk about it, and I wasn't included. One day I studied the teams and watched a game. I was glued to the screen, and I couldn't believe how much I had missed out on for so many years. Now I am a fanatic, but luckily, I love it so much. I can and do use it to banter with fellow workers and create relationships with them to gain influence with them. I have had employees do great feats for me because of our connection.

Developing social skills is a good way to get them up quickly. Many different times in my life where I have had people get into heated arguments have trained me to be a good problem solver. There is no single way to deal with conflict. Each encounter and different people react differently. But finding common ground between the two parties is the start. Allowing them to have their say and 'blow up' gives them a chance to release. Most arguments are caused because of other events. You got to work late because you didn't turn your alarm on, you're tired because your kid was up all night, and then when you got to work, you realized you forgot your belt, and someone noticed it and laughed at you and that was the final straw. On any normal day, that person would be fine, but today of all days, it blew out of proportion. If we are able to find commonality or even trace back to the real reason behind the conflict, we can then strip away at the levels of frustration.

Sometimes it isn't just that simple. Sometimes people have real outside of work dramas that are cause for grief or counseling. Sometimes it is just hearing the person out and letting them find someone who can listen that builds trust in the relationship. The most important tool someone can have socially is their ears—to listen is to let people express themselves. We all want to be heard or seen for what we stand for. In fact, we don't stand for the fun of it. We stand to be noticed, to be heard, to be seen. If you have been here before, then so has someone else. Be mindful and find common ground.

Being relatable is a strong tool. If you can find someone that is relatable or has common interests, it's because they have transferability. They can transfer a love or passion for one thing and understand your love or passion for another thing. To be mindful is to be open, and to be open is to let people see who you are because if you open up, they will open up to you, not straight away, and not instantly, but it will happen. The same as my bonsai plant continues to want to look like it is dying, and when I have almost given up, it starts to grow again.

We all learn about each other, and we all build relationships differently. What is important is understanding our differences and finding the points in which we can meet each other in the middle and harness these differences.

If you are progressing with your emotional intelligence and want to learn more, then, as I have said before, find many sources and absorb the opinions of many authors. To grasp a concept is to understand the good, the bad, and the ugly. To do this, you must understand the concept from all sides of the story. Most importantly, empower yourself with the decision to accept where you are at, who you are and what you want from your life. Yes, society will give us a set of instructions to follow, but we ultimately decide our direction and what we want from our lives. So, do it, be the person you want to be, and empower yourself each moment you get the opportunity to do so. And don't forget to have some fun along the journey.

Section Two - Accepting Who You Are

When I say it is the mortar that defines the leader, I don't just mean that it is someone's experiences. Mortar is not solely made up of one material. It is made up of a composition of materials, and it is the additives and the pieces put together that make it what it becomes. The same goes for a person or leader. The most important things that tie their great accomplishments together are the bits and pieces of their character that got them to this and these points in their lives. I didn't get here from my experiences alone. I also got here because of my studies, my choices to do things I didn't know, and be willing to fail. To choose to do things that scared me and that I couldn't see myself getting through. Whether I have failed or succeeded is not the point, the mortar is what defines who we are, and our accomplishments are reflections of this.

People who understand character don't see an award on a wall. That is who they are. It's how they treat people, how they want to be treated, and what they stand for that defines the character of a person. To think that the amount of money you have in the bank or most achievements make you a better leader or person is kidding themselves. Some people devote their lives to the background and make phenomenal gestures for the greater good of humanity that never get rewarded, yet they could have achieved all of the gold in the world.

Sometimes I try to be humble, but then I just bring myself back down and tell everyone what I did. Why? Because I want people to know what I have achieved. We all have our own ways, but what is most important is that judging the mortar of someone comes from what surrounds their achievements, not the achievement on its own. Each day that I grow older and wiser, I become more appreciative of the below understanding of age by Carl Jung.

"Our lives are like the course of the sun. In the morning, it gains continually in strength until it reaches the zenith-heat of high noon. Then comes the enantiodromia: the steady forward movement no longer denotes an increase, but a decrease, in strength. But it is a great mistake to suppose that the meaning of life is exhausted with the period of youth and expansion; that, for example, a woman who has passed the menopause is 'finished.' The afternoon of life is just as full

of meaning as the morning; only, its meaning and purpose are different." (Jung, 1967, p. 74)

Don't Change Who You Are

I went into an interview, and I was quite frank with what I wanted from the role. I explained where I was at and where I want to be. Let's just say I didn't get the job. Was I disappointed? Yes, I was, but you know what, I was also content that I had said what I believed. I have learned that being honest with yourself and others is important to the sense of fulfillment in our lives. I could have easily answered their questions exactly as they wanted it to be and potentially had a better chance at getting the job. But why bother, because then I wouldn't be happy with where I was. Sometimes things will take longer, but it is worth the way. And when you look back, you will appreciate the process that you went through to achieve what matters most in life.

Life is made up of many seasons—the long cold, the transitory times, and the long-awaited summer that brings vibrance, warmth, passion, and life. But the long winter should be respected for the lessons that it teaches us. Its ability to take us deep and to learn graciousness from the absence of light. Nothing stays the same. But we continue to move along life's path, side to side. Forwards and backward. But all along the way, our spirit and our decisions continually move us forward. We decide on the course, just like the sun. We rise and fall. And each evening, the sun sets. And each morning. The sun rises once again. Life is a gift. And it is meant to be shared for the rest of our lives.

Sometimes when you look in the mirror, it is hard to appreciate who you are. You might think you are being disciplined and doing all the necessary things that everyone else is doing, yet they are succeeding, and you just aren't. It's the same as the internet today, you will look at someone's post, and all you see is their lavish lives. But what you need to understand is we only present what we want people to see on these systems. They don't post a picture of themselves when they first wake up in the morning, and luckily too. It depends on your values and your upbringing to help define how you feel about yourself but consider that each little part between the good achievements in your life is the mortar. That each little step you take, whether it be getting ready, and even when you feel terrible you preserver, and yet you finish the day and feel exhausted. You will respect yourself because you got through the day.

And these are milestones. These are the things you need to reward yourself for. As we went through in conditioning, if you overcome something, reward yourself accordingly. Don't go overboard, but don't go underboard too. If you don't reward yourself for doing the things that are hardest, your mindset each time you do it will slowly crumble, and you will be less likely to preserver next time. It is, of course, easy to say, but we need to appreciate the little things. When I look back at some large tasks I have overcome, it was the daily work I put in that amounted to the finality of the task.

You will also find that you will change over time. You will mirror people in the media or the ones that you associate with. If you are not happy with the today you, be prepared to meet tomorrow you each day also. The changes are generally incremental and therefore unnoticeable. But I am sure you have had a friend or colleague say to you that you have changed so much since they have last seen you. You might admit to them that you don't know if anything has changed, but they point out features or mannerisms, and then it clicks to you that maybe they are right. Then you think how long it has been since you haven't seen them. And it could have been a short or long time. We continue to grow. If we don't grow, we decline.

I think though it's important that you are not content with the norm every day, you need to understand and accept yourself for who you are, but also you need to have a desire to become better each and every day. This is done by completing little bits and pieces every single day for your long-term vision. You need to embody the future you, the person that you want to be, is the person that you need to start acting like today.

Being Introspective

Consider your strengths. Yes, you might think you have a lot of weaknesses but consider what you can do well. What is it? How do you use your strengths? I am sure that you have talent that other people around you don't have, or you might have something that people are not always aware of. But I can guarantee that you are great at something that you know you are great at. Part of accepting yourself is understanding your strengths so that you can use your strengths to complement your strategy.

What about your weaknesses? If you are aware of your weaknesses, I would say that you are pretty observant. If you can see them, you are aware. Well, put that onto the strengths list. Now tell me, how can you use your strengths to improve your weaknesses? They might stay weaknesses for your entire life. Superman couldn't overcome kryptonite, but he made up for it with super strength and his unrelenting determination to overcome evil. There are things we just cannot change. But what we can do is continue to combat them for the rest of our lives. And that is not a terrible thing. In our lives, we are always coming up against conflict, challenges, and stone walls, but that is the interesting part of what we do. If we don't overcome great odds, then the finish line isn't worth it.

We also find it easy to criticize ourselves, and we are, in fact, our worst critics. If we put our lives into perspective, what we think is a big problem, most likely isn't. A great leader is able to weigh up their circumstances and those of other people and grasp the reality of the situation.

We all get anxious, and things get the best of us at times. But it's how we get through it each time that makes us the better person. A leader who is able to preserver and shows other people how to get through things will ultimately teach other people to be better at themselves. There is no harm in being annoyed at yourself for not achieving things because this will condition you for the next attempt. But you will need to ensure you learn from your circumstances and use the 'sharpened' tool that is your mind to overcome the challenges for next time. You will be the deciding factor in your own success, and it is you who will either make or break at every turn you come to.

To be successful is to have the mindset that you will continue to try until you succeed, 'winners never lose, and losers never win' is one way to think about it. It doesn't mean that you cannot lose because that is impossible, but what it means is that you have the mindset. You set yourself into a space where you decide that you will always win, and therefore in every situation, you will do so. That might mean falling short of the end goal, but you win because you got something else from experience. It comes down to a matter of perspective. Your perspective sets the tone for how you want to succeed.

Walking Away

Also, don't be afraid to let things go. I have said this before, but don't be afraid to walk away from things if you frame it in your mind as a decision to go about continuing to win, and doing this will result in failure. You are setting yourself up for future success. Sometimes some things in life are just not worth the effort that you could be putting into something else. If you see value in what you are doing, but it is hard, that is a different circumstance. Don't get confused between what is hard and what should be walked away from. This you must decide alone, of course, or with the support of a mentor or friend you might get some guidance on the subject.

Suppose you need to let something go. You need to take some time to grieve. But make it short, don't get stuck in a position where you are held up from your long-term vision. People tend to get into a place where they find it hard to get out of. Focus on a short burst of pain, take it in one go, and move forward. If you operate differently, you could even it out over time. It could even help to motivate you with your passions. I have had a bad issue that I couldn't force myself to get over in a short period. So, I found time on the drive home to talk to myself about it and break out, but then I would feel so much better a couple of days later.

Don't repress your problems because they will manifest and come back to you later in life. Trust me. Try to overcome them, some things you cannot, but try to tick off what you can as you go. Sounds easy, but it is no easy feat. Even take some time for a walk and talk to yourself about what is most important in your life. Look at whether these failures or problems are what is holding you back. You need to make the conscious decision to overcome them. Otherwise, they will unconsciously eat you up.

With this, learn to forgive yourself. We have all made decisions and look back with wide eyes. Life happens, and mistakes happen. But these mistakes are opportunities to better ourselves. You hear of it all the time where someone has been addicted for many years to drugs and then in their later life become the greatest example of someone who has overcome their demons. It's a daily activity, and it isn't just something that happens by a miracle. It takes a conscious effort to decide each day that change is for the best. Part of forgiving yourself comes to paying it forward.

Paying It Forward

If you embrace that there is a higher cause, or there is a situation in which you are not the big player, you might find that giving back to people in your community or finding a charity that suits you best. It will give you a sense of fulfillment in yourself because you are able to appreciate that in all situations in life, your situation in reflection with another might not be as bad as you once thought. If you give yourself to something where you give your time to others to help them, it will give you a great sense of achievement within yourself. Because it is inherent within humans to help one another, regardless of how much we might like to get forward on our own merits. Helping others is a way to broaden ourselves from a humanity perspective, where we can find a sense of fulfillment in helping others selflessly whilst also building our character.

It is incredible how much you can learn from someone if you are open to the task of listening to others—especially people in hardship. I have had dealings with youth that require mentoring, and I have found that what they have gone through, what they have endured, puts my little concerns into life into the limelight. The hardship of others brings humility to our own circumstances. Now I am not saying that you go and pay it forward in a way that you are seeking development for yourself wholeheartedly. What you need to do is be open to the activity, but you can also understand that there are associated benefits with doing this. Paying it forward and helping other people is a way of finding deeper meaning and just a clear opportunity to give back to others.

You don't necessarily have to go and do a charity. You can do anything that you think is of benefit to other people. Paying it forward is a concept like Karma, where there is a belief that 'what goes around comes around.' Doing good deeds might not get you fame and money but what it might get you is a feeling of goodness within yourself or a reputation from the people you associate with that you are either trustworthy or worth what you say you are.

Compartment Our Fears

If you can pay it forward, you might be able to learn to forgive yourself for the things in life you have regret or feel as though you have personally or professionally fallen short of the mark. If you see a greater perspective on life and the problems other people are facing, you will have a greater appreciation of what really matters in life. And with that, you will learn to forgive yourself for some things that, when you initially thought held all the weight in your life, you are now able to compartment portions of your life into sections. Consider your personal circumstances and putting things into their areas of focus, to what level it is deemed:

1. High Priority – Does this affect my personal life right now? If I did nothing about fixing it, would it still be a problem in my life? If I ignore it, will it go away?

2. Medium Priority – Does this affect people that I associate with? If I don't get involved, will it be a problem in their life?

3. Low Priority – Does this affect people that I have not met before? If I get emotionally invested in the problem, what relevance would I have on changing it anyway?

If you compartment things in your life into these sections, you might find that things that are concerning you or things that you have felt badly about. You might find that when you really think about it, your involvement might make no difference anyway, so why get emotionally attached when you cannot do anything about changing it? I have struggled in the past with issues that I have been passionate about, but then someone who has done it all before reminds me, *Don't let it get to you. You can't change it anyway.* That is a good means test to determine the priority level. Now what you need to do is determine the level of angst or fear that you associate with each of these categories.

1. It causes me a high level of anxiety, and I have problems sleeping at night because of this.

2. It causes me quite a bit of problem, I think about it quite often, and I must try and think about other things to keep away from the subject.

3. It's not a bad influence on me, and I am easily able to forget about it.

Designator	High Stress	Medium Stress	Low Stress
High Priority	■	■	
Medium Priority			■
Low Priority	■		

■	Major Project at work
■	Having problems with having a baby
■	A family member just passed away
■	My boss is on my back about my results

I only used four examples in my boxes, now you might ask, what is the purpose of this exercise? Well, to answer your question, and my own. It's to let you visualize what is right in front of you. You need to be able to learn or develop your ability to compartmentalize your life so that you can separate the important parts of your life from each other. By breaking things down into pieces, you can see the visual lines or obstacles between each section. Don't combine your problems because then they will get a hold of you. By separating them visually, you will have a greater appreciation of each problem in its isolation.

Some people that I have met have astounded me by how easy it is for them to switch off and go to their happy place. This, I think, is again the debate between nature and nurture, where some people are born a certain way with an ability to disconnect from things whilst others learn to go either way in respect to their fears. I have found, though, that by writing your problems out and compartmentalizing them, that you get greater respect for the things you can control, and the things that are outside of your control. And if you don't have control over them, sometimes you need to find your own way of letting go.

Setting Routines

Many visionary conversationalists speak about daily routines or rituals. These are tools used to allow you to determine how your days and weeks will be played out. By doing a morning ritual, you are determining your frame of mind by your actions. If you choose to work out in the morning, you are deciding to shock your system into action, which will change your mindset. Some people chose to do this at different times. What is important is that you get a chance in the morning, before the chaos of your day begins to decide your mindset, to free yourself of what will be and appreciate the moment. Whether you do this consciously or not, if you are able to work out, you will get space in your mind to do the physical activity.

Your routine doesn't necessarily have to be a physical workout. It can be whatever is most appropriate to your circumstances. My six-step routine each morning and afternoon sets the tone for how I will broach the day and my night's sleep. It starts me off in a more considerate place. I have been doing my morning workout in the car on the way to work. I turn off the radio, I close my windows, and I go through the below process:

1. My daily prayer,

    - My daily prayer is something that I have been saying since I was quite young, it has evolved, and I have included new things to it, but this prayer, at least for me, is a way to remind myself that things in life come about and that some of it I will take control and guide it, whilst others come upon us that we must weather the storm. Regardless, there is someone at our side, dependent, of course, on your religion or none. There is someone physically, metaphysically, or emotionally there or around the corner from us that is on the same journey as I am.

2. Admiration for someone

    - I consider someone in my life that has done something courageous that I admire, it doesn't necessarily have to impact on me, but I hunt around for things that people have done, just one that is most notable for the day prior or what you know is going to happen. And I admire what they did and how they did it, so I could understand how I can do the same, but then, why they did it.

3. Be Grateful for something in my life

    - I think about what I have and how lucky I am, regardless of what is not so good in my life at present, and I remind myself what I have that matters most. Yes, there might be bad things happening, but we all have something in our life worth living for. It's just hard to realize how lucky we are when we are always in the now and forget about what we have right now and not what we are doing right now.

4. Accomplish today

- I consider what tasks I have for the day and what it means for me to accomplish them today—what do I need to do to feel like I have made a difference, that I have earned my place. It could be that there is a task you will easily get done today, but just thinking about it and telling yourself that you will accomplish this task or your day is a good mindset, to begin with.

5. Stretching,

- I physically alter my body's position, and I decide how I want to feel physically. Stretch my back, and I massage my neck with my hand. I physically alter the current and determine how I want to feel. This can also be translated into an intense physical workout. Sometimes I might hit the boxing bag and run around like mad in the evening in place of stretching.

6. Nutrition.

- The best thing in the world, right? Food is very important. Eating the right food determines how we will perform each day. You don't put tuna into your fuel tank: you put the best stuff in. Don't settle for cheap meals or the bare minimum. You need to fuel your body to get great output. Make sure your vessel is well prepared for the day ahead, and make sure that you continue to input if you're expecting a big day of outputs.

The order to this process is not an exact science. I eat first, and then I jumble the other parts around to fit the day that I am heading into. What I have found is that this routine is now the way I put myself to sleep each evening. I go through my set routine until I put myself to sleep. I don't even get time to worry about the next day because I am normally asleep by the time I reach what I am grateful for. I generally get carried away with what I am happy about in my life because I am trying to block out the problems from the day.

Don't think that I am running away from things, but I don't need to be worrying about things that won't change at eleven at night. I find that when I am most stressed in my life that I force myself to complete these routines religiously, but when things are in a better place, I start to be a bit more flexible with doing them.

What is most important about this is setting for yourself the compartments that you operate within. You need to learn to separate sections of your life from each other. You sometimes see people who put everything together, and each argument becomes a manifestation of the day's problems as well. For clarity's sake! Separate things, and the same goes with your partner. Let them tell you off if confusing a situation for your own benefit and not for group or your relationship, and it goes both ways of course. Within your support network, if you are working on something, let them know what your intentions are. You might be trying to separate parts of your life, normally work and personal. With this, let people know to call you out if you start to cross the lines. Your support network is there to support you.

The SWOT Analysis

Have you ever considered what your strengths, weaknesses, opportunities, and threats were? It is a standard business practice today to determine the SWOT for the business by Albert Humphrey, who was initially used to understanding where businesses had previously failed. But why don't we use it in our individual lives? Look at your life right now and fill in the below or on a piece of paper in whatever format works for you.

Strengths	Weaknesses
Opportunies	Threats

1. Strengths

    - Look at what you are strong at, and don't write anything down because that is impossible. If you have made it this far in the book, you will have realized a lot of your own potentials you didn't realize before.

    - Your strengths are part of what defines you, part of what you excel at, and where you will be able to find where you are most confident. These are good things.

2. Weaknesses

    - Understanding your weaknesses is very important. If you can see what you have difficulties with, you can adapt and overcome them. Your weaknesses can be combated by your strengths. I use the standard example that I have a bad memory when people tell me things on the fly. But I am a highly organized person, so I write everything down. This then shows people that I remember our conversations because I consciously forced myself to write everything down. Now subconsciously, this is something I just do by habit.

    - Your weaknesses can become your strengths. I bet that if you were asked if you could speak another language and you said no. Technically your ability to learn another language is a weakness. So how do you overcome this? You put into practice each day sometime aside to learn the language, and now you are on your way to making this a strength.

    - On the flip side, you might find that some things will remain weaknesses for the rest of your life. That is fine, but if you can identify them, you can combat them, and with each day, you can learn to overcome them.

3. Opportunities

- Much like the weaknesses, you can turn learning a weakness into an opportunity. You are visually linking your strengths to overcome your weaknesses. This is a clear example of an opportunity because it is now right in front of you.

- Other things in your life could be clear examples of opportunities. You might have a potential new role forming in a company you work within. Look at your strengths, how they can be mapped to assist you into this space, along what weaknesses you have that need to be refined for this space.

- Opportunities can include relocation, changes to your work-life balance, having a kid, or changing things in your home. You decide what an opportunity is. They can also be some of your goals you have set up while reading this book.

4. Threats

- Don't think threats are just other people trying to get what you have. The threats in your life are linked to your opportunities. If you don't take a chance and dive into an opportunity, how does that threaten what you want in your life? If you don't take a chance at something you really want, it is a threat to your well-being.

- It is a threat to your personality and parts of what you want to become. Your threats are the things that affect your 'why.' They are the things that will negate your ability to be who you are, and that is the 'why' of your life.

- Overcoming your threats takes your strengths, tackling your weaknesses, which form your opportunities to become better, which then set a statement for you, that these opportunities are ready for you, now don't let them go by. Take them away and run with them. Because if you don't. Then these threats will threaten your ability to accomplish your life's *why* you do it.

Section Three - A House Divided

Who you are is who you are, right? Don't think that you need to change who you are to succeed. Normally if you are someone that finds it hard to slot into the social norms, then that is a good place to be. Most of my success has come from being different, taking a different perspective, and providing it to the people that make the decisions. I've always been the guy in the meeting with happy socks, and I get plenty of stick for it. I must admit that certain situations call for a level of conformity, and if your empathy is good enough, you will determine this based on who is around you. But remember that you should be the best version of who you are and who you want to be. As I have said before, it is your *why* that matters most, and people will emulate you if they respect your *why*.

If you stand for something, people will want to understand your why. And rightly so, we are inquisitive people. If you don't believe in who you are, then you will not achieve the things you want to. Of course, within reason, I must press. You might also see someone who is not entirely sure why they do something, but they do it anyway. Subconsciously it could be in their nature or nurture, and although at the front of their mind they are not entirely sure, there is an underlying current that determines why they do what they do. If you are aware, you are more able to be flexible and adjust your plans to align with your goals. If you run without understanding your *why*, you might not have the same level of flexibility in your planning, but instinct can also have a very large effect on your plans.

Instinct is that nature versus nurture argument that we will have throughout the course of our lives. I think there is a level of understanding that they both have a lot to do with the person that you are and who you will become.

"Your whole life is about learning. You're not going to get to the point where you know all there is to know. That's the exciting part. You get to live each day discovering something new." (Peppernell, 2017, p. 163)

So even though you have more awareness of your circumstances, it does not give you the ultimate power because some people are so very determined to achieve things in their life without the awareness as to why they do what they do. Granted, having awareness will make you more alter and flexible, but some people have circumstances in their lives that mean that failure is not an option.

"To a surrounded enemy, you must leave a way of escape, show him there is a road to safety, and so create in his mind the idea there is an alternative to death." (Sun Tzu, B.C)

What I am trying to get to is, don't be arrogant or think that because you have an awareness of self and others that you will be superior. That would be a fatal error. What is important is that you know you have the power to change yourself and influence others. This in itself is a level of power that needs to be managed appropriately. With accountability comes the responsibility to help or support those around us that are not as aware—to provide awareness to them through developing their emotional intelligence. A great leader will create other leaders. If you do not, you will end up with all the work, and when you are not around, you will have people waiting at the door for you to return—not a good space to be in.

I had the opportunity to interview a senior military leader who I asked the below question.

- In Summary, how do you define leadership?

Answer: *"Overall, I have a very simple leadership philosophy: Don't be a knob. I know it sounds a bit blunt, and crude, but what I mean by this is that you should treat people the way you want to be treated, respect their experience and personal circumstances and respect them by communicating regularly with a clear intent for the organization (nobody likes to be kept in the dark)."*

Setting Boundaries

It is important in new and existing relationships, in work, and personally that you set your boundaries. Setting boundaries is a very clear way to exhibit to people and someone where they stand with you. If you stand in the gray area, you will have confusion as to how you can approach certain situations. I am sure you have had a colleague in the past where you have felt uncomfortable, and you end up avoiding them at all costs. It is awkward, and you find that you are continuing to run from the rooms in which they are. But as a leader, we must be more forward-thinking, we must approach these situations at the coal face (at the very front of the problem). If we do not, we lose our level of self-assurance, and people who see us in this situation will also judge our actions or in-actions during our leadership.

I am also sure that in your travels, you have experienced people that you would rate as abrupt, or you would initially think that they were rude? I was the same. I would complain that they were a rude person or too upfront. I used to think it was rude to be upfront, but I have come to respect the people that act in this manner. Consider this, do you know where you stand with this person? Do you know what they will do and won't do? Do you think that they will likely just change?

Well, we all know the answers to these questions. What do we look for in a leader? Along with all the other points we have previously discussed, we want someone who is upfront, honest, true to their work, sets boundaries, and is consistent in what they do. Now that is not to say that these people we have met in our travels are born leaders, but what I am saying is that they have the qualities of what we expect from leaders. And if we can take a certain percentage of their personalities, we can tailor it to ourselves. As I have said all throughout this book, we must continually be observant and learn from those around us. I myself have become more upfront with people, and although I am normally quite flexible, in some situations, I have laid down exactly what I can and cannot do. The amount of phone calls and questions I get around the gray area with these people has reduced, they know what to expect from me, and therefore, the wasted time in talking around the subject is significantly reduced.

How do we set boundaries, though? What do we need to consider? You need to look at your emotional intelligence, and you need to understand yourself and what your limitations are, along with what you are comfortable with. You need to understand your *what*, *how*, and *why* so that you do not overstep your bounds and stand outside the lines of your life vision. You also need to understand others. With some people, you will go beyond your normal boundaries, and with other people, you wouldn't even entertain the idea. You also need to know that if you do extend your boundaries, that you will be able to manage yourself. It is easy to see that someone will work for you, but you also need to ensure you consider managing your own self, managing how you will react or deal with the situation. Having the predetermination that you will do something means you must back it up with the management of yourself.

And finally, you need to understand the social situation and your engagement within that situation. You need to understand your level of influence on the person or persons and ensure that your boundaries are either consistent across the board or at least tailored to each person within the group. We all know that we treat everyone differently, but you need to ensure that the way in which you come across is consistent, with how you will treat each person 'equally.'

As an example, you might shove one of the guys in your workplace as a joke or a form of building rapport, but with one of the ladies, you might thank them and slightly touch their shoulder. The way in which you approach people needs to be consistent but also tailored to each person. If you swap them both around, you might end up with a visit to your human resources department. The world is changing, and the two situations could very well be swapped, but you need to understand your place in the social scene to decide your boundaries, but also their boundaries.

Once you understand your own emotional intelligence, or at least you can have the headings and some examples of what each means in front of you, I believe you can then set clear boundaries. You will need to be assertive in setting your boundaries, and if you are not, they may appear to be flimsy. Here is a process that I have continued to use:

1. Be direct in your approach, don't shy away from your boundaries
2. Do not fear guilt for standing up for yourself
3. Practice standing up for yourself (it gets easier each time, trust me)
4. You cannot directly change others, so learn to deal with it
5. Ensure that your core values align with your boundaries

I have also learned the hard way with setting boundaries. Empathy can be your enemy or your friend in setting boundaries. I worked at a site where I started as a trainee and then became the manager. I was originally friends with all the other workers, but then I became their subsequent boss. I was given some extraordinary targets that I had to achieve within my position, and it meant first, becoming somewhat enemies with my former friends and colleagues. I had to reduce cost, which meant, at this point in time, reduce headcount, and I had to get our efficiency rates extremely up. Before this change came, I used to go out drinking and party with the former team, which meant my boundaries were a lot more flexible and relaxed. But when I took on the new role, I didn't realize how much I would have to restart my boundaries with the team members.

I pulled the whole team together and assured them that I would be a better boss than the many priors and that we would work together collaboratively. I tried my hardest in this way, but what I had found was the team was using our friendship to gain leverage over their own situations. I had one employee to who I used to give a lift, and as his new boss, I found it very hard to be direct and say that I could no longer do this as it would seem out of character and somewhat unprofessional. I struggled with this as I had a good personal relationship, and my friend was using this to his advantage.

Long story short, I became the bad guy for some time, and even though I was collaborative, many of the former friends then became workers, and I had to pick my career over some of these partly personal relationships. It was very hard to do. I tried my hardest to stay in the gray and keep everyone happy, but what I have found is that if you try to keep everyone happy, you end up enraging the people you don't want to. I had to make a change and set clear expectations. I set a structure of boundaries. I even told all my employees that they would be fine to talk to me at work, but it had to be about work. I set clear boundaries as to which phone they could call me on and that I wouldn't treat them any differently.

In another workplace, I had a close relationship with my then colleague, who I then became his boss. I think I would treat him even more harshly than the other employees to offset the fact that people knew we were friends outside of work. Your situation is determined much differently than mine and anyone else's. What you need to do is to understand your emotional intelligence and apply it to your circumstances. With your emotional intelligence in mind, you will determine your structure. You will find it confronting to set boundaries in already existing relationships but trust me, and it gets easier as you do it more often. If you can do it in a pre-existing relationship, you will have no trouble doing it in future relationships. And of course, practice makes perfect, which is the very reason why the basic building block, conditioning, is used because if you continue to set boundaries, you will either reward yourself or punish yourself. It doesn't have to be physical.

The emotional response you get from successfully setting boundaries and working with them is fulfillment enough as a reward. But sitting in the awkward gray area is enough punishment for you to continue to avoid it to you must come to heads with it and make a change for the better. Be direct, be assertive and decide. Remember to put on your leader hat and know that you need to demonstrate the characteristics of what you would expect from your leaders. When you see a leader, you will copy some of their characteristics, part of your observational learning. As a leader yourself, you need to understand that people will also copy you. Don't let them copy an awkward person trying to escape a situation. Let them copy from you a strong and unrelenting character who will clearly establish their structures and, in turn, achieve their goals.

Core Values

Your hierarchy of needs should be considered. Your values will align with your self-actualization and the esteem that you hold for yourself. Your values are obviously psychological stances or pieces that hold the crux of who you are together. You need to understand what you want to achieve to become the vision that you seek for yourself. And what achievements you come to, and how you view them, as either achievement that needs to be celebrated or pinnacle points in your life that you will cherish in another way. That is your decision, but you need to align your psychological needs with your core values.

Anything and everything that you do should align with your core values. Your values, as we have discussed previously, are what determines what you will do, how you will do it, and why you will do it. Do you have values that aren't part of who you are yet? Are there things like contribution or dependability that you don't have yet you want them? Well, you need to determine what values you have and then what ones you want. The way in which you close the gap relies heavily on your current values. If you are honest or determined as an example, you can use these values to gain traction on becoming, say, more dependable. You need to set yourself some personal goals to achieve this step. You might also find that although you are honest, you cannot be relied on, maybe because you don't factor your time well or that you give yourself too many things. It might come back to being honest with yourself and cutting back at some of your commitments to achieve your values reset.

The way in which you approach it is insurmountable. There are many ways to approach this change, and you just need to determine how you are going to do it and how it aligns with your circumstances in your life. I hope with the goal-setting we used that you can refer back to this and apply it to better yourself.

Our core values should be a representation of who we are, and again why we do what we do. If you live and breathe your values, people will define you by what you have chosen to be. If you were to ask a friend to be honest with you and ask them what they thought your core values would be, if you are content with who you are, and it comes out differently, that is not a bad thing. It just means that in the situations in which you have both been together, they have seen snapshots of what they think you are. It is important to take into consideration their thoughts, but also, you need to put them into perspective with your own interpretation of their thoughts.

Don't, though, discredit what they have said. Try and use your emotional intelligence and understanding of others to grasp where their thoughts came from. You might find that in certain scenarios, you flex with your values, and potentially, for example, your exertion of passion could come across as aggressive. Don't, though, just change who you are. You need to be comfortable with who you are, and changing or altering your values must be done with careful consideration of your own situation and what you want. It will need to align with your vision, the day in and day out of who you aspire to be.

Success Is On Your Terms

Don't try to grasp what success is based on what your friends are doing. It is easy to say, hard even for me to do. But consider your life, your values, and you determine what you measure success as in your life. There are so many people that think to be successful is to be better than the people you know or reach their level. Then these same people wonder why they are in therapy or cannot figure out why they don't find fulfillment in their lives. They resort to alcohol, drugs, or smoking, and it just won't give that level of fulfillment they think they need. Don't let the walls cave in on you.

You need to realize that the only success in your life is what you determine it to be. That is why I have focused in this book so heavily on goal setting because when you tick those boxes of your goals, you will determine the satisfaction you acquire. If you base your life on others, you will never feel as though you are where you need to be, even when you one-up them. You are better than normal, and you will determine on what terms success is founded.

I have found some friends who started to climb the corporate ladder, followed in their fathers' footsteps and then one day moved to the country, and their life has so much more success and meaning than ever before. Why? Because they decided on their terms what their determination of success was and how it is to be measured. Of course, it is easy to say this again, but doing it is hard, but it is then so fulfilling. To grasp what really matters to you, well, some people take their whole life to get to this point. It happens to everyone when they are aware, and you start to really look at what you are setting for yourself.

If you are questioning how you do this, then just write down your values, your current life circumstances, what goals you have and then determine, do they all align. You can do this in many ways, but in your heart of hearts, you will know what goals you have set and which ones have been set for you. Don't delay the inevitable. Make a change, or don't. It's your choice in the end. But don't feel trapped. There is always a way out if it doesn't align with your life goals. Consider that you are just one person of five billion on a planet where you could move to another country and start again and never see the same people from where you came from again. If you can think of this, then you will know that you can change anything in your life. You just need to make the conscious decision to do as such.

So, remember that you don't have to align with other people's successes to be successful. Self-fulfillment is determined by what you set for yourself. Esteem and self-actualization are factors of the self. Your basic need is determined by what you set out for yourself. Your safety net is near to the bottom of your hierarchy of needs—personal and self-determination hold higher appreciation in your life. Your psychological well-being requires that you determine what you want for yourself, not the other way around.

If someone has something, and you want the same, then do it, but remember, you determine your success, and you do it on your terms, not anyone else's. My wife is someone who does everything on her terms. Yes, she compromises, but as a partnership, we are still two individuals with shared goals but also our own self-determining goals in life. It would be silly for us both to combine everything because we both also want different things—my level of success is different from my wife's. Finding the commonality is because we are both visual and aware of our circumstances, but where we both don't find the commonality, we keep these as individual goals.

As a leader, it is important to be acutely aware of your own successes and also your teams. They might find that the goals you have set them do not align with what they think are successes, so you need to find a way to tick all the boxes. What a leader needs to be good at is awareness and the ability to find commonality in the definition, reward and completion of goals.

Victory and Defeat

To suffer both victory and defeat is both a blessing and a curse. To learn from both is the greatest victory of all challenges in life. If you can learn to appreciate what both bring, you will certainly overcome future challenges in life and apply knowledge of these events to achieve future outcomes.

But how do we learn from our failures? Well, much like operant conditioning, when we fail, we are not rewarded, and therefore our response to future situations that fit the mold of our past failures will be a consideration. If you fall off your bike because you lost concentration, then next time you lose concentration, you might click yourself back into gear. More effectively than when you fell off the first time. It might even take several occurrences for you to finally overcome this issue. There is no exact amount of timeframe for your learning and prevention of future occurrences.

Easy to say and not so easy to just do. But how do we take what we have learned from our experiences and learn from them? The below are some effective ways to learn from your experiences, however good or bad:

1. I think one of the best ways to do this is to pass on your experiences to other people by talking about them with someone else. As you speak to someone about them, you are reinforcing them within yourself. By talking about them and telling someone the way you did, which either worked or didn't work, you are answering questions in your mind concurrently. I have even had the answer click in my head as I told someone, but before that, I still didn't understand what I learned from the experience. Sometimes these conversations come up when someone is in a similar situation as you have been in, and they call for your advice, or you give it without restraint. Sometimes, you might have someone that you talk to about life in general.

2. Writing things down helps to identify what you did, how you felt about it, and what you learned. If you look at a time where you had a significant challenge to overcome, you can learn to respect what you went through. I have looked back in my diary and found some challenges I have faced, and I have written about, even times that surprised me because I forgot about them and at that moment it brought back what happened, and then I am able to use my current understanding for past experiences. I'd even critique my writIng style, as I knew when I was frustrated because my writing style was rushed or overly messy. We are our greatest critic and our greatest appreciator.

3. When completing a task, having a section ready at the start of the task is a list that you can easily write or type dot points of things you realized either during or just after the task. The list will exponentially grow if you do it as part of your daily task. If it is an inclusion in the daily grind, it will capture so much more than if it was an afterthought. The lessons learned can then be cleared up, and a concise set of lessons can be displayed and evaluated in your next set of tasks that you can draw similarities to.

4. Remove your big head from the equation. Even I, of all people, forget my origins. There have been many occasions where I think of my title when someone speaks with me before looking at how I come across. My personality has changed between the roles I took

on, but my thoughts are that I should be treated differently based on my title. The same goes for challenges, and it is me who chooses to react or treat a situation differently. Consider when you want to learn from your experiences is that you must make the personal choice to change with these lessons learned. Just knowing they are there but not changing how you treat the situation is part of the problem.

5. The hardest part is to be open to change. You need to consider yourself as an empty cup when you enter this area of learning. If you come into the room with your ideas that you want to throw into the mix, you have already failed to learn. To truly absorb and learn from your experiences, you must be willing to accept that you do not have the answers. That the answers you seek are in front of you, not within you. We all have had this experience and experienced it when someone comes in knowing all the answers but not finding any of the solutions. This is a daily and lifelong challenge for us all. Be open to being the person in the room who knows the least but will end up knowing the most by the end of the journey or conversation.

When we lose, it leaves a sour taste in our mouths. I recall a conversation with a friend of mine in which I was going to call him, have a chat and then complain about my current circumstances. I was going through a rough period, and I wanted another opinion. But when I asked my friend how he was doing, for at least forty-five minutes, he told me all about the problems he was faced with. And let me tell you this, they were huge and life-changing events. Yet as he spoke about them, he continued to be proactive and was humble in everything he had to overcome. As he continued to speak, it put what I had in my mind into a greater perspective. It essentially humbled me in my situation and made me realize that my situation and that there is always someone in a worse situation than myself.

It really put into perspective that the fights and problems that are in my life are my own and that, yes, they are causing me significant problems. It is not the be-all and end-all. This, I think though is part of the aging process. I think once I am at an age where my personal life has had enough blows to it that my career and professional development won't cause me as much heartache and headache. But what is important is that we need to learn to put our challenges into perspective. Is our problem the size of an anthill or a mountain, and in comparison, to what?

I think the most important part of this section is to grasp that lessons in life come in all shapes and sizes, and the person who is most open to the experience of success and failure will ultimately gain the most out of each situation. In my case, I can be a bit of a pessimist at times, and much like my friend, he is someone who is guaranteed to overcome any challenges that life throws at him. Because he not only backs himself to overcome it, but he tells everyone the same thing. I being someone who can learn from this because I tend to dwell on the bad and not focus on where I have come from to be here today.

And I can assure myself, and you, that you could be in a much worse place than you are now. When they say you have hit rock bottom, start digging because you can always sink further. But the same goes for raising yourself up. The sky is definitely not the limit, we are a race that has ventured beyond the skies into space, so there is no limit to your opportunities. Your only boundaries are time and your mindset.

Section Four – The Wrap-Up

I think you will find that this chapter really focused on what you already know and applying it to your current circumstances. We all overcome great obstacles in life. Whether we measure it or not, we do. Taking stock and realizing this is part of our developing observation skills.

When the ship sails toward the sunset. Overcome obstacles, achieve goals, be who you choose to be. It is very important that you define what you want from your life because you ultimately determine your fate. Don't let other people choose your path, and it is up to you to decide what you consider success to be.

Consider this:

1. What will you focus on?
2. What does this mean to you, and what will it give you once you have it in your sights?
3. What obstacles do you have in the way that you will need to overcome?

Without evening knowing it, you are someone who has all the ability in the world to overcome great things in your life. We all have the potential, don't think, though because you have a rough day, you fall over and that this is the way it is always going to be. If life wasn't like a roller coaster, our great times would become the normal mundane days, and we would lose sight of what is important in our lives. Applying yourself requires you to take steps to overcome the challenges present in your life, daily or even when they appear from nowhere. The daily steps, the daily grind, is the training to help us appreciate the really good and ugly things that come along our path.

I cannot stress just how important it is that you use a diary or a form of measurement of your daily or weekly activities, it will provide insight into your past actions and challenges, and it is a great opportunity to go back and see how you deal with situations as compared to how you would deal with them now. Just reading how you wrote something or in the way that you wrote something will give you that feeling, the emotion and the memories will come back to you just like it was yesterday.

You need to look inwardly and see the man or woman behind your mask. What things do you present to people that tire you? Are there ways you present yourself that even you feel like you are fake, or is it becoming just too much to be this way? The concepts that I introduced in this book were designed to make you think about your situations and how you can react or treat your circumstances differently.

Our past has a lot to do with who we become. The nature and nurture debate will continue on throughout our generations, but there is validity to both mindsets. I am a firm believer that we can control our actions, but it depends on our level of control over our situations. I personally know that I have been overwhelmed in situations and tried to run for the hills, but something inside of me held me together. I also get itches and things that I would like to do, yet there is a part of me that stops me from thinking or doing things that I know are not acceptable to my family, friends, and society. As we all do, we all test our boundaries and consult the inner 'me' when we act out.

As a leader, people will love and hate you. Accepting this is a daily challenge but understanding the impact you have on the lives of people is a factor in the decisions that you make. A leader has the easy opportunity to make or breach any operation, and even when the people they manage are university-qualified operators, the manager could be just as simple as someone who knows someone in power. This is a scary thing, but being the wolf, which I don't associate with aggressive, the wolf is part of the pack that knows what decisions need to be made or acts with good intentions. That the pack, the group, is the focus of the leader and that to survive, we must work in collaboration but also in isolation. The leader must be aware of which situations require these choices to be made.

Exercise: Put together a SWOT analysis of your life at present, consider your work, family, friends, and things that are soon to come about. Considering your strengths, what do you excel at, and what would you and other people say are, in fact, your strengths. The same goes for the rest of the analysis. From there, you will have a visual grasp of your challenges and opportunities that are with you now or are soon to come. I am sure that from this experience you will learn something about yourself, if you didn't, then consider some opportunities you have in ten years. If you cannot look this far out, maybe one of your weaknesses is your foresight for future planning. What I am doing here is letting you know that with all that you know and what I know, there is always more to learn.

The Conclusion – The End – A New Beginning

> *"The end is the beginning is the end."*
>
> (The Smashing Pumpkins, 1998)

The End Is The Beginning Is The End, Is The Beginning

Firstly, if you made it this far, you are either very persistent or have enjoyed what you have read. I hope that you have learned from reading this book, and you know what, I can guarantee that you have, because just by going through this journey, you have learned about some of my experiences and the people that I have associated with that have taught me lessons in my life.

I think it is very important for me, and I hope for you to is that you have a desire to create a compelling future. That what you are doing each day, that what you do in each moment of your life is the stepping stones toward your vision or visions in life. But that you respect each individual moment for what it brings and that you somehow learn to find comfort in the present. Because we, and I know I do this too often is to look toward what our future holds but forget to grasp the 'now.' Not just in leadership, but in our lives overall this is something that we look back at events and aspire to have absorbed more of the present than we did at the time. So, with that knowledge and understanding in your mind now, don't let time slip by you.

Leadership is most times when it is done right, a thankless role.

"A leader is best when people barely know he exists when his work is done, his aim fulfilled, they will say: we did it ourselves." (Tzu, 2011)

We know that when we achieve something ourselves that we feel our internal fulfillment value increase. We will draw influence from the leadership that is around us, but if we are pushed into something, we don't foster it the same as if we do it on our own terms. The same as a child rebels against the parents who want what is best for the child, but there is still a rebellion and a want, a need to find our own way.

I think the most important concepts I tried to explore were the basic building blocks which are the foundation of a leader or any person in this world and their interaction with each element of the world. These blocks are the day in and day out of what we already do, and there is no hiding that. But understanding them at their core and how they relate to you is where you will learn the most about yourself—in that you will learn about your limitations, your strengths, and your abilities. Without seeing inwardly, you won't be able to test the boundaries of your current construct. Unless somehow your system gets a shake-up and you decide to make a change, this would be our nurture, and we are all affected by our environment in very different ways.

But if you can grasp these building blocks and learn to push your understanding beyond the mundane day to day and realize that you can use these concepts to better yourself and the people around you, then if I have led you to this conclusion, then I feel like my job has been done. Don't be fooled thinking that you should have by the end of this book had a revolution in your mind. It's the small steps toward the change in your reality that have the most effect. And if I was able to nudge you, then I will feel fulfilled in what I have myself also experienced, the same that I hope you do too.

Take this from me, that even if you reach a dead-end, and you think there is no way past it, just take a look up, you might find that the wall you have run into is actually quite short, and you can make the jump over it. There is always going to be a brake, a stop in the road, a nail on the train line. Something will try to stop you, but at each challenge you come to, it's your ability to apply yourself, not just using the concepts in this book, but to have an unrelenting pursuit for excellence in yourself and in what you do that will continue to propel you toward your end vision. Our goals will set the tracks for the train, but it's you who needs to shovel the steam into the engine to keep it rolling on.

I don't think that you will just have a smooth track all the way, I wish it was so, but then I also am glad it isn't because I have gone from strength to strength. Even on days when I have felt so down, the next day, the next month, maybe the next year, I bounce back, but even better than before. Just know that the end is just another beginning. Take the birth of a child. It's the end of the pregnancy, but guess what, it's the start of an entirely new chapter in your life. Every end comes up to a new beginning, and your ability or awareness to see this will show you that there are limitless possibilities in your future.

Sometimes the things we want in life must take a systematic hold on the backburner, sometimes to achieve our greatest desires, we must do the things that we don't necessarily love but don't think that this must be the norm. If we set in motion the daily goals and we can start to follow the stepping stones to our end goal, if there is a light at the end of the tunnel that the light is growing brighter, then we are in the right place. But don't think that we must bear the weight of the world just to get what we want. If you really wanted to, you could get on a flight and start anew tomorrow.

For every no that you get, there is another yes just awaiting your call. And I know that, of course, it is easy to say this, and it is even harder to do. I have never found it easy to be rejected on so many occasions, but having faith in myself and the support of my family, I know that I will achieve what I want, even if I continue to collide with dead ends. It's also a good opportunity for a wake-up call. Maybe my approach needs work, and maybe I think that what I have to give is actually not as amazing as it seems in my own head. These are the opportunities in our lives to take a step back and see why what we are doing is not working. Or it could, but we just need a different audience. Don't be afraid to fail, don't be afraid to try something, and have people underestimate you. Fear of failure will stunt you and cause you not to try at all. You can have a fear that you will have to keep trying till you succeed, but don't let the little voice inside your mind tell you that you cannot do what you want to do. Nothing is impossible. We see every day someone achieves something we didn't think was possible.

If we can land on the moon, where next? Who next? Is It you or me that will be that person in the history pages? It's up to you to decide what you want in life and don't let anyone tell you that you cannot—even that person sitting on your shoulder. It is no easy feat, don't get me wrong, but you decide how you live your life, don't look back in ten years and regret it all. Make a change now to better your life now. The same goes for a leader. It is our job to inspire people to be the best person that they can be. If we don't lead by example, how can we expect people to follow suit?

Don't wait for the right moment to achieve your life goals and dreams. Now is the time, there are three certainties in life, that time is never enough, and that we cannot get back what we have already had, that we all want to be a part of something no matter how much some people try to disassociate, we all want to love and to be held. And finally, that true success is not in the value of your wallet or your fancy house, and it is the fulfillment of your life as a whole. I have a good friend who is not wealthy, just owns a car, but has beautiful children, a kindred connection with his wife, a great work-life balance, and all the time in the world with his family.

Now to each their own, but seek out what gives you the most fulfillment in your life. It's not all about being the richest or strongest. It's about what you want because there are many people out there that can earn a million, yet they still don't feel fulfilled. Don't do it because someone else sets your benchmark, do it because you set your benchmark. You alone decide what success is, and you alone will fail or succeed to achieve what you set for yourself. Knowing how to do this, well, I reckon if you've made it this far, you well on your way.

Remember, and lastly, great leaders are not just born. We are made, and what makes a great leader is not the shining star that they hold out for everyone to see. It is their experiences, their values, their basic building blocks, and it is their mortar that makes them who they are. It is their mortar that strings all their achievements together, and it is their mortar that makes them overcome the challenges that come their way. The challenges that come your way. Don't be surprised when you suffer hardship and feel like you cannot carry on. This is part of being human. But persevere, adapt, and overcome, and you will always win. The mortar that defines you is right now, in this book, and what you do each day to become who you are now and who you will become one day. For every setback, take two steps forward because the end is only just the beginning.

...Vivas Sperandum...

(Niven Motto)

References

Abraham Lincoln, N/A. Sharpen the Axe [Interview] (N/A N/A N/A).

Adler, A., 2012. Theories Of Personality. In: TBA, ed. Individual Psychology. TBA: TBA, p. 50.

Aesop, (. A., 6th Century B.C. jonathanbecher. [Online]
Available at: http://jonathanbecher.com/2014/06/15/four-oxen-lion/
[Accessed 11 July 2018].

Aesop, 2014. The Ass and the Sick Lion. In: Aesop's Illustrated Fables. New York: Barnes and Noble, p. 200.

Alex Hamilton, 1978. 1978 radio broadcast. [Sound Recording] (Radio broadcast).

Amish Proverb, n.d. Unknown. s.l.:s.n.

Anderson, S. M., 2015. Blessings. [Sound Recording] (Dark Sky Paradise).

Ashton, M. J., 1992. The Tongue Can Be a Sharp Sword. [Sound Recording] (General Conference).

Bardell, A., 2018. Dow / Dupont Meeting. Melbourne, N/A.

Bernard Montgomery, 1942. Leadership, s.l.: s.n.

Branson, R., 2014. Virgin. [Online]
Available at: https://www.virgin.com/richard-branson/hire-attitudes
[Accessed 12 October 2018].

Bridge, A., 2004. In Loving Memory. [Sound Recording] (Wind Up).

Bruce Lee, N/A. N/A [Interview] (N/A N/A N/A).

Chomsky, N., 2001. Global Issues. The World After Sept. 11, 1(1), p. 4.

Churchill, W., 1948. Speech in House of Commons. [Sound Recording].

Colin Powell, 2017. Read Anyone Like a Book, s.l.: Chapter 3: Associates and Associations.

Coutu, D., 2018. How Resilience Works. In: H. B. Review, ed. Resilience. Boston: Harvard Business Review, p. 128.

Covey, S. R., 1989. Inside-Out. In: S. &. S. U. Ltd, ed. The 7 Habits of Highly Effective People. Great Britain: Franklin Covey Co, p. 391.

David O. Mckay, 2004. The 7 Habits of Highly Effective People - Stephen R. Covey. In: F. Covey, ed. Habit 7: Sharpen the Saw. New York: Free Press, p. 380.

DiCaprio, L., 2013. The Wolf of Wall Street. [Sound Recording] (Martin Scorsese).

Douglas, J., 2017. Sometimes the Dragon Wins. In: M. tie-in, ed. Mindhunter. Quantico: Cornerstone , Arrow Books Ltd, p. 409.

Eisenberg & Fabes, 1999. Consistency and Development of Prosocial Dispositions. A Longitudinal Study, 1(1), p. 15.

Field Marshal Bernard Montgomery, n.d. s.l.: s.n.

Gandhi, M., 1936. Ghandhism [Interview] 1936.

Gitomer, J., 2015. Twitter [Interview] (27 November 2015).

Goldsmith, O., 1760. The Public Ledger. London: The Citizen of the World.

Goleman, D., 2016. The 3 Types Of Empathy You Need To Strengthen Your Relationships [Interview] (22 March 2016).

Govindarajan, V., 2016. A Strategy For Leading Innovation. In: A. N. Standards, ed. The Three Box Solution. Boston: Harvard Business Review, p. 240.

Greene & 50 Cent, 2016. The New Fearless Type. In: Greene, ed. The 50th Law. Queens: Joost, p. 398.

hammarskjold, D., 1963. Markings. In: V. S. Classics, ed. Vägmärken. New York: Random House USA Inc, p. 222.

Hayes, D., 2014. Perceptions. Sydney, Linfox.

Hemingway, E., 1996. In: Across the River and into the Trees. s.l.:Scribner, p. 288.

Henry T Ford, 1923. Business Competition. Ford News, p. 2, Volume 2, p. 1.

Hunt, J., 2015. Senior Pastor of First Baptist Church Woodstock. [Sound Recording] (First Baptist Church).

Hyatt, M., 2018. Daily Pages. In: Full Focus Planner. s.l.:Michael Hyatt & Co, p. 304.

Jans, N., 2018. Mission-Team-Me. In: A. &. Unwin, ed. Leadership Secrets of the Australian Army. Sydney: Allen & Unwin, p. 188.

Jung, C., 1957. The Dilemma of the individual in modern society. In: The Undiscovered Self. s.l.:Signet, p. 112.

Jung, C., 1967. Volume 7 – Two Essays on Analytical Psychology. In: Collected Works. Princeton: Princeton University Press, p. 376.

Lewis, M., 2011. Memoirs of an addicted brain. In: G. Press, ed. A NEUROBIOGRAPHY OF ADDICTION. Doubleday Canada: Scribe Publications, p. 311.

Limp Bizkit, 1999. Re-Arranged. [Sound Recording] (Limp Bizkit).

Machiavelli, N., 1532. Concerning new principalities which are acquired by one's own arms and ability. In: N. Machiavelli, ed. The Prince. Italy: Antonio Blado d'Asola, p. 114.

Maslow, A., 1943. Hierarchy of Needs. In: B. Hergenhahn, ed. Theories of Personality. New Jersey: Prentice Hall, p. 614.

Matthew 7:12, 2000. World English Bible. In: C. . d. (. waived), ed. The Bible. s.l.:Rainbow Missions, p. 798.

Megginson, L. C., 1963. The Convention of the Southwestern Social Science Association. Louisiana: Louisiana State University.

Miller, F. T., 2016. Power Corrupts [Interview] (16 April 2016).

Miller, R., 1972. ABC late-night, San Diego: TV-Radio editor at "The San Diego Union."

Miroslav, H., 2006. The Door. In: C. E. translations, ed. Poems Before & After. Prague: Bloodaxe Books, p. 50.

Musashi, M., 1645. In: T. Cleary, ed. The Book of Five Rings. Boston: Shambhala Publications Inc, p. 75.

Mylett, E., 2018. What Everyone Struggling Needs to Know Right Now. [Sound Recording] (Impact Theory).

Narcotics Anonymous, 1981. The Ultimate Quotable Einstein. s.l.:s.n.

Niven Motto, Unknown. Scotland. [Sound Recording] (N/A).

Niven, G., 2017. Life Lessons. [Sound Recording] (N/A).

O'Loughlin, D., 2014. The Failings of Leadership. Sydney, Linfox Logistics.

Pacino, A., 1996. City Hall. [Sound Recording] (Metro Goldwyn).

Parton, D., 2015. find-out-who-you-are-and-then-be-it-on-purpose. [Online]
Available at: https://medium.com/@timleroyis/find-out-who-you-are-and-then-be-it-on-purpose-12141970f1d3
[Accessed 19 January 2019].

Peck, M. S., 1978. Discipline. In: N. W. Nelson, ed. The Road Less Travelled. Great Britain: Ebury Publishing , p. 320.

Peppernell, C., 2017. The Road. 1st ed. Missouri: Andrews Mcmeel.

Plutarch, 1958. The Lion's Lair. In: R. Warner, ed. Fall of the Roman Republic. Rome: Penguin Classics, p. 365.

Proverbs 16:18, B.C. The Bible. In: TBA, ed. The Bible. Jerouseleum: King James, p. 2000.

Renatus, P. F. V., 4th Century. Dispositions for Action. Book III, 1(1), p. 50.

Robbins, A., 2013. Whats Your Mission. [Sound Recording].

Romans 12:4, B.C. The Bible. In: TBA, ed. TBA. Jerusaleum: King James, p. 2000.

Sharma, R., 2012. RobinSharma. [Online]
Available at: https://www.robinsharma.com/article/there-are-no-mistakes
[Accessed 15 September 2018].

Sherrilyn, K., 2007. Dark Hunter #11. In: 0312369506, ed. Devil May Cry. New York: St. Martin's Press, p. 320.

Sinek, S., 2014. Why Some Teams Pull Together and Others Don't. In: TBA, ed. Leaders Eat Last. Boston: Penguin Books, p. 234.

Skinner, B., 1938. Operant Conditioning. In: Theories of Personality. s.l.:Duane P. Schultz, Sydney Ellen Schultz, p. 516.

Stanley, A., 2001. N/A. In: Visioneering. s.l.:Multnomah Books, p. 314.

Sun Tzu, B.C. The Art Of War. In: China: s.n., p. 62.

Tennyson, A. L., 1861. Alfred Lord Tennyson Quotes. [Online]
Available at: https://www.brainyquote.com/quotes/alfred_lord_tennyson_153702
[Accessed 15 April 2019].

The Smashing Pumpkins, 1998. Adore. [Sound Recording] (The Smashing Pumpkins).

Tucic, D., 2016. Smart Man / Wise Man [Interview] 2016.

Twain, M., 1870. The Galaxy.

Tzu, L., 2011. The book of the way. In: S. Mitchell, ed. Tao Te Ching. s.l.:Octopus Publishing Group, p. 128.

Unknown, 2009. Minimum Wage. Wollongong, Snap Printing.

Vince Lombardi, 1970. The Will To Win Speech. [Sound Recording].

Will Rogers, n.d. [Interview] n.d.

About the Author

I was born in Auburn in Sydney, Australia. To two parents, funnily enough! My mother's background is Dutch, and my father's is English/Scottish.

Having lived on this planet for only a short period of time, I have had an extraordinary amount of challenges, triumphs, tributes, hostilities, be-all and end-all situations, and my fair share of learning experiences. I think by the end of this book, I will look back and think I could have done so much better in all my life experiences. But I guess that's why they call it hindsight, right? I think what I have that other people don't is that I am able to absorb moments in my life and translate them into where they fit in the greater picture of my life.

I believe that I am a capable leader with a great insight into the personal and professional development of those around me, not something I have learnt overnight either. I am aware and able to pick up on people's idiosyncrasies, and I find myself staring through people sometimes, to the point where their habits are what I look at rather than their faces.

Funnily enough, I thought when I was younger that my future career would be as a superstar musician. I began to lose interest in education (school) as I thought at the time that I didn't need it. But later in life, I realized that it wasn't only due to me thinking education had nothing to do with my success as a musician. It was due to the teachers that I had and the people that surround me.

I recall some special teachers, albeit few and far between whom I can still remember having a vested interest in my development. We cannot blame our lack of ability in education or a profession on ourselves. It comes down to the leadership of people who hold positions of authority. Much like myself, there have been times where I would have found it easier not to get involved or take the easy route. But a sturdy and stubborn values system instilled in me from day dot reminds me that because I am aware, that I have a responsibility to help those who are around me.

It's funny that I wanted to be a musician. I lacked a decent amount of self-confidence. Even more surprising is I still lack a decent amount of self-confidence. This would surprise the people that I associate myself with. I am quite outspoken and generally am willing to jump up and do things, even when I have considered the risk, such as karaoke or making a speech in front of more than two hundred people in one sitting. My poor dear wife must deal with it every day. There doesn't go a day where I don't look in the mirror and complain about my size, my lack of motivation, or the fact that I don't feel fulfilled doing what I am doing.

Again, the people that I know would be surprised by this. And now that I am writing this, I think, "Hmm, is this something I really want to add to my introduction?"

It's not to say that my confidence hasn't grown, but it started from a low point. Part of this issue with my confidence, initially, is due, in part, to my parent's divorce. I was quite young when it happened. I can just remember being in my family home. My mother was pulling me by my ankles while I held on tightly to the leg of the kitchen table. Whilst my parents argued above the table, my two brothers were in the adjacent room near the staircase, watching on. Not able to get involved, this was beyond their comprehension. And from that point on, I don't remember anything on the rest of that day. I can see it clearly in my mind. It's not a gray image. It's in color, and it's alive.

I am not old enough or wise enough just yet to fully understand the impact of this event and its influence on the course of my life and its trajectory. But I am aware that this event has caused me to act in the way that I do, presently, at the time of writing this book, at least. I can be easily cold to others. My wife reminds me of this quite often that I could make (her) someone feel as though they mean nothing to me. But that is a feeling, a reaction to my persona or projection. This is not to say that this is solely who I am.

In my own self-defense, I have the ability to overly care for people in my life. But it is a reflection that I can attribute, some, in part, the blame toward this single point in my life. Developmental Psychologist Alfred Adler states, "Children who were neglected or rejected by their parents develop feelings of worthlessness". This is just one example that I will talk about later in the book, but regarding childhood experiences, assumptions can be made. Our earliest memories of childhood can help reveal or characterize our habits or motivations in life.

Part of my childhood has led me to become a highly determined person. I think that in everything I do, I try to complete it at 100%. People get overwhelmed by my level of enthusiasm regarding projects, activities, or even fitness. Somewhere along the line, I realized that I wanted to reach a level of comfort that was well beyond my reach. I was aware that I had to work hard now so that when I am marginally older, I will have the capability to slow down at some point.

I try so hard to prove myself to others, though I feel like as I am getting older, or wiser, that this is no longer the biggest focus for me, that which I want to achieve is because of what I want for myself based on my vision. I think I am shifting from proving myself to others to aligning with my vision, though it can be seen as a very similar approach.

When everyone was leaving school at the end of year twelve, there were several of my co-students who were earmarked for university. In conversations, I would overhear that they would solely focus on university and that their parents could help them whilst they go through this process. I was let down by the fact that no one told me I could get financial aid, also known as hex-debt in Australia. I thought that once I left school, I was completely on my own. So, despite this, I did what I thought was best: work and work hard.

I will reflect on this later in the book, but it is a leader's responsibility to make their teams aware of how we are perceived, how we present ourselves and what the end goal is. Communication is key. I know firsthand what it is like to not be informed and do just what I think is right. Had I known that there were other options available, maybe I would have gone down a different path. Much the same in the workplace, people expect that everyone knows what they should be doing. Or we assume that people have just made the wrong decision because they chose to. All too often, it's because the leaders of organizations or societies don't provide enough options, and these options are always there. It is just up to the leaders to inform and consult on the availabilities.

After leaving school, I had little awareness of what I could do. I didn't have experience, or so I thought at the time, I went to a job agency with my mother to find a job. After some searching, there was an opportunity. I was at a crossroads. I was offered two jobs. One of the jobs was as a warehouse hand (technically a trainee) in a printing company in Wollongong or as a trainee nurse in Helensburgh.

My brother was living with my mother and me during this time. Ben is a person that is hard to figure out and the wisest man I have ever met. He is like a sponge, remembering the details of every formula or complex theory. I turned to him for advice. But Ben, someone from whom I have learned a lot, doesn't make the decision for you. Ben is a listener who provides pros and cons for all arguments. So, he doesn't make it easy for me to decide, still to this day. But what he did was inform me of all the options. Now my brother Ben is not a 'technical' leader, he doesn't have employees that work for him, and in a group, he doesn't take the lead. But what he does is complement the mix of the group.

Not wanting to rock the boat and take a leap, I took the warehouse hand role. For me, Helensburgh was too far away, and the new job was in an industry I knew nothing about. As a warehouse hand, I knew it would be partly in an office and in a warehouse. But not to take away from my decision, I still took a leap in this role. Whilst most of my friends were working casually and studying, I thought from day one that a full-time job is where the money is at. I will speak more about my experiences in this role within the book.

I must admit that I own a great debt of gratitude to my brothers. Christopher David Niven and Benjamin Reuben Niven. Both of my brothers have supported me in my youth, both paying money and emotional time to my endeavors. Both of my brothers supported me in their own way when I was aspiring to be a superstar musician. The returns on that venture didn't come to fruition but what I got out of it was the experience. I think that it would be hard to find three brothers with a bond as close as ours. We have helped each other through many great and woeful experiences and have continued to develop our invisible bond.

Both of my brothers are older than me, the smallest age gap being seven years. My older brothers are my best friends and I have grown up to their maturity level quickly. People that I associate with describe me as an old soul. But what I think is the case is that I am acting, embodying the age of my older brothers. My parent's divorce, along with all the other hard moments, is what made us who we are today.

And if you asked me if I could change any of it, would I? I wouldn't in a million years. I am the person I am today due to my experiences. A depiction of how I interpret adversity can be understood by the following text:

"Strength through adversity. The strongest steel is forged by the fires of hell. It is pounded and struck repeatedly before it's plunged back into the molten fire. The fire gives it power and flexibility, and the blows give it strength. Those two things make the metal pliable and able to withstand every battle it's called upon to fight." (Sherrilyn, 2007)

"It is not the bricks, but the mortar that defines the leader." (Pacino, 1996)

Although the original quote is slightly different, what this one line did for me was put my actions into perspective. It is surprising how powerful a sentence can be and so insightful at certain times of our lives. What I see in this is that it is not all the glitz and glamour that makes you who you are—it's what you did, how you did it and in which direction you are headed.

People don't achieve great things all the time via honorable actions, sometimes they can achieve great things via the wrong route. In leadership people can see through the fifteen seconds of fame. The ones that last are the ones that have built the mortar around their bricks, so well that the bricks or achievements can only come down if you break the whole wall down. But even still, the mortar sticks to the brick. What am I saying?

I have been very blessed over the past years to have been awarded quite generously for some of the projects or tasks that I have been in control or involved in. But I try to remind myself to be humble, especially to my wife, who is quite good at keeping me grounded when my head fills up with hot air.

Why do I get so much praise from those around me? Because I suggest that I am quite effective at sharing the success of things that I am involved in. I found in business and in life that people focused more on getting the job done than worrying about prevention for future events. But it is pleasing to see that society is trending in the direction of sustainability and true accountability.

What I hope that people get out of this book is some insight into what a leader should exude, along with ways in which you can find the good and the bad of my approach, and mold it into a new perspective, a better way of thinking—and ultimately leading people effectively. Because when it is all said and done, a leader could make or break people's perspectives, a bad manager can affect a person's home life and add to the problems that someone might already be enduring.

It could potentially be the straw that broke the camel's back. It is in the best interest of the leader's conscience that we try to develop pro-social behaviors, and the best way to develop them is by being the embodiment of these behaviors.

I have in me a strong sense of service now, and I recall when I was a kid that I played with Army men and dressed up as a soldier. In games, I would do basic training, yet I was sitting behind my computer screen when the backyard of my parents' home was completely unused. I am in the process of joining the Reserve Army, and I feel a huge sense of pride in going through these motions. In my next book, I will be reflecting on this and what it will bring to my life.

My values are summarized as strength, determination, service, and awareness.

My Ode

And Lord, please still the clamor of our days

And help calm our anxious rushing ways

In silence teach us how to praise

And find peace within your love

Because sometimes I think to myself

But my thoughts they'll escape with the train

They'll make their new life on the light side

But I'll stay in the dark until the rain pours down

It'll wash away the hate and burn out the darkness

And Lord, I know that things are in motion as you allow them to be

And I know that if I am hurting, you'll be there right beside me

Against unrelenting odds

I will do just the same

No matter its size

Not accounting its number

I will increase just the same

No matter its fear

Not shrouding it in my darkness

I will stand just the same

And always it will be there

And always I will be here

Just the same

www.ingramcontent.com/pod-product-compliance
Lightning Source LLC
Chambersburg PA
CBHW070618170426
43200CB00010B/1834